LIVING THELEMA

A PRACTICAL GUIDE TO ATTAINMENT IN ALEISTER CROWLEY'S SYSTEM OF MAGICK

DAVID SHOEMAKER

LIVING THELEMA

A PRACTICAL GUIDE TO ATTAINMENT IN ALEISTER CROWLEY'S SYSTEM OF MAGICK

DAVID SHOEMAKER

Originally published in 2013 by

Anima Solis Books
P.O. Box 215483
Sacramento, California 95821, USA

First reprinting, March 2017

www.livingthelema.com

Cover design by Frater Julianus

Illustrations © Thomas Nelson Stewart IV
Solve et Coagula Design
www.solve-et-coagula.us/design.php

ISBN: 0989384411
ISBN-13: 978-0-9893844-1-4

A∴A∴
Publication in Class B

Imprimatur:

N. Fra. A∴A∴   **PRO COLL. SUMM.**

I.   7°=4□   **PRO COLL. INT.**
V.V.   6°=5□

I.   Praem.   **PRO COLL. EXT.**
R.O.   Imp.
L.L.L.   Canc.

Unto Thee, my Lord Σ……,
This kiss,
This soul,
This heart!

"Thou shalt mingle thy life with the universal life."
-*Liber Cheth vel Vallum Abiegni*

TABLE OF CONTENTS

Acknowledgements

I would like to thank my wife and my son for their love and support, and for tolerating the many hours I was absent as I worked on this material. Thanks also to my parents, my sisters, and my extended family, for a lifetime of support and encouragement. I am sure I have not expressed my appreciation for your presence in my life nearly enough. To my spiritual forebears in A∴A∴, Soror Meral, Soror Estai, Frater Saturnus, and Frater To Mega Therion—I owe much gratitude for even being allowed to dip my toes into the current of wisdom they initiated and nurtured over many decades. Special thanks to my students, for teaching *me* so much every single time we interact. I hope that in return, I have given you some measure of sustenance for your spiritual journey.

Finally, I wish to acknowledge the following for their support, encouragement, wisdom, and friendship across the years: Lon Milo DuQuette, Richard Kaczynski, Craig Berry, Frater Sabazius, Soror Helena, Frater Puck, Howard and Amy Wuelfing, Kim Knight, Geoff Leibinger, Robie Schriber, Vere and Lita Chappell, James Fairman, Robert Fripp, Joseph Thiebes, Frater IAO131, Anna-Kria King, Andrew Ferrell, Gregory Peters, Joseph Larabell, Frater Sohum, Robbi Robb, Charlotte Moore, Monika Mayer-Kielmann, and Edward Mason.

For technical support on this project, many thanks go to: Frater Julianus, for the beautiful cover design; Thomas Stewart, for his detailed illustrations; Kelli Patton, Britta Cox, Monika Mayer-Kielmann, and Thomas Stewart, for transcription assistance; John G. Bell, for all manner of online support; and Charlotte Moore, Frater IAO131, and Anna Tsu, for proofreading and editorial suggestions.

INTRODUCTION

Do what thou wilt shall be the whole of the Law.

Looking back over the past 20 years of my involvement with Thelema, I have often reflected on what exactly drew me to the Great Work. Life is simpler (at least superficially) without all the self-discipline required of initiates, and one can easily find a spiritual path with more cultural acceptance and societal support mechanisms. There's a church, mosque, ashram, and new age guru on practically every block in today's world, but I had a pretty tall order for any spiritual system: Give me wonder and mystery, but don't make me check my brain at the door!

This spiritual and intellectual dilemma was more-or-less foreordained for me. My father was an atheist philosophy professor, while my mother was a musician and theologian from a deeply religious upbringing. I had to make sense of this somehow—to find a way to reconcile these divergent worldviews and appreciate the positive contributions each perspective had brought to my life. Luckily, my parents were both open-minded enough to give me space to find my own answers.

After graduating from college as a psychology major, I set off for graduate school to become a psychotherapist. I learned all about the mainstream cognitive-behavioral approaches to therapy, but the work of Carl Jung and other so-called 'depth' psychologists was always tugging at my sleeve. After a few years of exploration, I stumbled upon the work of Israel Regardie and, shortly thereafter, Aleister Crowley and Thelema. I had finally found the solution to my spiritual dilemma. Here was a path of passion, devotion, mystery and transcendence; yet it was to be executed with scientific rigor and a healthy dose of skepticism. "The Method of Science, The Aim of Religion." Here I could unify the best parts of the divergent perspectives my parents had shown to me into a coherent whole, and forge a path uniquely my own. I immediately set about contacting all the Thelemic groups I could find in those pre-internet days, and in the fall of 1993 my journey into initiation formally began. I joined Ordo Templi Orientis, and I committed myself to the student path of A∴A∴.

Before long, I found myself in the position of assisting in the training of more junior initiates, reviewing their assignments, teaching and testing them on various magical techniques, and evaluating their diaries. I moved to California and began to work under the direct tutelage of Phyllis Seckler (Soror Meral). Within a few months, I had advanced to various administrative positions in the orders with which I was working, and was spending about as much time with my magical pursuits as my day job. I have seen several generations of students succeed and fail, and entire magical orders come and go. I have consulted with students on the mechanics of ritual, as well as the triumphs and tragedies of their personal lives. In writing this book, it is my hope that I can communicate the insights I've gained over the past twenty years, as I've witnessed the day-to-day strivings of modern magical aspirants. I have learned from experience what works and what doesn't, and the pitfalls that face seekers in our tradition.

I have designed this book to be a useful reference at every stage of the path. Once you've read the source materials from Crowley and others, you should be able to pick up this book and get valuable advice on how best to *execute* those source materials, whatever your level of experience. Beginning students can learn how to get the most out of basic rituals like *Liber Resh*, and how to understand concepts like the True Will; while intermediate and advanced magicians can get helpful advice on pursuing the deeper work of A∴A∴, and discover ways to enrich their existing practice with new perspectives on the foundational materials.

How to Use this Book

This book is not intended to be a comprehensive survey of all the concepts and practices of the Thelemic path of attainment. Rather, I have chosen those topics where I felt there was the greatest need for practical commentary, and where I could offer a unique perspective on the material. I certainly have no illusions that my take on all these topics is the best or the only way to think about them. Accordingly, I encourage you to approach everything in this book with your critical thinking skills fully engaged, and with an attitude of balanced skepticism.

I am assuming that the reader has a basic grounding in the fundamental principles and commonly used terms relevant to the Thelemic worldview. I am also assuming that you will have copies (printed or online) of the relevant source texts available. Rituals and other instructions will not usually be reprinted in full. Please refer to the multimedia resources available at **livingthelema.com** and the **Living Thelema YouTube channel** for demonstrations and additional instruction.

I have included performance notes and other comments concerning a few of the basic rituals you are likely to encounter in your magical path. While some minimal ritual outlines are provided, I have elected to emphasize the various experiential aspects of ritual performance rather than focusing primarily on the mechanics of the ritual. As with much of the rest of this book, my aim is to help you deepen your practice of these rituals, to give a greater context for their use, and to enhance the inner energetic patterns that make them come to life in your daily work. Even where I delve into theory, I have tried to emphasize how the theory can inform your practice, and help you understand the experiences likely awaiting you on your path.

There is no substitute for working with a competent personal teacher within a structured training system. A basic course of training within a well-run magical order will give you a solid, internally consistent foundation on which to build all your later work. The Temple of the Silver Star, Ordo Templi Orientis, and A∴A∴ are designed to accomplish such goals, and I encourage you to explore the training offered by these organizations using the contact information given at the end of this book.

If you belong to a magical order that teaches its own versions of the rituals and other practices discussed in this book, I suggest that you consult with your assigned teacher before incorporating any of this material into your daily practice. One of the benefits of being in such an order is the internal consistency of ritual practices, gestures, and symbol sets, and you shouldn't complicate your progress with clashing systems and practices.

Let's take a look at the different sections of the book, so you'll know what to expect. Each section approaches the Thelemic path of attainment from a slightly different vantage point.

Part One

In Part One, we will review some of the underlying principles of Thelemic attainment, and discuss an array of practical tools you can use as you progress in your path. Some of you may be relatively new to the concepts of Qabalah, so I have included an introductory essay on this topic as the first chapter. If you have a solid grounding in Qabalistic theory, you can safely skip this chapter and move on to the more advanced material beyond.

Included in Part One are practical discussions concerning many of the foundational ritual and meditative practices of Thelemic magick and mysticism, as well as a review of associated tools such as astral projection, devotional practices, and sexual magick. If you are new to magical practice, these chapters will give you plenty of material for months or years of experimentation. Experienced practitioners will, I hope, find their work refreshed with new perspectives on these tools. In keeping with my aim for this book, I have avoided undue emphasis on historical or philosophical details in favor of practical and experientially useful guidance.

Additional audio/visual materials, including demonstrations of some of the basic practices presented here as well as additional rituals, are available at livingthelema.com and the Living Thelema YouTube channel.

Part Two

In Part Two, we take a step back from the specific tools discussed in Part One, and focus on broader conceptualizations of the magical path itself. Here, we will discuss the path of attainment in light of the training methodologies of A∴A∴, the Trumps of the Tarot, the chakras, and a number of other symbolic templates that give unique perspectives on the path.

This section of the book will give you an opportunity to 'pull back the camera' a bit, so that you may better understand the transformative processes taking place within you as you progress in the Great Work. Special emphasis is given to various ways of understanding the path toward the Knowledge and Conversation of the Holy Guardian Angel, and the later ordeal of 'crossing the Abyss,' as these are the critical events in the magical career of any seeker.

Part Three

In the final section of the book, we will bring our discussion to a close with a review of various techniques and tools for managing the challenges of everyday life. To a great extent, these tools reflect an integration of my experiences as a Jungian and cognitive-behavioral therapist with the principles of magick. After twenty years of treating patients *and* training magicians, I think I have a few useful tricks up my sleeve!

Love is the law, love under will.

Sacramento, California
Summer Solstice, 2013 e.v.

Part One:

Tools for the Journey

1

An Introduction to the Qabalah

{A different version of this essay originally appeared in the Instructor's Manual of Fadiman and Frager's *Personality and Personal Growth*, an undergraduate psychology textbook. As such, it was designed to introduce the Qabalah to a lay audience with no prior exposure to the material, with an emphasis on practical application in a psychotherapeutic setting. While it does not utilize explicitly Thelemic terminology, it describes universal processes that form the foundation of Thelemic magical and mystical practice. It is included here as a basic introduction to Qabalistic concepts, particularly the psychological aspects of Qabalah which you may find especially useful as you progress. As it was written more than fifteen years ago, it does not reflect my most developed thinking on the matter, but I offer it here in the hope that it may be helpful for beginners.}

INTRODUCTION

The past few decades have seen the increasing acceptance of Eastern philosophies into the mainstream of Western thought and culture. The importance of this trend to the field of psychology has been passionately and effectively argued in the present textbook and elsewhere. While the text focuses specifically on the psychological aspects of Sufi, Buddhist, and Yoga traditions, the latter part of the 20th century saw yet another mystical system come into mainstream awareness: the Qabalah. The Qabalah expounds a remarkably rich and complex transpersonal psychology; a psychology which has much to offer this modern society in search of depth, meaning and purpose in life.

The Qabalah is the name for the mystical branch of the Jewish tradition. The word Qabalah itself is derived from the Hebrew linguistic root *kabal*, which literally means "to receive" (Kaplan, 1991). The Qabalistic goal was therefore to receive illumination and wisdom from the divine. Much of the Qabalistic teachings and methodology involved understanding this process of divine transmission and developing the spiritual capacity to retain and integrate the divine influx. This was accomplished through various practices designed to help create and strengthen a spiritual "receptacle," often referred to in Qabalistic literature as a *keli*—a spiritual vessel.

MAJOR CONCEPTS, STRUCTURE, AND DYNAMICS

The Qabalah simultaneously describes (a) the process of the divine creation of the universe, and the Mind of God, (b) the structure and function of the human psyche, and (c) the "Way of Return" which reunites the human psyche and soul with their divine source.

The Creation of the Universe

Qabalistic traditions describe the creation of the universe as a series of progressive emanations of deity. They originate in the great nothingness, *ain*, and gradually take the form of ten *sephiroth* (spheres), and the twenty-two paths that connect them. Together, the *sephiroth* and the connecting paths form the *etz chayim*, or Tree of Life—a map of all universal possibilities. The Tree of Life not only represents the process of creation—it is also a depiction of the "mind of God," and by coming into an understanding of its varied aspects, Qabalists believe they draw closer to divinity itself.

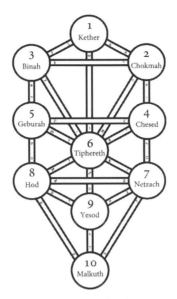

The Tree of Life

The ten *sephiroth* describe the process of universal creation through increasingly complex and diversified forms. They symbolize all possible states of being, and they form an all-inclusive catalog of the ideas and manifestations of the divine Mind. The paths, meanwhile, show the states of change and flux between these states of being. The process of creation moves down the Tree corresponding to the numerical order of the *sephiroth*. Although the ideas associated with the spheres and paths are extremely complex and far-reaching, the names of the *sephiroth* give a good indication of the basic concepts involved. These names and their English translations are given below.

1	Kether	Crown
2	Chokmah	Wisdom
3	Binah	Understanding
4	Chesed	Mercy
5	Geburah	Strength
6	Tiphereth	Beauty
7	Netzach	Victory
8	Hod	Splendor
9	Yesod	Foundation
10	Malkuth	Kingdom

Essentially, the progression from Kether to Malkuth involves the descent of the divine from the primal, singular point of Kether, through the archetypal realities associated with the spheres of Chokmah through

Yesod, and culminating in the physical, manifest universe at Malkuth. With each step downward, the divine becomes increasingly dense and multi-faceted, as it takes on the characteristics of each successive sephira.

> …imagine a ray of sunlight shining through a stained-glass window of ten different colors. The sunlight possesses no color at all but appears to change hue as it passes through the different colors of glass. Colored light radiates through the window. The light has not essentially changed, though so it seems to the viewer. Just so with the sefirot. The light that clothes itself in the vessels of the sefirot is the essence, like the ray of sunlight. That essence does not change color at all, neither judgment nor compassion, neither right nor left. Yet by emanating through the sefirot—the variegated stained glass— judgment or compassion prevails (Matt, 1994, p.38).

The Human Psyche

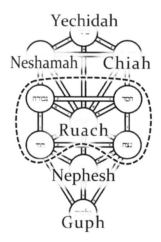

The Qabalistic 'Parts of the Soul' on the Tree of Life

The highest, most spiritual aspect of the psyche is known as *yechidah* (yeh-khee-dah). This is the essence of Spirit, and is our primary linkage to collective consciousness and universal energies. As such, it is akin to the Jungian concept of the Self. Much of the psychospiritual work in Qabalistic psychology is directed toward a conscious union of the "lower" aspects of ourselves with this inner spark of Spirit. On the Tree of Life, *yechidah* resides at Kether, the point from which all creation emanates. This parallel between the Source of universal creation, and the

Source of individual consciousness, is of paramount importance, as we will see in the discussion of the Way of Return below.

Emerging from *yechidah* are the complementary principles of *chiah* (khee-ah), the life-force and spiritual Will, and *neshamah* (neh-shah-mah), the receptive, intuitive faculty which gives shape and meaning to this life force. *Chiah* is assigned to the sephira of Chokmah, and *neshamah* to Binah. The *neshamah* is the spiritual intuition, the enlightening and awakening energy that descends from pure spirit to those who are ready to receive it. Stated in more conventional psychological terms: to promote psychospiritual growth, we must tap into the divine, intuitive wisdom of the Self by forging a link between it and our conscious ego.

The conscious mind is made up of a number of energies collectively known as the *ruach* (roo-akh), which literally means "breath," but implies the idea of the vital life force as well. Compare this with the Latin *spiritus*, Greek *pneuma*, Chinese *chi* and Sanskrit *prana*, all of which equate the breath with the life-force. The implication is that the mind, the *ruach*, is ever-flowing and full of life-energy, like the air we breathe. The *ruach* is analogous to the Jungian ego in its fullest sense— the totality of conscious self-awareness. Shaping the *ruach* into a fit vessel for the influx of spiritual insight from "above" is the characteristic work of a number of systems of transpersonal psychology as well as many mystical traditions. This is akin to the ego-Self linkage described above. As another metaphorical example of this process, consider the Sufi concept of being filled with the "wine" of God.

The *ruach* is composed of five sephiroth on the Tree of Life, each representing a specific component of human ego-consciousness. These components are summarized in the table below, along with the sephira to which they are attributed.

Memory	Chesed
Will	Geburah
Imagination	Tiphereth
Desire/Emotion	Netzach
Intellect	Hod

The Qabalah teaches that our subconscious, instinctual drives and energies reside in the *nephesh* (neh-fesh). The *nephesh* is associated with the sephira *Yesod*, and is very much like the Jungian personal unconscious, or the Freudian *id*. It is a wellspring of powerful energy, which must be examined, explored, and put to constructive use to avoid blockage, repression, obsession, and illness. That is, the *ruach* must be the master of these energies, and not the other way around. The vital, instinctual forces of the *nephesh* must be harnessed to constructive, conscious direction by the *ruach*, so they may be applied to the work of psychospiritual growth and balance. This process is not unlike that described in some yoga traditions, with their emphasis on utilizing the kundalini for personal transformation.

Finally, the human body itself is often called the *guph* (goof) in Qabalistic traditions. On the Tree of Life, the *guph* is placed at *Malkuth*. Not accidentally, the *guph* and the *nephesh* are adjacent, suggesting their intimately intertwined functions. That is, there are close connections between the autonomic nervous system, the instincts, the unconscious mind, and the entire human body. To the human being in his or her natural state, these bodily and instinctual aspects of self, and not the *ruach*, are the most directly receptive to spiritually informed intuitive insights. Accordingly, it is taught within some Qabalistic traditions that our spirit is more immediately and closely tied to our bodies, our instincts and our unconscious minds than to our conscious minds. It is only when we have progressed on the Way of Return that the link between the conscious *ruach* and the super-conscious *neshamah* is solidified.

The Way of Return

The Way of Return is the Qabalistic term describing the process of reuniting the incarnate human personality with its divine Source. Just as the universe (and each human being) was created in a "top down" process descending from Kether, so must each human seek to return to God in an upward path from Malkuth. This is an elegant and uniquely Qabalistic restatement of the mystical path common to all esoteric traditions. That is, by retracing the process through which we came into being, we may discover the divine nature within us, and transcend the limitations of physical existence.

The beginnings of the Way of Return may be visualized as the construction of a cup or similar vessel. The raw material of this cup is, of course, the human personality in its inert, unexalted state—the sheet metal from which the cup will be fashioned, if you will. Just as any cup's purpose is to contain a liquid, the purpose of the human personality is to become a literal container for the "liquid" of divine inspiration—that which the Sufis might describe as the wine of God. Yet we must fashion ourselves as a balanced, stable cup, with no holes and a sturdy base, if we are to be successful. Therefore, much of the psychospiritual work of the first steps on the Way of Return consists of equilibrating our personality, and eliminating those defects in "construction" which would hamper our receptivity to the divine.

Carl Jung believed we should strive for balance of the four functions of personality: thinking, feeling, sensation, and intuition. Similarly, the first four steps on the Way of Return—that is, the passage through the spheres of Malkuth, Yesod, Hod and Netzach—can be seen as an equilibration of the aspects of human existence to which they correspond. In the Hermetic Qabalah, these spheres are attributed to Earth, Air, Water and Fire, respectively. Psychologically speaking, these represent the faculties of sensation, common intuition, intellect, and emotion or desire, paralleling Jung's functions mentioned above. It is only when these aspects of the lower human personality are brought into balance that the vessel is prepared for the *conscious* influx of the divine light.

The fifth step on the Way of Return brings the Qabalist to the sphere of Tiphereth, at the center of the Tree of Life. This stage marks the literal dawning of the spiritual light, for indeed Tiphereth is the sphere attributed to the sun in Hermetic Qabalah. Having fashioned a suitable vessel, the Qabalist has in essence performed an invocation to the highest forces within himself or herself, inviting that divine light to take up residence in the formerly mundane human life. Another appropriate metaphor for this process is that of the lightning rod. If it is built correctly, its *very nature* is to bring forth the surge of electricity from above. Similarly, the equilibrated human psyche is a lightning rod for the divine presence. If correctly formed, it cannot help but bring forth spiritual enlightenment.

The Way of Return beyond Tiphereth is marked by a progressively more intimate relationship between the lower human personality and the divine. If the steps before Tiphereth were somewhat like a courtship, and the attainment of Tiphereth a wedding, then the remaining Way of Return can be likened to the ongoing marital relationship. The ultimate goal is to be wholly reunited with God at the sphere of Kether.

In the Hermetic Qabalah, tradition holds that this ongoing relationship between the personality and the divine brings all the benefits associated with psychological and spiritual growth: a sense of purpose and meaning, inner peace, harmony between the self and the world, and the ability to mobilize more fully our inner resources in service of our life goals, for the benefit of ourselves and humanity.

Gematria and the Esoteric Interpretation of Scripture

One important practice within Qabalistic traditions is the esoteric interpretation of scripture through the use of *gematria*, a means of translating any Hebrew word or phrase into a numerical value. This practice is rooted in the fact that the ancient Hebrew culture did not possess a separate number system; each letter of the Hebrew alphabet represented a particular number, and therefore any representation of numbers involved an alphabetic expression. Conversely, any word or phrase had an implied numerical value. By examining the numerical values of key words and phrases in scripture, Qabalists are able to extract relationships between concepts that otherwise would remain invisible. To give one simple example, the Hebrew words for "love" (*ehebah*) and "unity" (*achad*) both have the numerical value of 13. A Qabalist might therefore conclude that there is a particular esoteric relationship between these concepts, and this insight might allow for certain texts to be interpreted in ways far deeper than their surface meaning would suggest.

PRACTICAL APPLICATIONS

Even in a purely secular context, the Qabalah lends itself readily to an array of applications, including therapeutic and "self-help" interventions. Let us first examine applications in psychotherapy settings. As you will have noted from the discussion above, Qabalistic theory overlaps nicely with depth psychology approaches such as those of Freud and Jung. Furthermore, Qabalah's integrative psychospiritual perspective resonates well with modern transpersonal approaches such as those of Roberto Assagioli and others. A therapist well-versed in Qabalistic theory and practice will be able to use his or her understanding of the Way of Return, as it relates to the balancing of the personality and the search for meaning and purpose, to aid clients in need of guidance.

Furthermore, the sephirothic model of human consciousness, as well as the nature of the paths between the spheres, can guide the therapist in understanding the particular life transitions, challenges, and obstacles facing the client at any given time. For example, we have seen that the sphere of Hod is associated with the human intellect, and the sphere of Netzach with emotion. A therapist working with a client who seems to be overly intellectual might diagnose a need to increase the Netzach/emotional focus in the client's life. This might be accomplished by utilizing the many traditional characteristics of Netzach, such as the ideas of love, desire, and devotion, in the design of a meditative or ritual program. The client might be encouraged to meditate on the above ideas as they apply to his or her relationships, or to undertake a walking meditation through a place of beauty such as a garden or other natural setting. The possibilities for applications of this sort are only limited by the creativity and experience of the therapist.

It is important to note that while it may seem otherwise, the Qabalah is not a rigidly linear model. The tradition holds that in the course of human life, an individual will find themselves at various 'places' on the Tree of Life on many different occasions. For example, we do not experience the sphere of Hod only once as we ascend the Tree, but each and every time the intellectual aspect of our personality is activated. Furthermore, the processes of change represented by the paths between the spheres on the Tree appear as the various life challenges, obstacles, and opportunities for growth that confront us in any manner of ways throughout our lives. To give another example, the path connecting the spheres of Hod and Netzach is seen as a symbol of the challenge of balancing intellect and emotion. It is easy to see how such a challenge presents itself time and time again in our lives, and "traversing" this path is therefore a repeated and lifelong process. The therapist's task in such a case is to be sensitive to this ongoing flux in the client's growth process, and guide the client toward equilibrium and insight at every step of the way. The therapist is a guide and coach, but does not take responsibility for the client's own choices and actions. Rather, the therapist encourages the client to assume full responsibility for his or her own destiny. It is her task to make choices and create desired realities as her/his life path unfolds itself, bringing with it a sense of greater meaning and purpose.

Another application of the Qabalah is in a self-help context. As shown above, the model of the Tree of Life, with all its paths and spheres, is a complex and flexible symbolic system. Since each path and sphere embodies a certain quality or process, it is possible to develop a personal system of classification of life experiences based on the Tree. For example, a student of the Qabalah might wish to gain greater understanding of the workings of his or her personality. To accomplish this, s/he might begin a daily journal in which he monitors her/his daily experiences and classifies them according to the four lowest sephiroth on the Tree, which were shown above to roughly correspond to the four Jungian functions. So for each daily entry, he would record the extent to which the natures of Malkuth, Yesod, Hod, and Netzach were prominent in his experience that day. After a few days or weeks of this monitoring, it is likely that patterns, biases, overemphasized tendencies would become apparent, and corrective steps could be taken.

Another student might wish to gain insight into the higher principles of Mercy (Chesed) and Severity (Geburah) operative in her life. She or he would monitor outer and inner experiences and classify each as either expansive, peaceful and growth-promoting (Chesed), or as energetic, severe and seemingly restrictive (Geburah). Thus, s/he might gain a greater appreciation for the ebb and flow of these opposing forces not only in his or her own personality, but also in the life events that shape her experience each day. This type of practice, when pursued with brutal honesty and conscious intent, can potentially lead to even more exalted levels of consciousness—direct awareness the spiritual self within, of the nature of life, and of the interconnectedness of the universe as a whole. In other words, what begins as a psychological exploration may open the door to mystical experience itself.

Recommended Reading:

Epstein, P. (1988). *Qabalah: The Way of the Jewish Mystic.* Boston, MA: Shambhala Publishing.

Fortune, D. (1999). *The Mystical Qabalah.* York Beach, ME: Samuel Weiser, Inc.

Halevi, Z.B.S. (1994). *Psychology and Kabbalah.* York Beach, ME: Samuel Weiser, Inc.

Idel, M. (1990). *Kabbalah: New Perspectives.* New Haven, CT: Yale University Press.

Kaplan, A. (1985). *Meditation and Kabbalah.* York Beach, ME: Samuel Weiser, Inc.

Kaplan, A. (Ed.) (1990). *Sefer Yetzirah.* York Beach, ME: Samuel Weiser, Inc.

Kaplan, A. (1991). *Inner Space.* Abraham Sutton (Ed.) Brooklyn, NY: Moznaim Publishing.

Matt, D. (1994). *The Essential Kabbalah.* New York, NY: Harper Collins.

Regardie, I. (1992). *A Garden of Pomegranates.* St. Paul, MN: Llewellyn Publications.

Regardie, I. (1970). *The Middle Pillar.* St. Paul, MN: Llewellyn Publications.

Scholem, G. (1974). *Major Trends in Jewish Mysticism.* New York, NY: Schocken Books, Inc.

Seckler, P. (2012). *The Kabbalah, Magick, and Thelema. Selected Writings Volume II.* D. Shoemaker, G. Peters & R. Johnson (Eds.) York Beach, ME: The Teitan Press.

Seckler, P. (2010). *The Thoth Tarot, Astrology, & Other Selected Writings.* D. Shoemaker, G. Peters & R. Johnson (Eds.) York Beach, ME: The Teitan Press.

2

THE HOLY GUARDIAN ANGEL

The Holy Guardian Angel is Crowley's term for that force, aspect of consciousness, or external entity that many other traditions have spoken of as the Higher Self, the Augoeides, the Higher Genius, and innumerable other names. Crowley discussed the Holy Guardian Angel in different ways at various stages of his life, and with considerable variation depending on his audience and his intention. At some points, he described the Holy Guardian Angel as if it were synonymous with the Higher Self—an aspect of our own conscious or unconscious existence. At other times, he quite definitively characterized the Holy Guardian Angel as an external entity of some sort. For example, his experience with his own Holy Guardian Angel, Aiwass, was of such a quality during the dictation of *The Book of the Law*, that he perceived it as an external voice dictating to him. Given all of this, the HGA is one of the most difficult things for a magician to explain or discuss, so please bear with me as I attempt to use inevitably inadequate language to delve into these matters.

In the system of A∴A∴, from the very beginning, the path towards Knowledge and Conversation is of singular importance. All of the tasks in the A∴A∴ curriculum up to the Adeptus Minor grade are designed to be stepping stones towards Knowledge and Conversation. These tools come in several varieties: magical rituals, meditation, the gradual raising of the *kundalini* through various practices, devotional practices, and so on; but the important thing to note here is that all of these really are simply tools to be used to attain Knowledge and Conversation. After the K & C, when the knowledge of the True Will is consciously and deeply ingrained in our everyday living, we can choose to do a magical ritual and be assured that it is in line with our True Will. This is rarely the case before Knowledge and Conversation.

Unfortunately, this fact has often caused people to ignore basic training in ritual and other practices because they believe that they are not going to "get it right" until they've had Knowledge and Conversation. It is essential to remember that the only way we learn to do things is through experimentation. No one at the beginning of the path is going to have the level of insight into their tools, their methods, or their True Will that further attainments will bring. So start wherever you are, practice, make mistakes, learn from them…and write it all down in your diary!

Let's look at the building experience of the Holy Guardian Angel as it tends to manifest in the lives of aspirants. One of the most common misconceptions about the way this typically occurs is that there is no knowledge of the Holy Guardian Angel—no conscious connection—then one attains to the Adeptus Minor grade of A∴A∴ and in a single flash of light it's suddenly there. For most people I've supervised, as well as in my own path, that's not the way it tends to unfold. Generally, there is a gradually increasing intimacy of communication and understanding that begins far earlier on the path than Adeptus Minor. We feel the impulses and subtle urgings of the Angel in dreams, intuitive flashes, and synchronistic events. In those moments, when we seem to be receiving impulses from a deep level of consciousness or we have an abiding sense of the *rightness* of a certain choice, we are seeing a glimmer of the HGA. Likewise, our strivings for beauty in our lives, our drive to be enraptured in the things and the people we love—all of these are glimmers of the Angel as well.

There is communication with the HGA well before Adeptus Minor, to be sure, but it tends to come through our own unconscious mind, and in the language of symbol. Our experience of this is such that we may not sense a conscious communication at all for quite some time, but we gradually improve our ability to speak in the language of symbol. Hence, the requirement in A∴A∴ and other orders to memorize the various correspondences, for such symbols are in one sense the 'native tongue' of the Angel.

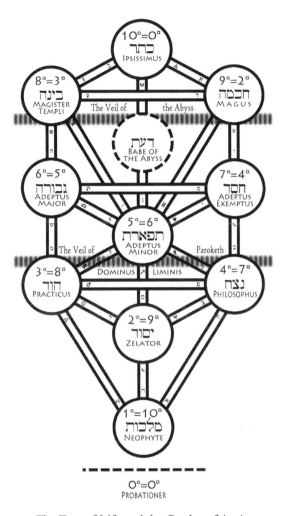

The Tree of Life and the Grades of A∴A∴

Eventually, we begin to perceive these communications in a much more direct and conscious manner. In the system of A∴A∴, the so-called Vision of the Holy Guardian Angel is attributed to Malkuth, which is the sephira of the Neophyte (1°=10□) grade. It is often in the Neophyte grade that aspirants begin to have more of these conscious communications, sometimes even the name of the Angel. It is a courtship —a gradually increasing and intensifying intimacy, a gradual improving of our ability to perceive the language of the HGA in our lives. Finally, at the Adeptus Minor (5°=6□) grade, the breakthrough of Briatic consciousness into our previously Yetzirah-bound mind forges a conscious link.

The defining characteristic of the adept is that he or she can communicate with the Angel consciously and at will. What is this process like? It is essentially the ability to differentiate that one voice of the HGA from all the other voices that speak to us in various ways in our lives. In many ways, it is like a radio receiver. Our conscious mind is the radio; we turn the dial trying to find that *one* particular station we're looking for. In the pre-adept stage of the work, we sweep the dial, searching somewhat blindly for the station. Occasionally we move past it and get a little snippet of the Angel's voice, but then we have trouble finding it again. The goal is to develop the ability to quickly, precisely and reliably tune in to that station, and keep it there.

Another metaphor may be useful here. As shown above, the sphere of Tiphereth represents the Adeptus Minor grade of the A∴A∴ where conscious communion with the Angel is attained. Tiphereth is like the head of the king, and Kether is the crown. The Great Work, quite simply, is all about getting your head in the right place—the receptive awareness of Tiphereth—so that the crown can be placed on your head. In other words, it is less about 'going somewhere' looking for the Angel and more about refining your awareness such that you are ready to receive what is *right there waiting for you.* Perhaps this is one way of understanding the import of *Liber LXV*, Cap. II, where we read, "to await Thee is the end, not the beginning."

Many aspirants find that the process of moving towards Knowledge and Conversation consists of successive layers of instruction in the *methods* of properly invoking the angel. You will very likely discover that everything you are, everything you have been, and everything you love and find beautiful, will be utilized as a tool in the invocation of your HGA. As you move through the grades of the A∴A∴ below Tiphereth, you will likely receive successive layers of instruction in how to hone and finely tune your ability to embark on the final invocation process.

As long as you are forging ahead with the great tasks, as long as you are enflaming yourself in prayer, invoking often, devoting yourself to pushing ahead on the path towards Knowledge and Conversation, you will undergo these successive layers of instruction from the HGA. You will get a name, an impulse to pursue a particular line of work, a mode of meditation, or other such tools. You may find that later on, you receive additional instruction that supersedes or completely overturns what was given to you before. That's the nature of this Work: as you refine your tools of reception, as you get better at tuning that radio dial, and finding that one voice, you will quite naturally cast aside some of the things that you've been given earlier. If you persist, you will refine your own tools to enable you to hear and recognize the voice of the Angel clearly, and at exactly the right time. In fact, such progress is *inevitable* if you follow the path as instructed.

While no one can tell you exactly what your path may bring, and how it may unfold, it is useful to ponder the experience of adepts who have walked similar roads. I'd like you to consider something my teacher Phyllis Seckler (Soror Meral) wrote late in her life about her own Holy Guardian Angel experience:

> The first stirrings of the angelic voice may come to us through intuition. If a person isn't open to relying on this deep intuition, it may not be evident that the Holy Guardian Angel can speak through the same voice. It is entirely possible to turn one's back on such whisperings and inspirations, especially when one's concerns are mostly materialistic, emotional, or intellectual. But the Holy Guardian Angel's lessons persist. If one becomes upset, unhappy, or miserable due to some behavior, it is certainly the Holy Guardian Angel dealing out tough love so that one will make changes. All of this I have observed in myself and when trying to understand others. It provides a preamble as I try to write of my own experiences with the Holy Guardian Angel.
>
> It was July 1, 1952 when my first acquaintance with the Holy Guardian Angel occurred. I was raising my three children alone. Once they were in school, I was also in college, training to become an art teacher. I had also been typing Crowley manuscripts for Karl Germer, so they would not become lost. I was awakened by a light up my spine. I could vaguely understand that instructions had been given to me for some time before my awakening. What I could remember of this was the name of the Holy Guardian Angel and his instructions to enumerate this name with the aid of the Hebrew alphabet. Understanding this name took quite a few years, but the voice never really left me after this incident. There have been many occasions when I have had help from the voice when it was obviously needed. One goes on living a normal life, working and doing all of the things to support oneself and one's children. The voice of the Holy Guardian Angel is not needed in everyday circumstances. One must go on refining one's self and one's reactions. One must study and learn about magical and mystical processes. The God will not indwell a vehicle poorly prepared, as the ultimate advice states. Once major lessons or ordeals were needed, they were supplied in order to continue this growth and refinement.
>
> Prior to this first awakening, I'd been writing poetry inspired by various sorts of love, shadowed forth by the major direction of my soul. Karl Germer thought that the Knowledge and Conversation of the Holy Guardian Angel happened in my case because I had pure aspiration. The event of the night, which I only too plainly described above, left me with such awe that I could scarcely speak of it without an inner

trembling. It was six months before I could even write of it to Karl. Yet he knew from the tenor of my letters that this event surely must have happened.[1]

In a letter dated July 7, 1952, Karl Germer (who was at the time the head of A∴A∴ and, with Jane Wolfe, one of Seckler's primary magical teachers) wrote to Seckler:

> Dear child, your questions go to the bottom of one of the deepest problems that has puzzled and troubled all initiated men and women in memorial, as you could find out from reading the records of the Saints, men or women, the great men of genius and so forth. I suppose it is the conflict with being human with the body of flesh and the fact that you have risen to or above Tiphereth, where the voice of the secret guide is gradually taking over and begins to speak to your soul.
> The 20th Aethyr, I think it is, initiates this phase. I'm a very poor teacher along these lines. I had this experience in 1927 but I am so dull and dumb. Have you seen my horoscope? If not, I'll send you the main data with so much earth weighing it down, but I paid no attention to the guide and its voice until, let me say 1947 or 1948. This may sound unbelievable to you, but then my case may be different. My connection with A.C. the man was so close and intimate, that I all the time thought that the impulses came from the man A.C. and thinking so, I obstructed. The moment the man died the interpretation changed. Do not follow me. Obstruction to the impulses and the voice has become second nature to me through so many years and I may have suffered from this obstruction badly, very badly and made my life miserable without need. Learn to follow the voice instantly without questioning unduly. I quote that old saying of mystics, 'perinde ac cadaver'.
> [...] the idea is that once one has heard the voice of the Holy Guardian Angel, one must learn to follow instantly, even to the perishing of the cadaver which is the mere body and the rational mind which reasons against it. I believe this is the hardest lesson to learn. I shall be happy if I can make one human's life happier for teaching the lesson, which I have too much failed to learn. As you progress in the typing of *Liber 418*, you will discover that the Holy Guardian Angel grows

---

[1] Seckler, P. (2010). *The Thoth Tarot, Astrology, & Other Selected Writings.* D. Shoemaker, G. Peters & R. Johnson (Eds.) York Beach, ME: The Teitan Press.

ever more and more. In other words, the path is unending. Your views and your understanding at this moment will not be the same as years hence. Do not think for one moment that A.C.'s conceptions about this problem were the same when he was 50 as at 70. Strive ever to more, and if thou art truly mine, etc.

All you can do is to remain in the intimacy of your Holy Guardian Angel. Train your finer senses and your soul to receive ever finer and subtler impulses. Sometimes, they appear or may appear atrocious as you grow. Never mind, your Holy Guardian Angel looks farther ahead than mortals can. The only danger is that there are other beings in this invisible universe who are sent to test or thwart your true path. That is where constant inflaming yourself in prayer is so important, by the method that your Holy Guardian Angel will indicate to you. Yes, one is alone in this task, it seems, as long as one does not fully realize the intimacy with ones constant companion. See *Liber 65*, Chapter 1. "There was a maiden and therein she forgot her sighing and loneliness." That particular verse in that form may apply to a special case, but it is universal in the general way.[2]

As I noted above, no one can tell you the particulars of *your* path, or predict the twists and turns that you will encounter as you walk it. But the system of A∴A∴ exists so that those a few paces ahead of us can light beacons for those who follow, as has occurred throughout the full span of human history. It is my hope that the words in this chapter may serve as one such beacon. May you attain to the Knowledge and Conversation of the Holy Guardian Angel!

---

[2] Seckler, P. (2010). *The Thoth Tarot, Astrology, & Other Selected Writings.* D. Shoemaker, G. Peters & R. Johnson (Eds.) York Beach, ME: The Teitan Press.

3

THE TRUE WILL

In this chapter, we'll explore what the True Will means in daily life, in magical practice, and in spiritual advancement. In doing so, we will unveil some of the mystery in the way the True Will actually unfolds in a human life—especially, of course, for someone trying to build their *conscious understanding* of the True Will, such as many of you reading this book.

I'm sure many of you have some basic familiarity with the term 'True Will,' but just in case, I want to define it here briefly. First of all, the 'will' in question is the same as the will implied by the word *thelema* itself, which is the Greek word for will. This is not the simple will of the ego or the whim of the personality. This is not merely "wanting something." It is a deeper level of life purpose, and the living out of that purpose in an individual lifetime and across multiple incarnations.

The True Will is the will of the deepest inmost Self—the core of who you really are as a spiritual being. Also, and importantly, it is an expression of the *universal* will, as particularized and expressed in your *individual* life. This is why, when we are living in accordance with our True Will, we find that much of the time the universe seems to open up a path right in front of us, as if in sympathy with our aims. Likewise, when we feel as though we are swimming upstream against life it is very often the case that we have veered a bit from the path of our True Will; or perhaps we're receiving a lesson from the HGA and/or the universe itself that is helping to nudge us back onto the path.

The understanding of the True Will is dramatically enhanced with the Knowledge and Conversation of the Holy Guardian Angel; but much like the ongoing intimacy of the courtship of adept and Angel as the adept moves across the grades of the first order of A∴A∴, the knowledge of the True Will unfolds in a progressive manner as we peel back the layers of our personality to discover what is at its core.

All too often, the True Will is erroneously conceptualized as a singular choice of a career or a single task to be accomplished in life. This is far too restrictive. The True Will is the essence of your Self. It encompasses you, your actions, your thoughts, your feelings, and your behaviors; and it pertains to the way you live, moment-to-moment, as well as the entire arc of your life itself—and even beyond one life into other incarnations. As you can see, it's really much, much more than a choice of career or a single task to complete. There is often, however, a great deal of *overlap* between the True Will and what one chooses to spend one's time doing in life—one's occupation or favorite hobbies, for example.

The True Will is very likely to overlap with your passions, your interests and your preferences, but not always. On the other hand, we've established that this is not the simple will of the ego-personality (or, in the terms of Qabalistic psychology, the *ruach*.) Sometimes we find that our True Will—which ideally our ego is here to facilitate—is not necessarily something that is going to be comfortable and perfectly harmonious with the ego's conceptions of itself. You may find yourself, at times, feeling surprised by what you discover about your True Will. But even more frequently, you may find that the discovery of the True Will forces you to make painful choices about lifestyle, priorities, career, relationships, and many other things. Such growth processes are painful precisely *because* they make us stretch outside our comfort zone; but in this case, it's all in service of making these egoic choices in our day-to-day lives harmonize with the deeper needs of our soul and the commandments of the HGA. Yes, stretching hurts, but if we can come to experience this pain as a marker of deep growth, we may come to a greater sense of peace about the process. Just as physical pain points us to the area in need of healing, so does this psychological pain inform us about areas in need of growth.

As I said earlier, the True Will should equally explain your choices in any given moment, and in any given situation, just as well as it explains the overall path that you take in your life. When you contemplate your True Will, you should try to take a step back from your everyday circumstances, career and life choices and think about it this way: the True Will will explain the way you affect the universe, the choices you

22

make and the paths you tend to take, whether you happen to be a stock broker in New York City, a fisherman in Malaysia, or anything else. In other words, this central truth of who you are will express itself in a certain way regardless of the mundane situation in which you find yourself—your place of birth, occupation, family situation, and so on.

Much of the time, the discovery of the True Will is a slow and gradual process, occasionally punctuated by breakthroughs of insight. For example, you may have been reflecting on your life choices over the past several years and discover that there has been a certain trend that had escaped your notice at the time; but then, in looking back on it, you gain some insight into the True Will. In contrast, there are those moments when you'll simply be stopped in your tracks when a realization appears as an instantaneous flash, causing you to laugh or cry (or both) with the clarity of the insight.

The process is incredibly individualized, and no two seekers will experience its peaks and valleys in the same way. To put it somewhat poetically: Think of yourself as the prophet of your own Angel—as the high priest or priestess of a religion you are developing that is yours alone. The aim of that religion is to deepen, intensify, and delineate with ever-increasing clarity the mystical and magical procedures that effectively invoke your Holy Guardian Angel.

The development of this religion is essentially the work of the aspirant in the pre-Adeptus Minor stage of the work of A∴A∴. Your body and mind are the vessel in which your Angel abides. The purpose of this vessel is to live out the True Will, which is the voice of your Angel in your everyday life. Many find that the name of the Angel itself reveals a certain formula that is one very important key to the True Will. This name, perhaps by the arrangement of the letters, perhaps by some other associations that you develop over time, is a road map of sorts to the right living of your life.

As I mentioned earlier, the understanding of the True Will takes a quantum leap forward with the Knowledge and Conversation of the Holy Guardian Angel, which occurs at the Adeptus Minor grade of A∴A∴ corresponding to the sphere of Tiphereth. This stage represents the breakthrough of Briatic consciousness into the Yetziratic ego-mind. With this attainment, the supernal realm of the *neshamah*—the spiritual intuition and the voice of the Angel itself—becomes apprehensible to the *ruach* for the first time. The adept's awareness of the Angel's voice is no longer limited to the symbolic language of the nepheshic subconscious; rather, he or she can receive the instruction of the Angel directly into the conscious mind.

Let's review a few practical tools you can use to enhance your understanding of the True Will. In some ways, these are almost like mental games to play with yourself as you examine your life and attempt to get a grasp of the Will. Ask yourself these questions: How do you change a room when you walk into it? What affect do you have on the world around you and on the people in your world? There is something unique about you that will tend to affect the world in fairly predictable ways. Throughout your life, embodied in your moment-to-moment choices, there is some quintessential "you-ness" that impacts the world around you—an energetic *signature* which you leave wherever you go. For example, when you walk into a party, the people in the room are impacted in a certain way because it was *you* specifically that walked in. What is the specific nature of that impact? Alternatively, think about yourself as a force of nature: wind blows, water flows, fire burns, and acid corrodes. What is it that *you* do to the world?

Ask people who know you fairly well about your strengths and weaknesses. What are your talents in their view? Ask a friend. Ask an enemy. Ultimately, anyone else's opinion of you or your True Will doesn't matter a fraction as much as your own—but you'll get some really interesting feedback this way; and if nothing else, it's certainly an entertaining exercise!

Another one of my favorite techniques involves looking at your life retrospectively as a story or myth. What myth are you living out? One of the ways to examine this is to divide your life into, say, five year segments from age five onward. Next, reflect on what your passions were during each particular phase of life. Let's say you're looking at age five to age ten. What were your favorite books, movies, heroes, or songs? Repeat this process for each five year span and then try to abstract the broader themes. What sorts of stories have tended to capture you? Slaying dragons? Or perhaps solving mysteries? What was the *nature* of the heroes that captivated you when you were younger? Did you identify with the wizard or the warrior? The prodigal son, or the wandering hermit? And so on.

Looking across your entire lifetime, you may see these themes develop. Consider the following list of Georges Polti's "36 Dramatic Situations." Polti developed this list to aid writers, but you may find it interesting to look through the different stories he identifies and see if you can spot a few that have relevance to your life. This will not necessarily be synonymous with the True Will by any means, but it may give you some powerful clues. In some cases, the 'story' best matching the course of your life will reflect those obstacles in your personality that have actually *limited* your ability to tap into True Will. This information is no less useful! When you understand the ways in which your ego traps or blinds you, you have a powerful tool for seeing past such blockages and perceiving the reality of the Will.

The 36 Dramatic Situations[3]

1. Supplication (in which the Supplicant must beg something from Power in authority)
2. Deliverance
3. Crime Pursued by Vengeance
4. Vengeance taken for kindred upon kindred
5. Pursuit
6. Disaster
7. Falling Prey to Cruelty of Misfortune
8. Revolt
9. Daring Enterprise
10. Abduction
11. The Enigma (temptation or a riddle)
12. Obtaining
13. Enmity of Kinsmen
14. Rivalry of Kinsmen
15. Murderous Adultery
16. Madness
17. Fatal Imprudence
18. Involuntary Crimes of Love (example: discovery that one has married one's mother, sister, etc.)
19. Slaying of a Kinsman Unrecognized
20. Self-Sacrificing for an Ideal
21. Self-Sacrifice for Kindred
22. All Sacrificed for Passion
23. Necessity of Sacrificing Loved Ones
24. Rivalry of Superior and Inferior
25. Adultery
26. Crimes of Love
27. Discovery of the Dishonor of a Loved One
28. Obstacles to Love
29. An Enemy Loved
30. Ambition
31. Conflict with a God
32. Mistaken Jealousy
33. Erroneous Judgment
34. Remorse
35. Recovery of a Lost One
36. Loss of Loved Ones

---

[3] Polti, G. (1921). *The Thirty-Six Dramatic Situations*. Franklin, OH: James Knapp Reeve., p. 3.

Many aspirants will arrive at a place of certainty about their True Will, yet when they proclaim this discovery to a friend or family member, it hits with a resounding thud. Why? Because it is something that has seemed perfectly obvious to everyone but them! Naturally, your own insight into your True Will is going to be much more complex and intricate than what someone else will be able to tell you; but don't be surprised if you come to a sense of clarity about your True Will and it is much less impressive to everyone else than it is to you!

Regardless of the particular twists and turns of your path, I am sure you will find the journey toward understanding the True Will one of the most beguiling, fascinating, frustrating, but ultimately satisfying tasks you will ever undertake.

Recommended Reading:

Hillman, J. (1996). *The Soul's Code: In Search of Character and Calling.* New York, NY: Random House.

Palmer, P. (2000). *Let Your Life Speak: Listening for the Voice of Vocation.* San Francisco, CA: Jossey-Bass, Inc.

4

GETTING STARTED WITH
A BASIC MAGICAL REGIMEN

I realize that many of you likely began your own daily magical practice long ago. Nevertheless, it is useful to give an overview of the practices available to the beginner and to discuss the reasons why you might choose one practice over another. In other words, what are your training goals? What specific skills are you trying to build as a beginning magician, and how might these aims guide your choice of practices to undertake? For many aspiring magicians, the goal can be summed up as follows: "Be an incredibly powerful magician!" Unfortunately, a goal this vague may not be the most useful way of getting started with *any* endeavor. The advice I give in this chapter assumes that you are not already working in a magical order that has assigned (not merely recommended) specific tasks and practices. If you *are* working in such an order, then you should consult with your teacher before altering your training program in the ways I suggest here.

Here are the training goals that I believe are most essential for the beginning and intermediate magician.

1.You need a set of practices that will ensure magical 'hygiene'—the magical equivalent of brushing your teeth. You need to be able to cleanse and strengthen your energy system; to undertake what we might traditionally call fortifying the aura, or charging the body of light.

2.You need to build your ability to call forth magical force, and to healthfully tolerate this force in ever-increasing levels of intensity. Furthermore, you need to strengthen your ability to *direct* the magical force toward any desired aim.

3.You need to have the basics of yoga in your practice; specifically, asana (posture) and dharana (concentration). These practices will aid in focusing the mind. If you haven't developed the requisite level of mental control *outside* of a ritual context, you're certainly not going to suddenly gain the ability to focus your mind appropriately when you're in a magical ritual; and you're unlikely to be able to direct the force to the desired aim.

4.You need to begin internalizing symbol systems, such as the Qabalistic Tree of Life as a model for your psyche. To do this, you must begin memorizing the correspondences related to the sephiroth and the paths on the Tree of Life, as found in *777* and elsewhere (see *Liber O* for a list of correspondences to get you started). Ultimately, the goal is to build these symbol systems into your daily work so that you truly live and breathe them, and so you can call upon them with precision and power when constructing and executing a magical ritual.

5.You need to develop the discipline of the magical diary. Frankly, this is just an extension of the self-discipline that's required for all the above tasks; but the diary in particular is so fundamental and so important in terms of your future work that you simply *must* be diligent in its practice right from the outset of your magical career. Get into the daily rhythm of writing in your diary, no matter what!

6.Last, but certainly not least, your basic training in magick should begin to forge a conscious link to the Holy Guardian Angel through enflaming yourself in prayer, however you may define it. The exact form is unimportant. The HGA itself will gradually reveal all the specifics you need. The real key is in the enflaming. To this end, every magician should include some sort of devotional and aspirational practices in his or her daily regimen.

Now, let's take a look at how you're going to achieve these goals, by walking through the different phases of your training and reviewing how these goals might unfold. For the purposes of this discussion, I have divided the basic training into four phases. Some of these may be as brief as a few weeks or less, and some may take months or much longer; but even by phase four this is still just basic work. These steps will get you started, but there's a lifetime of work to explore!

Phase One

In Phase One, you're brand new to magical practice. The most fundamental and important practice of all is your ability to let go of outside distractions and relax your body. Admittedly, it is not very exciting to aspiring magicians when they are told that their first course of training is simply to relax; but believe me, if you can't control your level of bodily arousal, how can you possibly expect to control the far more subtle components of your nature? I can't emphasize this point strongly enough.

So, in Phase One, you're going to start every practice session by simply sitting quietly for a few minutes and letting go of any cares and concerns of the outer world. Simply *be* in your body and in your temple. Once you've settled into a comfortable posture, perhaps one of the asanas illustrated in *Liber E* or elsewhere, you will begin to work with some form of breathing practice. This is done not only to deepen the relaxation, but also to form the basic foundations of pranayama practice that may come later.

Israel Regardie suggests a 'fourfold' breathing pattern, where you have an evenly spaced breathing pattern of in, hold, out, hold—just for a few seconds each direction. Simply witness the breath, making it regular and rhythmic. At this stage, don't worry about breathing slowly or deeply. Just breathe at a natural rate and depth, and focus on getting that air to the diaphragm and getting into a regular pattern. Learning to regularize the breathing in this way enhances your ability to control the energy residing in the breath—an essential skill for any success in magick (you'll read much more about this in the chapter on asana and pranayama).

Also in Phase One, I suggest you memorize and begin working with *Liber Resh vel Helios* (see Chapter 7) and begin the practice of saying Will at meals. And that's it for Phase One. No pentagram rituals, no evocations of cool-looking Goetic demons—nothing fancy. Just relaxation, fourfold breathing, *Liber Resh*, and Will, for *at least* several weeks. Do your practices at least six days per week, and record everything meticulously in your magical diary.

Again, I recognize that this will likely be a bit anticlimactic to someone who's excited to get started with magick; but I assure you, what you're doing right now – psychologically, magically, and physically—will form the foundation for every single thing you will *ever* do in your magical career, so please don't attempt any short cuts! (Besides, if you jump ahead to more advanced practices without forming a strong foundation in the basics, you'll ultimately just slow yourself down, because you'll have to come back later to correct the gaps and imbalances. Hardly a 'short cut'!) After at least a few weeks of Phase One, you're ready to move on to Phase Two.

Phase Two
At this point, I suggest that you add the Lesser Ritual of the Pentagram in both its Banishing and Invoking forms (see Chapter 5). You may also wish to experiment with the ritual of the Star Ruby.

The reason you should work with both the invoking *and* banishing forms of the LRP is that the banishing form will help with magical cleansing, while the invoking form is very effective in building your tolerance for magical force, and your ability to call it forth and control it. Both forms of the ritual help you build the skill of visualization—the visualizations of the archangels and the drawing of the pentagrams, for example.

All of the ritual practices discussed so far will help you begin to internalize the symbol systems most relevant to the Thelemic magician, such as the pantheon of Nuit, Hadit, and Ra-Hoor-Khuit, the Hebrew hierarchies, the elemental archangels and so on. For example, you will learn to associate the elemental quarters with the subjective experience of those specific types of energy, thereby building your own inner energetic 'language'—an essential tool for any magician.

Also in Phase Two, you might wish to add some formal *asana* (posture) and *dharana* (concentration) practices (see Chapter 9). Pick any posture, and sit still in that posture while you begin basic dharana practices. At this stage, I suggest a simple visual focus, such as *tejas* (a red, upward-pointing equilateral triangle). Simply hold the visualization as best you can and count the breaks in concentration. As always, keep good diary records of the conditions and results of these experiments.

Stay in Phase Two for at least a month. As before, you should always feel free to extend this period. When you are ready, move to Phase Three.

Phase Three
At this stage I suggest that you add some form of the Middle Pillar exercise as described by Regardie, including the circulations. In my experience, practices such as the Middle Pillar increase ability to call forth, contain, and tolerate magical force. Furthermore, since this practice utilizes the divine names associated with certain sephiroth (seen at the various energy centers of the body) you will reinforce these important correspondences. Finally, and most importantly, the Middle Pillar practice gives you another opportunity to enflame yourself in aspiration to the divine.

While the pentagram ritual certainly offers opportunities for enflaming yourself in prayer, such as experiencing the awe of an encounter with an archangel, or the feeling and visualization of the pentagram flaming about you and the hexagram at your heart, the Middle Pillar gives you an important new key: the visualization of the Crown center as a sphere above your head. You can aspire forcefully to that center as a symbol of Kether—the light of your Holy Guardian Angel itself—thereby strengthening the muscles of aspiration to the most sublime energies of which you can conceive. The practice thus becomes a true aspirational and devotional exercise, ideally performed daily, empowering everything else you do. Later, having trained yourself in this manner, you will be able to use the Middle Pillar ritual *within* the structure of a larger working as a general invocation, any time you need an influx of power to fuel your ritual (see Chapter 8).

Also in Phase Three, I suggest that you begin various meditations on the sephiroth and the paths below Tiphereth. Refer to the material toward the end of *The Book of Thoth* for suggestive themes and phrases associated with the 22 paths. The point here is to intensify your work with the correspondences, most relevant to the work ahead you as you 'climb the Tree' along these paths. The better acquainted you are with the terrain, the more effective and empowering your exploration will be. Spend at least six months in Phase Three, and then move on to Phase Four.

Phase Four

Here, I suggest that you add the Lesser Ritual of the Hexagram (see Chapter 6). In many Golden Dawn-derived systems, the hexagram ritual is undertaken at the Second Order level, *after* the initiate has symbolically traversed the sephiroth and paths below Tiphereth. This is why I suggested in Phase Three that you focus your meditations on these sephiroth and paths—so that you can bring a greater sense of meaning and relevance to the hexagram ritual when you actually begin practicing it. Those of you who are working in a Golden Dawn-patterned order (such as the Temple of the Silver Star) will be at an advantage here; but if not, you can replicate that for yourself to some extent by aligning yourself with the sub-Tiphereth regions before moving on to work with the hexagram ritual.

You may wish to experiment with the ritual of the Star Sapphire as an alternate form of hexagram ritual, but remember that the Star Sapphire has no banishing form, and in my experience it brings in a much more exalted level of force than the 'classic' Lesser Ritual of the Hexagram. It should, therefore, be used mindfully and judiciously when a more intense degree of magical force is required.

Additional Recommended Practices

The Eucharist

In *Magick in Theory and Practice*, Cap. 20, Crowley writes:

> Of the Eucharist and of the Art of Alchemy. One of the simplest and most completive magical ceremonies is the Eucharist. It consists in taking common things, transmuting them into things divine and consuming them. So far, it is a type of every magic ceremony for the reabsorption of the force is a kind of consumption but it has a more restricted application as follows: Take a substance, symbolic of the whole course of nature, make it God and consume it. [...]

> The circle and other furniture of the temple should receive the usual benefit of the banishings and consecrations. The oath should be taken and the invocations made. When the divine force manifests in the elements, they should be solemnly consumed. [...]

> A Eucharist of some sort should most assuredly be consummated daily by every magician and he should regard it as the main sustenance of his magical life. It is of more importance than any other magical ceremony because it is a complete circle. The whole of the force expended is completely reabsorbed. If the virtue is that vast gain represented by the abyss between man and God, the magician becomes filled with God, fed upon God, intoxicated with God. Little by little his body will become purified by the internal lustration of God. Day-by-day his mortal frame shedding its earthly elements will become in very truth the temple of the holy ghost. Day-by-day matter is replaced by spirit, the human by the divine. Ultimately the change will be complete. God manifest in flesh will be his name. This is the most important of all magical secrets that ever were, or are, or can be. To a magician thus renewed the attainment of the knowledge and conversation of the Holy Guardian Angel (HGA), becomes an inevitable task. Every force of his nature, unhindered tends to that aim and goal of whose nature neither man nor God may speak for that it is infinitely beyond speech,

or thought, or ecstasy, or silence. Samadhi and the Guna are but its shadows cast upon the universe.[4]

There is really no limit to the ways you can integrate eucharists into your daily magical work, but let me give a couple of examples. One approach is to extract a personal 'ritual of two elements' from *Liber XV*, the Gnostic Mass. If you consider the structure of the Mass, it's not hard to see how you might be able to turn this into a ritual you could use on your own, or perhaps with a partner. Start with Section VI, the consecration of the elements. With your wine and host handy, move through the procedures of consecrating the elements, invoking the divine force, locking it into the elements, combining them and consuming them (see Sections VI-VIII).

Much as in the Gnostic Mass itself, there is an opportunity here to use visualization and other inner work to amplify the magical benefit of performing this ceremony, or other similar personal rites. Hold in mind a specific magical goal throughout the ritual process: the building of intensity, the consecration of the elements, the invocation of the force, and finally the climactic uniting of the elements, and their consumption. When you consume the eucharist, be mindful of the fact that you now *embody* the magical goal. You are like a computer that is ready to be programmed with the right software. The software that you have created is the mental form of the desired magical goal; it's the program you are giving to your 'new self' to run. The more intensely and vividly you can visualize the desired outcome, the more effective it will be. Make it as vivid as possible in terms of the psychological realities of the desired outcome—the way you will feel and think about yourself, and the way your life itself will take shape when you have attained the outcome. The more you make that goal 'come alive' within you, the more magical momentum you will bring to the ritual.

Mindfulness Practices

Some mindfulness practices appear in the core curriculum of A∴A∴, such as *Liber Jugorum*, and *Liber Resh* (which is a mindfulness practice inasmuch as one must remember to perform the four daily adorations). The practice of Will at meals is another common example. Here, you are bringing your attention to the fact that the consumption of food fortifies

---

[4] Crowley, A. (1997). *Magick: Liber ABA*. Hymenaeus Beta (Ed.). York Beach, ME: Samuel Weiser, Inc.

your body for the performance of the Great Work. This sort of mindfulness is hardly limited to mealtime—you can extend this concept to *any* task. Anything that you are doing during the day can and should be recognized as a contribution to the execution of your Great Work and your True Will. To take an everyday example: "It is my will to get into the car and drive to work, so that I may earn money, so that I may have shelter and free time in order to pursue the Great Work." And so on.

If, for any specific behavior, you find that you are having difficulty explaining to yourself why the behavior is in service to your will, you may need to rethink your priorities and your time management in this regard! Naturally, not every individual behavior in your daily life will be experienced as important, willful and magical. However, to the extent that you can maintain mindfulness of your entire life as a structure within which you strive to attain that universal goal of all who begin the path of the Great Work—the K & C of the HGA—you will cultivate an ability to *feel* will in action, even in the smallest choices and behaviors.

Another useful practice is to maintain mindfulness of yourself as a balanced microcosm, and one method of doing this is to strive to *embody the pentagram* each day; that is, to live each day, to the extent possible, as a balanced expression of the four elements and spirit. Make a daily diary entry where you record your success at living out each of the elements fully in your life. You can use a code to simplify this: S is spirit, F is fire, W is water, A is air and E is earth. At the end of each day, simply write those five letters and then a number from 1-10 to indicate how successfully you embodied that aspect of self. I'm using the sephirothic attributions of the elements here, but you can define them and arrange them however you like. For earth, how well did you take care of your body that day? For air, how well did you attend to the aspects of your subconscious through dreams and awareness of intuitive impulses, and monitoring of your psychological projections? For water, how well were you functioning intellectually? For fire, how did you do in terms of devotion to your magical goals, and aspiration to the HGA? For spirit, how receptive were you to the light of spirit manifesting in your life? As with many such self-monitoring practices, the mere act of *watching* these aspects of our lives will tend to push us toward healthier choices and more balanced living in this regard.

Breath Awareness

Various pranayama techniques may take on elements of mindfulness as well. For example, the simple process of breath awareness is very powerful when done mindfully and diligently. The practice called *mahasatipatthana* begins with a simple, silent, mantra-like observance as you breathe: "The breath is moving in; the breath is moving out." With repeated practice, you will find that your awareness has actually shifted; you realize that it is more accurate to say that you are aware of a *sensation* of the passage of air, and you adjust your mantra accordingly, i.e. "There is a sensation that the breath is moving in…" With further practice you become aware that it is really a *perception* of a sensation that the breath is moving in and out, then a *tendency* to perceive a sensation, and so on. The deeper purpose of this practice is to dis-identify with the ego as the center of consciousness, gradually refocusing your everyday experience on the *real* center of who you are—the divine star within, the khabs. By backing away, step-by-step, from the habitual ego-based center of consciousness, you become aware of entirely new vantage points from which to view your reality.

General Recommendations

So those are the four phrases of our 'basic training.' Now, let's review some general recommendations that will be broadly useful regardless of your stage of training. Firstly, *rhythm* and *regularity* is very important in daily work. As I've noted elsewhere, rhythm is one of the natural languages of the unconscious. If you can begin to prove to your unconscious that you are committed to 'tuning in' to its language on a consistent basis each day, your whole spiritual system will tend to get into 'sync.' This is much more difficult if you're doing practices at random times, skipping days, and engaging in other similarly sloppy behaviors.

Secondly, I suggest six days a week of practice, with vigilant diarizing. Take the seventh day off. Don't set yourself up for failure by setting unrealistic goals at the beginning, such as doing four hours of ritual, seven days a week, and so on. That would be far too strenuous and unrealistic for a beginner. Plan for six days a week of practice, following the gradually building curriculum that I've described here. That said, everybody is going to mess up and have days where they simply don't do anything. In such cases, it is far better to have a diary entry for that day that simply says, "I didn't do my work today," "I got distracted," or "My pet goat ate my pantacle" rather than nothing at all. Don't apologize for it or beat yourself up about it, but *do* record it!

You might wish to review diaries from the Thelemic tradition to get an idea for what to include in your record-keeping. Some of the best include *John St. John* (Crowley), and *A Master of the Temple* (Frater Achad), as well as Jane Wolfe's diaries from the Abbey of Thelema in Cefalu, Sicily. All of these provide interesting insights into the content, tone, and scope of a well-done magical diary.

Thirdly, you may wish to consider keeping your diary electronically. There is, of course, great beauty in a nicely bound journal. On the other hand, an electronic diary makes it much easier to search for certain passages and keywords. There may be times when one might wish to retrieve and collate all the diary entries pertaining to a series of practices which spread out intermittently across many weeks or months. For example, some years ago I undertook a series of scryings of the thirty Enochian Aethyrs and I wanted to extract those into a separate document. My electronic diary made quick work of this.

Fourthly, I suggest that you make your diary entry as soon as possible after concluding your work, and preferably in the same space where the work occurred. You will surely retain more vivid details of your magical or meditative results if you record them immediately, before you've had a chance to go eat pizza, pet the cat, and talk to your roommate.

Finally, and quite importantly, please remember (especially at this early stage!) that fear is never helpful; nor is beating yourself up for what you did or didn't do. Don't be afraid to experiment—to learn from trial and error. When you fall down, pick yourself back up and keep going. The only real failure is the failure to *persevere.*

Recommended Reading:

Crowley, A. (2006). John St. John. In J. Wasserman (Ed.), *Aleister Crowley and the Practice of the Magical Diary.* York Beach, ME: Red Wheel Weiser.

Crowley, A. (1992). Liber E. In I. Regardie (Ed.), *Gems from the Equinox.* Scottsdale, AZ: New Falcon Publications.

Crowley, A. (1992). Liber O. In I. Regardie (Ed.), *Gems from the Equinox.* Scottsdale, AZ: New Falcon Publications.

Crowley, A. (1997). *Magick: Liber ABA.* Hymenaeus Beta (Ed.). York Beach, ME: Samuel Weiser, Inc.

Crowley, A. (1993). *The Book of Lies.* York Beach, ME: Samuel Weiser, Inc. [Particularly the chapters on the rituals of the Star Ruby and Star Sapphire]

Frater Achad. (2006). A Master of the Temple. In J. Wasserman (Ed.), *Aleister Crowley and the Practice of the Magical Diary.* York Beach, ME: Red Wheel Weiser.

Wolfe, J. (2008). *Jane Wolfe: The Cefalu Diaries: 1920-1923.* D. Shoemaker (Ed.). Sacramento, CA: College of Thelema of Northern California.

5

THE LESSER RITUAL OF THE PENTAGRAM

The Lesser Ritual of the Pentagram (LRP) should be the foundation of any magician's ritual practice. In spite of its origins prior to the Aeon of Horus, Crowley recommended its performance twice a day, to the end of his life. Likewise, many teachers and magical orders include it in their basic curricula.

What is the effect of the ritual? Ultimately, you will have to answer that question for yourself through daily practice, taking careful note of other factors that may be influencing the effect of the ritual. That said, the effects generally fall into a few basic categories. The LRP tends to clear the physical, psychological and magical 'space' of the magician. It is also an invocation of the four archangels traditionally attributed to the four elements and the four quarters. Many people use the LRP as their daily 'hygienic' practice, as it includes the cleansing effect of the banishing form of the ritual as well as the energizing and sanctifying effect of the invoking form. In addition to this hygienic function, the banishing form is often used to prepare the temple for elemental invocations, or as a general banishing prior to other work (see Chapter 8 for more on ritual construction methods).

It is important to note that while the LRP uses the 'earth' form of the pentagram, the purpose of the basic ritual is not specifically to banish or invoke earth as an element. Rather, as noted above, it is used as a generic cleansing and space preparation. There would be differences in intention and in some performance details if you were doing a specific invocation or banishing of earth (or any other specific element). The Greater Ritual of the Pentagram (see *Liber O*) may also be adapted for such purposes. The Temple of the Silver Star has its own distinctive method of approaching specific elemental invocations and banishings, and other magical orders have constructed techniques along similar lines in the many years since this material was originally developed.

As will be explained below, the version of the ritual presented here varies slightly from what you will find in *Liber O* or other published sources. As with many rituals, begin by relaxing and regularizing the breath. When you are ready to begin the ritual, you should move to the center of the room where you may have an altar set up. On the altar should be, minimally, your magical implement of choice. This might be a Geburah-keyed dagger or sword, or any other dagger or wand; or you can simply use your finger as a ritual 'implement.'

The ritual begins with a set of gestures and words called the *Qabalistic Cross*:

1. Touching your forehead with your right forefinger, intone: **ATAH.**
2. Touching your heart, intone: **AIWASS.**
3. Touching your genitals, intone: **MALKUTH.**
4. Touching your right shoulder, intone: **VE-GEBURAH.**
5. Touching your left shoulder, intone: **VE-GEDULAH.**
6. Clasp your hands upon your breast, then intone: **LE-OLAHM. AMEN.**

When you learn the name of your own HGA, you should replace 'Aiwass' with that name. Some magicians have objected that since Aiwass was Crowley's HGA, we shouldn't use that name in our own practice. While that would be a reasonable objection under most circumstances, keep in mind that Aiwass was not only Crowley's HGA, but also the very intelligence that inaugurated the Aeon of Horus. Accordingly, by intoning 'Aiwass' at the heart, you link yourself to the energies of the Aeon itself.

The key to the successful performance of the Qabalistic Cross is a quiet intensity of vibration and energy flow at each of the body areas touched. You should feel the force moving with your hand as you physically move from point to point. Each time you vibrate a word or phrase, you should feel the energy intensify at the point of the body where you are touching. Also, as with any such vibration, you should conceive that the word is echoing to the far reaches of the universe, and the universe itself is resonating in sympathy with your will. Each of the words should be vibrated on a full exhalation; that is, you take a full in-breath and then on the exhalation the word is vibrated with approximately equal time and emphasis on each letter of the word. The last syllable will sometimes be elongated slightly (see *Liber O* and the additional audio/visual resources for more on the vibration of divine names).

After performing the Qabalistic Cross at the center of the temple, you then move to the east and draw the first pentagram.

THE PENTAGRAMS & THE DIVINE NAMES

The invoking form of the pentagram begins with a downward stroke starting at the top point and moving toward the lower left point. The banishing form begins at the lower left point with an upward stroke, moving toward the top point. **Be sure to close each pentagram at its starting point.**

1. Facing east, trace the pentagram in the air in front of you. See the pentagram flaming in a bright blue-white light. Point your implement of choice toward the center of the pentagram, and intone: **YOD HEH VAV HEH.**

2. Extend your arm and turn south, drawing a connecting line of blue-white light to the point that will be the center of the next pentagram. Facing south, draw the pentagram, and intone: **ADONAI.**

3. Repeat as above, moving to the west, and intone: **EHEIEH.**

4. Repeat as above, moving to the north, and intone: **ATAH GIBBOR LE-OLAHM ADONAI.**[5]

5. Return to the east, completing the connecting line to the original pentagram, and thus sealing the circle.

When drawing the pentagrams, I suggest that you aim for approximately hip level for the lower points, and shoulder level for the upper points (except the top point, which should be above the height of your head). This is probably one of the least awkward ways of tracing them, as the movements are naturally within the reach of your arm.

---

[5] Many published sources use *"AGLA"* at this point. *AGLA* is simply a word comprised of the initials of the phrase, "Atah Gibbor Le-Olahm Adonai."

THE INVOCATION OF THE ARCHANGELS

Face east. Extend your arms to your sides so that your body forms a cross. Say:

Before me, RAPHÆL.
Behind me, GABRIEL.
On my right hand, MIKHÆL.
On my left hand, URIEL.[6]
For about me flames the Pentagram,
And in the Column shines the six-rayed star.

The archangels are seen as huge, winged figures of great majesty, robed and armed as follows:

Raphael: Yellow robe with violet trim. Bears a sword or dagger.
Gabriel: Blue robe with orange trim. Bears a cup.
Mikhael: Red robe with green trim. Bears a wand.
Uriel: Black robe with white trim. Bears a disk (pantacle).

Repeat the formula of the Qabalistic Cross, which brings the ritual to a close.

The invocation of the archangels is definitely one of those moments where you can amplify the effect of the ritual through visualizations and other inner work. With each of these archangels, you have an opportunity to emphasize the corresponding element within your being. For example, when you invoke Raphael, you aren't merely seeing a great archangel robed in yellow—you are experiencing the element of air itself as it manifests in you. You might amplify this by feeling a great cleansing wind from the east. Similarly, when you invoke Gabriel in the west, you could feel a wave of blue water purifying you; a consecrating fire from Michael in the south; and a preserving solidity and groundedness from Uriel in the north. Amplify, elaborate, or customize this part however you like. Your own experience will be your best teacher.

As you say the words, "for about me flames the pentagram" visualize a large pentagram surrounding your body, affirming yourself as a perfected microcosm; but also understand and experience this point of the ritual to be a statement of the truth that the entirety of your earthbound experience—the material universe itself—is truly flaming around you like a pentagram. When you say, "and in the column shines the six rayed star," you might wish to visualize a hexagram at the heart,

---

[6] The names of the archangels should be intoned, not merely spoken.

symbolizing the light of the HGA burning there—the true spiritual seed at your very core.

I recommend performance of the LRP twice daily in the early stages of magical practice—one invoking and one banishing. Since the invoking form can be energizing enough to cause sleeplessness in some people, I suggest you try invoking in the morning and banishing in the evening. You can also experiment with banishing and invoking on alternate days, or testing the effects of using only one or the other for several days in a row (if you try this, I suggest that you go no longer than three or four days without banishing, to ensure adequate magical hygiene).

If, on occasion, you need to be quiet when you do the ritual, it is acceptable to whisper, or to perform it completely silently. You may even find that such variations take on a unique, quiet intensity that differs in effect from a full-throated performance. Furthermore, you may experiment with astral (or at least purely mental) performance, which will strengthen your 'muscles' of visualization and, in theory, your astral body's ability to perform this ritual on its own plane.

The deeper secrets of this ritual, many uniquely your own, will be revealed over the months and years of your subsequent practice, as you integrate and harmonize the ritual's symbols with the inner landscape of your mind, body and spirit.

6

THE LESSER & GREATER RITUALS
OF THE HEXAGRAM

The Lesser Ritual of the Hexagram (LRH) should be learned and used after the Lesser Ritual of the Pentagram has been mastered and practiced regularly for some time. The combination of the LRP and LRH is strongly recommended as a daily practice suitable for maintaining the magical hygiene of the aspirant. As with the pentagram ritual, some aspirants have found that use of the invoking form of the hexagram ritual at the end of the day can lead to sleeplessness. Therefore, I suggest using the invoking form earlier in the day and the banishing form in the evening.

The Lesser Banishing Ritual of the Hexagram (LBRH) is used to clear the magician's aura and the temple of unwanted macrocosmic influence (that is, those forces pertaining to the sephiroth above Tiphereth), and to assert the magician's lordship over these realms. Aside from its hygienic function, the LBRH would typically be used before invoking any specific planetary, sephirothic, or zodiacal force.

The Lesser Invoking Ritual of the Hexagram (LIRH) can be used to invoke macrocosmic forces, and to create a magical working space that approximates the energies of a Second Order Temple. Indeed, the LRH has traditionally been practiced by Second Order initiates of Golden

Dawn-derived mystery schools. Unfortunately, it is partly for this reason that most published versions of the ritual are incorrect. Published versions, including the one given by Crowley in *Liber O*, use the elemental attributions to the quarters that would have been used only *within second order Vault*—that is, fire, water, air and earth, counterclockwise starting from the east. (You will note this arrangement on depictions of the circular altar within the G.D. Vault, for example.) For most daily use, the elemental attributions are exactly as used in the LRP—air in the east, fire in the south, water in the west, and earth in the north. The various forms of the hexagrams given in published versions of the LRH *are* correct—they simply need to be moved to the correct quarters when performing the ritual outside the Vault.

A note on pronunciation of "ARARITA": The full phrase, which has now been openly published in several places, is *ekhud rosh, ekhudotho rosh yekudotho, temuratho ekhud.* If you wish to intone this phrase in place of "ARARITA" you may do so. A traditional method of intoning the full phrase is taught within the Second Order of the Temple of the Silver Star.

The so-called 'Analysis of the Keyword' presented in most published versions of the LRH relies on certain traditional formulæ that some Thelemic practitioners may find unsuitable (i.e. formulæ which focus on the symbolism of the Dying God). The Analysis given here is one possible Thelemic variant.[7] Other distinctive versions of the Analysis are taught privately within the Second Order of the Temple of the Silver Star and elsewhere.

Ritual Outline

1. Stand upright in the center of the temple, facing east. The wand is held in the right hand on the center line of the body.

2. Perform the "Analysis of the Keyword," saying:

    I.N.R.I.
    Yod, Nun, Resh, Yod.
    Virgo, Isis, Holy Mother.

---

[7] See Chapter V of *Magick in Theory and Practice*, where Crowley comments in a footnote: "There is a quite different formula in which I is the Father, O the Mother, A the Child—and yet another, in which I.A.O. are all fathers of different kinds balanced by H.H.H., 3 Mothers, to complete the Universe. In a third, the true formula of the Beast 666, I and O are the opposites which form the field for the operation of A. But this is a higher matter unsuited for this elementary handbook. See, however, *Liber Samekh*, Point II, Section J."

Scorpio, Apophis, Destroyer.
Sol, Osiris, Holy Father.
Isis, Apophis, Osiris, IAO.[8]

3. Give the appropriate sign, keeping the point of the Wand upright, and say: **"The Sign of Osiris."**

4. Give the appropriate sign, weapon pointing upward, and say: **"The Sign of the Dance of Isis."**

5. Give the appropriate sign, and say: **"The Sign of the Ecstasy of Apophis."**

6. Give the appropriate sign, and say: **"The Sign of the Shining Star."**

7. Extend the arms again as in step 3 above, and then cross them again as in step 6, saying: **"L.V.X., Lux,**[9] **the Light of the True Cross."**

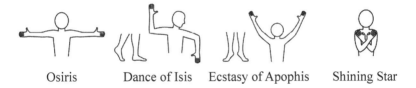

| Osiris | Dance of Isis | Ecstasy of Apophis | Shining Star |

The L.V.X. Signs (with modified names)

8. With the wand, trace the hexagram of air in the east in golden light. Point the wand to the center of the line where the two triangles meet, and intone "**ARARITA**."

9. Turn, or move, to the south, tracing a connecting line in golden light. Trace the hexagram of fire. Point the wand at the center of the base of the upper triangle, and intone "**ARARITA**."

---

[8] The name IAO is intoned, not spoken. The correct pronunciation is "ee-ah-oh."

[9] Pronounced "looks."

10. Continue to the west, and trace the hexagram of water. Point the wand at the place where the two triangles meet, and intone "**ARARITA**."

11. Continue to the north, and trace the hexagram of earth. Point the wand at the center of the hexagram, and intone "**ARARITA**."

12. Continue to the east, connecting and thus completing the circle, and repeat the signs and words of steps 1-7.

The Banishing Ritual is identical, but the direction of the hexagrams is reversed.

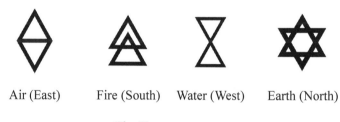

Air (East)   Fire (South)   Water (West)   Earth (North)

The Hexagrams

The Greater Ritual of the Hexagram (GRH), which is used for invoking or banishing specific planetary or zodiacal forces, can be adapted from the material given in *Liber O* as you see fit, but I will give a few basic suggestions here.

Begin with the Analysis of the Keyword, exactly as in the LRH. The Hexagrams are all drawn using the 'earth' form; that is, interlocking upward and downward facing triangles, as shown above. At each quarter you will draw the hexagram in a different pattern, depending on which planet or zodiacal region you wish to invoke or banish (see *Liber O*). The unicursal hexagram may be used in place of the overly complex solar hexagram, if desired. Invoking hexagrams consist of triangles drawn clockwise; banishing forms are drawn counterclockwise. The unicursal hexagram, if used, is always drawn starting from the top point. The same form of the hexagram is drawn at each quarter.

Draw the hexagram, then draw the planetary or zodiacal sigil in the center of the hexagram. Point to the center and vibrate the divine name of the planet or ruling planet (in the case of the zodiacal region); then the archangel of the planet (or ruling planet); then ARARITA. You may draw the figures in the specific colors corresponding to the forces desired, to enhance the power of the ritual.

Some traditions recommend concluding this portion of the ritual by drawing a fifth hexagram in the direction of the actual astronomical placement of the planet or zodiacal region at the moment of the working. To do this you'll need an accurate sidereal astrological chart or some other method of calculating the exact placement. There are a number of excellent software applications, including very useful mobile versions, for accomplishing this task.

Close with the *Analysis of the Keyword,* as in the LRH.

7

LIBER RESH VEL HELIOS

Liber Resh vel Helios, a Class D ritual of A∴A∴, is one of the foundational practices of Thelemic magick. Along with the LRP and LRH, it will likely be one of the core hygienic, devotional and consciousness-attuning practices you use daily throughout your life. Daily performance of *Liber Resh* has a number of magical and psychological benefits. By identifying yourself with the sun in its four 'stations' throughout the day, you forge a conscious link to the energies represented by the sun. Some assert that this manifests as a direct energetic effect upon the initiate; others feel the benefit is primarily symbolic and psychological—that is, we benefit from the symbolic alignment of our consciousness with the undying cycle of the sun, and the mindfulness of this alignment throughout the day. I encourage you to experiment with the ritual and come to your own conclusions. In addition to the benefits of mindfulness and magical identification with the sun, you get regular practice in the assumption of God-forms, fortifying the so-called "aura" with multiple instances of the Sign of Silence (corresponding to Harpocrates), and a chance to build an overall sense of connection to the Thelemic current.

It is common for A∴A∴ initiates to begin working with this practice during their Probationer phase, and several other Thelemic training systems assign one or another version of the practice to their initiates in the early stages of the work. While the basic text of the ritual, as written by Crowley, has been published and discussed in many places, there are a number of performance details taught in A∴A∴ which seem appropriate to present here.

Students often ask about the importance of the timing of the ritual throughout the day. As noted above, some teachers believe that the closer you are to the exact time of the station of the sun, the more effective the ritual will be. This may very well be true, but I encourage you not to let your attempts at perfect timing distract you from simply getting the ritual done. If you sleep past dawn, as many of us often do, perform the Dawn adoration upon arising. If you go to bed before midnight, do the Midnight adoration before retiring. If you miss the exact time of a planned adoration, do the adoration whenever you catch that you've missed it. Nevertheless, I suggest you do *strive* to be as exact as possible with your timing. Consult the many websites which provide exact times for solar dawn, noon, etc. on any given day and location, and don't forget to take into account the one-hour offset due to Daylight Savings Time.

Another common question involves privacy during the ritual. What do you do if you're in your cubicle at work and it's time for an adoration? What if you're in a meeting? Crowley clearly intended the ritual to be performed publicly or privately, depending on where one is at the given hour. My stance on this issue is simple: it's better to do it inwardly, via visualization and silent recitation, or to do it later than planned, than to skip it. If you're at work and you need privacy, excuse yourself to the restroom and do the adoration in a stall, silently if need be. If you can't excuse yourself from your desk or other workplace, do the ritual mentally and silently, visualizing yourself in the appropriate physical postures and God-forms. If nothing else, such situations give you valuable practice in the yoga of mental control, and a chance to get more comfortable in the so-called astral body.

The ritual begins by facing the appropriate quarter: east at dawn, south at noon, west at dusk, and north at midnight. Imagine yourself to be standing at the junction of the paths of *peh* and *samekh* on the Tree of Life. From this vantage point, you will have the sephiroth of Tiphereth, Netzach, Yesod, and Hod surrounding you, in the east, south, west, and north, respectively. Position your physical body according to the corresponding A∴A∴ grade signs. [Note: If you are an initiate of A∴A∴, you may also simply give the sign of your grade at each quarter.] These are:

Dawn: Osiris Slain (a stand-in for all of the so-called "L.V.X. Signs" corresponding to the Adeptus Minor grade of Tiphereth.)

Noon: Thoum-aesh-neith (a sign of fire corresponding to the Philosophus grade of Netzach)

Dusk: Shu (a sign of air corresponding to the Zelator grade of Yesod)

Midnight: Khephra (a sign of water corresponding to the Practicus grade of Hod)

Dawn   Noon   Dusk   Midnight

The Signs for *Liber Resh*

Next, you visualize yourself in the appropriate God-form. The basic technique and God-forms to be used are as follows:

1. For each God-form, drape your physical form with that of the visualized forms described below. (Imagine that if you looked into a mirror, you would not see your physical body, but only the God-form.)

2. RA (Dawn): Humanoid male body in Egyptian garb. Hawk head. Red solar disk above head. Uraeus serpent (a cobra's head) rising at brow. Left foot placed slightly forward. Left arm extended forward, bearing a Phoenix wand. Right hand slightly forward, bearing a golden ankh.

3. AHATHOOR (Noon): Humanoid female body in Egyptian garb. Cow head (or female human head with cow horns). Red solar disk above head. Left foot placed slightly forward. Left arm extended forward, bearing a Phoenix wand. Right hand slightly forward, bearing a golden ankh.

4. TUM (Dusk): Male human body in Egyptian garb. Stylized Egyptian beard. Nemyss on head. Left foot placed slightly forward. Left arm extended forward, bearing a Phoenix wand. Right hand slightly forward, bearing a golden ankh.

5. KHEPHRA (Midnight): Full body of scarab beetle. Wings stretching outward and curving upward. Front legs bent upward, bearing the disk of the sun.

6.   Maintain these God-forms only during the first "elemental" adoration of the quarter. That is, drop the visualization before moving on to the "Unity" Adoration.

So, at this point, you are standing facing the appropriate quarter, with your physical body in your chosen grade sign, and an astral "overlay" of the appropriate God-form. You then recite the particular adoration which is keyed to the time of day, as given in the text of *Liber Resh* itself, followed by the Sign of Silence (the right forefinger touching the closed lips). I suggest you couple the Sign of Silence with a visualization the God-form of Harpocrates, as depicted the Aeon Atu of the Thoth tarot deck. As you perform the adoration, attempt to throw yourself into ecstatic spiritual communion with the forces represented. For example, at dawn, you can feel yourself as a solar being, rising from slumber to begin consciously shedding light upon your world throughout the day; and at midnight, you can identify with that secret solar source within, which is ever-burning even when unseen (as with the sun during the night). When giving the Sign of Silence, seek to strengthen and sharpen the visualization of the energetic aura around the physical body. As with all such magical signs, repeated practice of this sign, with this particular intention, helps to make it a truly efficacious gesture, and not merely a ritual formality.

Next, you are instructed to "perform the adoration that is taught thee by thy Superior." The following adoration is one traditional form used in the beginning stages of A∴A∴. Additional material is added at a later stage.

After performing the solar invocation and giving the Sign of Silence, stand in the Sign of Osiris Risen, or the Shining Star (your arms crossed upon your upper torso, right over left, fingertips touching the collarbones) recite the following from Chapter III of *The Book of the Law*.

> Unity uttermost showed!
>   I adore the might of Thy breath,
> Supreme and terrible God,
>   Who makest the gods and death
> To tremble before Thee:
>   I, I adore thee!
>
> Appear on the throne of Ra!
> Open the ways of the Khu!
> Lighten the ways of the Ka!
>   The ways of the Khabs run through

To stir me or still me!
  Aum! Let it fill me![10]

The light is mine; its rays consume
  Me: I have made a secret door
Into the House of Ra and Tum,
  Of Khephra and of Ahathoor.
I am thy Theban, O Mentu,
  The prophet Ankh-af-na-khonsu!

By Bes-na-Maut my breast I beat;
By wise Ta-Nech I weave my spell.
Show thy star-splendour, O Nuit!
  Bid me within thine House to dwell,
O winged snake of light, Hadit!
  Abide with me, Ra-Hoor-Khuit!

Follow this, again, with the Sign of Silence.

There are a few additional techniques that may enable you to maximize the magical benefits of this Adoration.

First, recognize that in performing this Adoration you are paying homage to that unity that is beyond the four separate manifestations of solar energy worshipped in the preliminary adorations of the quarters. Along with other potential interpretations, this symbolizes the spiritual unity of each initiate (Tiphereth) which lies beyond the apparent elemental divisions of the psycho-spiritual being (Malkuth-earth, Yesod-air, Hod-water, Netzach-fire). As it is written in *The Book of the Law* (I: 51): "There are four gates to one palace..."

Second, intone the "Aum!" in the last line of the second stanza fully, slowly, and forcefully. After finishing the line, take a deep breath, feeling the light of the crown center flooding down into the aura. Having done this, you will likely find that your recitation of the next line ("The light is mine...") will reflect a true magical reality—an actual shift in available energy brought forth by virtue of your mindful performance of these ritual lines.

Finally, as you deliver the final lines of the Adoration, visualize yourself as Ankh-af-na-khonsu within the Stele of Revealing, as follows: With the line, "Show thy star-splendour, O Nuit!" see the body of the star-goddess arched above you; her feet in front of you and her hands

---

[10]This line of text has appeared in various places as either 'let it fill me' or 'let it kill me.' I encourage you to use either reading according to your personal preference.

behind. With the line, "Bid me within thine House to dwell, O winged snake of light, Hadit!" see the winged globe at the center-top of the scene. With the line, "Abide with me, Ra-Hoor-Khuit!" see the hawk-headed Lord seated upon the throne facing you. At the conclusion of these lines, pause for a moment to allow the entirety of the scene to "lock in" to your consciousness. By placing yourself in the midst of these powerful archetypes, you strengthen your link to the Thelemic current itself.

As instructed in the text of the liber, you may wish to follow the final Adoration with a period of meditation. Many students take advantage of this opportunity to accomplish whatever meditative tasks they happen to be working on at the time. No particular style or focus of meditation is required, however.

8

METHODS OF RITUAL CONSTRUCTION

This chapter will give you a sense of the basic components of a well-constructed ritual, using Crowley's comments in *Magick in Theory and Practice*[11] as the primary source material. After reading this chapter, you should be able to choose a ritual aim and assemble a well-designed and powerful ritual to achieve your goal. Naturally, like many of the things discussed in this book, repeated practice really does bring greater strength, clarity, focus, and efficacy to your work. Hopefully, you'll be constructing and executing rituals for the rest of your life, and getting better at each step of the way.

Before we talk about the components and stages of effective ritual, I want to review the theory of magick itself, and consider the question: Why would you even bother to do ritual at all? You are likely aware of Crowley's definition of magick as "the Science and Art of causing Change to occur in conformity with Will." Consider also these further words from *Liber Libræ*:

> 16. To obtain Magical Power, learn to control thought; admit only those ideas that are in harmony with the end

---

11 Crowley, A. (1997). *Magick: Liber ABA*. Hymenaeus Beta (Ed.). York Beach, ME: Samuel Weiser, Inc.

desired, and not every stray and contradictory Idea that presents itself.

17. Fixed thought is a means to an end. Therefore pay attention to the power of silent thought and meditation. The material act is but the outward expression of thy thought, and therefore hath it been said that "the thought of foolishness is sin." Thought is the commencement of action, and if a chance thought can produce much effect, what cannot fixed thought do?[12]

So, with these words in mind, let us first consider ritual as a technique of *focusing attention*. This perspective partially explains the importance of the training of the mind through raja yoga that is so prominent in the system of A∴A∴ and elsewhere in Crowley's body of work. When we ritualize our intention—focusing our thought into word, and our word into deed—we create a form that is keyed to our ritual goal. It is a law of nature that force follows form. Force will only manifest where a suitable form exists to contain it. If you build the physical components of an electrical circuit (i.e. a network of connected wires) and connect it to a power source, the power flows. If the form of the wires is not correct— that is, if it does not 'invoke' the desired force—that force will simply not manifest.

Accordingly, we must set up our ritual to be a form that will invite a certain force. The effectiveness with which we can do this will depend on our ability to focus our attention and *intention,* via symbol, ritualized actions, and all of the other correspondences and associations we may have with a particular idea. These may take the form of incense, colors, magical implements, sigils and talismans, and so on. Intelligent and practiced use of these ritual forms will create very precise changes in consciousness that match our ritual aim. Through ritual, we construct a psychological environment for building up these associations, and then we find a way to tap into the necessary ecstatic force that can charge that form. Here again is that union of thought, word, and deed which completes the ritual action.

There are different types of ritual, of course. We have dramatic ritual, such as the Rites of Eleusis, where the energetic effect of the ritual is accomplished through the dramatic narrative, and the embodiment of the particular energies in the characters and their interplay. We also have what I would call 'unconscious ritual' embedded in our culture, where we collectively engage in ritualized behaviors that tend to have a

---

[12] Crowley, A. (1992). Liber Librae. In I. Regardie (Ed.), *Gems from the Equinox.* Scottsdale, AZ: New Falcon Publications.

psychological or energetic effect. This includes constructing and participating in the modern mythology embodied in films, music and other cultural forms, as well as our collective celebration of various holidays and their associated customs.

What we're going to focus on in this chapter, however, is the classical ceremonial approach to ritual. This is a fairly structured method that Crowley would have learned in his early association with the Hermetic Order of the Golden Dawn, and which many magical orders have adopted and elaborated since the late 19th century.

Preliminary Considerations

The first step is to take a look at the reason you're doing the ritual. Explore conscious or unconscious blockages to the success of the ritual. There may be ego-based influences on the desired goal, including the dreaded 'lust of result,' that may interfere with the proper execution of the ritual. If you are ambivalent about the outcome in some way, even unconsciously—if there's any part of you that doesn't actually *want* the ritual to succeed—you may find that it leeches power out of the ritual. No matter how perfectly you execute it, if your mind's working against you and against itself, you will be much less likely to succeed.

Next, take practical steps to achieve the aim. If you need to put out a fire, reach for a fire extinguisher before you invoke the fire elementals for aid! If you want a job, put in some applications before doing a formal ritual. These practical steps become a part of the overall ritual, when understood broadly. One way of understanding this process is to view it in terms of the Qabalistic 'Four Worlds' (see Chapter 17 if you are unfamiliar with this conceptual model). What you're doing here, in essence, is shaping your magical goals in the world of Yetzirah (thought and word) through your conception of the ritual aim, and then linking that goal to the world of Assiah (deed). And that deed, such as putting in the job applications, becomes a concrete magical link to the desired goal.

Once you have decided to do the ritual, I recommend that you do a brief ceremony or meditation to purify and consecrate your aim. You may recall that in *Liber CL,* Crowley defines purity as a state where 'no alien element' intrudes—the thing is 'purely' itself. With purification of your intention, you're simply washing away any undesirable accretions to the central, pure aim of the Will. One of the ways you do this is through the process of looking for counter-impulses and ambivalence about the outcome, as discussed above. Another approach would be to undertake an exercise where you mentally visualize the magical aim as a symbolic object of your own devising, then see the object being cleansed and made pure. The consecration of the ritual aim simply involves bringing a sense of sacredness to it. Perform a meditation wherein you link the ritual aim to your True Will, seeing it as an extension of the will of your Holy Guardian Angel, and a step in your path toward union with the HGA.

Having completed these preliminaries, you are now ready to construct the formal ritual. Choose the sephira or path on the Tree of Life that best matches your ritual aim, and look up the correspondences from *777* or other sources.[13] These may include incenses, colors, sigils, deities associated with the goal, as well as the Qabalistic hierarchies of the divine names, archangels, angels, and the 'Palaces of Assiah,' corresponding to the Four Worlds, or any other correspondences you are moved to incorporate.

Next, consider the timing of the ritual. Let's say you've decided that Mars is an appropriate planet for the ritual intention. Consult your astronomical references (or draw up a sidereal astrological chart) and choose a day and time when Mars is prominently placed in the heavens. For example, you might choose a moment when Mars is on the horizon; or you can simply choose a Tuesday—the day of the week attributed to Mars. You can also base the precise timing of the ritual on the traditional Tattva tides (see below), which are cycles of five twenty-four minute periods starting at sunrise, and corresponding to the four elements and spirit. Our Mars ritual might be well-suited to the fire Tattva. Some people choose to use the traditional 'magical hours' where specific times of the day that correspond to certain certain planets, magical goals, and so on; but I have found little use for these in my own magical work.

Akasha	Spirit
Vayu	Air
Tejas	Fire
Apas	Water
Prithivi	Earth

The Tattvas

Let's review the overall structure of an effective ritual, and the building blocks that make it work. As I said earlier, *Magick in Theory and Practice* is our primary source material, but I've supplemented Crowley's ideas with conclusions drawn from my own experience doing ritual, as well as that of the students I have supervised.

---

[13] Crowley, A. (1986). *777*. York Beach, ME: Red Wheel/Weiser.

Banishing, Purification and Consecration

First, we have the banishing, purification, and consecration of the space, and of the consciousness of the magician. Some of the options for banishing are fairly obvious, such as the classic lesser rituals of the pentagram and hexagram, the Star Ruby, and the like. Alternatively, you can banish 'by fiat,' where you simply declare that the temple is appropriately banished. There are also traditional forms of banishing like clattering swords together, hitting gongs, widdershins circles, and so on. The purification and consecration discussed here are slightly different from what I described above; here we ritualize these steps with a purification of the space with water and a consecration of the space with fire (typically incense). The underlying theory is, however, the same: we cleanse the space of all extraneous influences, and then imbue it with sacredness.

General Invocation

Next comes the General Invocation. I liken this to plugging a T.V. into the wall socket and turning it on. Later, you'll concern yourself with tuning to a particular station, but for now you simply want to make sure it's powered up. Accordingly, the general invocation should be powerful, but non-specific. Examples would be the preliminary invocation from the Goetia, also seen in a different form in *Liber Samekh*, the first Enochian call, some sort of middle pillar variation, the Nuit invocation from the Gnostic Mass, and so on. Anything that gets the power flowing *for you* is a good candidate.

The Oath or Proclamation

After the General Invocation, make the Oath or Proclamation; that is, state the purpose of the rite. You have formulated the intention of the ritual (thought), and now you consciously formulate this intention via the word. It is a microcosm of the idea of the Logos and the effect of the Logos in the world; the word that embodies the primal will-force and takes it out into the world. The Oath or Proclamation could be as simple as a sentence or two, such as, "I am Frater or Soror so-and-so, and it is my will to create a talisman of Mars so that I may obtain magical power to execute my True Will." There is no need to be overly wordy, or to belabor the point.

Specific Invocation

After this, we move into the Specific Invocation. Here is where we tune that T.V. to the particular channel we want to watch, and of course, this will be the 'channel' that corresponds to the aim of our ritual and the symbolic correspondences we have chosen. An excellent example of a specific invocation in poetic form is *Liber Israfel,* which is designed to be an invocation of Tahuti.[14] Other options for a specific invocation would be the Greater Pentagram or Hexagram rituals of the particular element or planet or zodiacal region you wish to invoke (see Chapters 5 and 6 for details).

Bringing Down the Magical Force

Now that you have turned on the primary power with the General Invocation, declared the aim of the rite with the Oath or Proclamation, and performed the requisite Specific Invocations, you must find a way to bring the force down into manifestation. As noted earlier, this process mirrors the doctrine of the Qabalistic Four Worlds: You are attempting to bring an ineffable energy down through increasingly concrete levels of form, so that it can bring tangible results in your outer and inner life. There are a few neat tricks for doing this, such as using the four color scales for visualizations as you bring the force down, or 'personifying' interactions between the levels of the hierarchy. For example, if you're using a certain Qabalistic hierarchy of divine names, archangels, angels, and so on, you can implore each 'entity' to send forth the next, and use the color transitions to accentuate each successive level.

At each stage, try to identify as fully as possible with the nature of the entity that you're addressing. By the time you're done you will have completed all the links in the chain, and brought the hierarchy down to a manifest level. This is one aspect of ritual construction where you can unleash your creativity and have some fun. For example, I was teaching a ritual design class a few years ago, and our aim was to consecrate a Jupiter/Chesed talisman. Several of us had constructed a ritual with various specific invocations of Jupiter, including the appropriate Greater Hexagram ritual, but we didn't stop there. The climax of the ritual, and the final method of bringing down the force, was to draw a large Tree of Life on the floor, and then have all the ritual participants walk the path of the 'Lighting Flash' on the Tree while chanting the hierarchy of divine names, archangels, and angelic choir. We made several passes down the Tree, finally concluding in the West, where the talisman rested on an altar symbolizing manifestation in Malkuth. We brought the energy down, and then all of us simultaneously projected the force onto the talisman using the Sign of the Enterer, sealing it with the name of Chesed according to the 'Palaces of Assiah,' completing the magical link. Thus, the ritualized actions themselves *physically* embodied the descent of the magical force (an outline of this ritual is given at the end of this chapter).

---

[14] Crowley, A. (1992). *Liber Israfel*. In I. Regardie (Ed.), *Gems from the Equinox*. Scottsdale, AZ: New Falcon Publications.

The Completion of the Magical Link

The next phase of the ritual, and a very important one at that, is to find a way to *lock in* the force invoked, to ensure its effective action on the desired plane. One of the most common ways of doing this is to consecrate a talisman (as in the above example) or to consecrate a eucharist of some kind. Common choices for a eucharist might be some sort of food corresponding to the invoked force, a Cake of Light and goblet of wine, and any number of other options (see Chapter 4 for more details). In the case of a talisman, you can then carry that talisman with you as an embodiment of the force; with a eucharist, you lock the force into the physical substance and then consume it, taking the force directly into your body. "...[F]orasmuch as meat and drink are transmuted in us daily into spiritual substance, I believe in the Miracle of the Mass."[15]

Once you've charged the magical link, you want to take great care to protect it so it will retain its charge. In the case of a eucharist, this means that you remain very mindful of the magical aim, and that you are taking the force into yourself as you consume it. In the case of a talisman, the tradition is to wrap it in silk as soon as it has been charged, and before the invoked force has been banished from the temple. Otherwise, you risk banishing the charge right back out of the talisman you have so painstakingly created!

Closing and License to Depart

Before closing the temple, you must banish any specific forces invoked. Generally, this would be the complementary banishing form of whatever pentagram or hexagram rituals were done, but a banishing by fiat is another option. Some version of the classic 'license to depart' works well here, e.g., "In the name of Heru-Ra-Ha, I now set free any spirits which may have been imprisoned by this ceremony. Depart ye in peace unto your abodes and habitations, harm none in your going, be there peace between us, and be ye ready to come when called." Once the temple has been ceremonially closed, and preferably before you do anything else—even before you leave the room—enter the results of the ritual into your magical diary.

I know this chapter has been something of a whirlwind tour, but I think you will find the material here is a useful framework that you can expand infinitely as you grow in experience. Continued experimentation will teach you which options and approaches work best for you, and in the process you will have become a much more powerful magician.

Following are several examples of simple rituals exemplifying the structure outlined in this chapter. I have chosen to include three fairly

---

[15] *Liber XV, The Gnostic Mass.*

similar rituals—all of them talisman consecrations—to make it easier to see how the basic structure can be adapted for various ritual goals, e.g., using different correspondences and divine and angelic hierarchies. Note how the various components of the overall ritual framework can be interchanged (using poetic invocations vs. specific pentagram or hexagram rituals, etc.) and how identical formulae, such as the tenfold sephirothic invocations, can be used in different ways.

All capitalized divine names, etc., are vibrated, not merely spoken (refer to the audio-visual resources for examples of the vibration of divine names).

Sample Rituals

A Ritual of Chesed

The Temple is empty except for a black double-cube altar in the East (Kether-of-Chesed), draped in blue cloth. The paths and *sephiroth* of the Flaming Sword, descending from the altar, are marked in tape on the floor. Lights are dim. Hand drums are placed wherever the drummer(s) will be seated. In the extreme west (Malkuth-of-Chesed) is a smaller altar on which are placed individual items for consecration, and a black silk cloth large enough to cover the entire top surface of the altar. Chairs for attendees line the north and south walls.

The Altar in the East: Cup of water, censer, incense and charcoal, single lighted white taper; talisman with sigils created from the Kamea of Jupiter; *The Book of the Law.*

Incense: Cedar or other resinous wood

The officiants and **attendees** are dressed in white robes with blue sashes or similar color charges; or, a base of black or white street clothes with blue as the primary additional color; or, the violet robe of an Adeptus Exemptus may be worn, as corresponding to Chesed. Otherwise, plain black or white clothing is acceptable.

The officiants are seated in a circle of chairs surrounding the altar. Other attendees sit outside this circle, as convenient.

Preliminaries

Magus: Lead attendees in Rhythmic Breathing for approximately 5 minutes, for relaxation and centering.

Banishings, Purification and Consecration

Officiant 2: Perform the Lesser Banishing Ritual of the Pentagram. Return to chair and sit.

Officiant 3: Perform the Lesser Banishing Ritual of the Hexagram. Return to chair and sit.

Officiant 4: Move to altar, take up cup, and turning in place, sprinkle water to east, south, west, north in sequence. With each sprinkle, visualize a wave of purifying water spreading out to the quarter. Finish by saying, **"The Temple is Purified."** Replace cup on altar, return to chair, and sit.

Officiant 5: Move to altar, take up censer, and turning in place, cense to east, south, west, north in sequence. With each censing, visualize a wall of consecrating fire spreading out to the quarter. Finish by saying, **"The Temple is Consecrated."** Replace censer on altar, return to chair, and sit.

General Invocation

ALL remain seated.

Magus: Move to altar. Perform the Priest's portion of the Anthem from *Liber XV*, beginning with **"Thou who art I, beyond all I am..."** and concluding with **"...in thy Child."**

Statement of Purpose

Magus: (Still at altar.) Say: **"In the name of HERU-RA-HA, Lord of the Universe, I declare that it is our purpose to invoke the powers and beings of Chesed, so that all present may find prosperity and ease of circumstances, for the performance of their Great Work!"**

"The Temple is duly opened!" Knock on altar: **** (4)

ALL: "So mote it be!"

Magus: Return to chair and sit.

Specific Invocations and Bringing Down the Magical Force

ALL: **All** stand, move to form a line that begins near the altar, with **Magus** at the front, and begin to chant as taught: **EL, TZADKIEL, KHASMALIM**, repeatedly. (**Drums** are played in rhythm with the chanting.)

The line moves down the path of the Flaming Sword to Malkuth, and then circles back clockwise to the Kether point. This may at times evolve into a gentle dance, as desired.

When **Magus** reaches the Kether point, the movement and chanting stop, and the powers of Kether-of-Chesed are invoked:

Magus: (elevates talisman) **"May the One Source blaze brightly within this talisman!"**

Repeat the chanting and movement down the Flaming Sword, circling back to Kether. **ALL** formulate the intention of charging the talisman, which remains elevated, with the Kether-energy. This time, **Magus** stops at Chokmah for the next invocation:

Magus: "May the Universal Will be this talisman's Force!"

The pattern is repeated for each of the remaining sephiroth. The invocations are as follows:

Binah: **"May the Great Mother enwomb this talisman with perfect Form!"**
Chesed: **"May this talisman enjoy the bounty of Right Rulership!"**
Geburah: **"May this talisman achieve its aim with Strength!"**
Tiphereth: **"May Beauty flower in the lives of all who look upon this talisman!"**
Netzach: **"May this talisman find Victory in its Desired Aim!"**
Hod: **"May this talisman be a perfect receptacle of its Higher Form!"**
Yesod: **"May this talisman stand on the stable Foundation of its Purpose!"**
Malkuth: **"May all its Force find perfect Form, as this talisman manifests its Kingdom!"**

The Completion of the Magical Link
(Charging the Talisman and other items)

After the Malkuth invocation, the chanting begins but instead of moving back to the east, the participants fan out to have a clear view of the Malkuth altar. On **Magus**' signal, **ALL** turn to face the Malkuth altar, and give the Sign of the Enterer toward the altar, feeling the accumulated energy flowing from the fingertips and charging the talisman and other items, while vibrating together: **TZEDEQ**. Retire in the Sign of Silence, the right forefinger to the lips. Remain standing in place.

Magus: Holding hands over talisman and other items, performs the final sealing with appropriate names. Knock *** ***** *** (3-5-3) The talisman and other items are covered with the black cloth.

ALL: Sit peacefully and silently in the invoked atmosphere. **All spend 5-10 minutes scrying the astral atmosphere of the Temple**, using whatever techniques they may choose (any such techniques should be accomplished silently, and without any movements that would distract other attendees). **Magus** signals quietly to bring the scrying to a close, when appropriate.

Banishing Specific Invoked Energies

ALL circle counter-clockwise around temple, three times, while chanting **HERU-RA-HA**, with the intention of banishing the invoked energies of Chesed kept firmly in mind. **Drums** are played with the rhythm of the chanting.

License to Depart

Magus: In the Name of HERU-RA-HA, I now set free any spirits imprisoned by this ceremony. Depart ye in peace unto your abodes and habitations. Be there peace between us, and be ye ready to come when called. May the blessings of EL be upon you. Knock * (1)

A Ritual of Kether

The Temple is empty except for a white double-cube altar in the east (Kether). Chairs for attendees line the north and south walls. Temple lights are at approximately half-intensity.

The Altar: Cup of water, censer, incense and charcoal, single lighted white taper; *The Book of the Law*

Incense: Ambergris, or Jerusalem (Half frankincense, half myrrh)

The officiants and **attendees** are dressed in white robes; or white street clothes; or any clothes accented by a white sash or other color charge. Each attendee holds his or her chosen talisman. The officiants are seated in a row of chairs to the west of the altar. Other attendees sit on the sides of the temple, as convenient.

Preliminaries

Magus: Lead attendees in relaxation for approximately 3-5 minutes.

Banishings, Purification and Consecration

Officiant 1: Perform the Star Ruby. Return to chair and sit.

Officiant 2: Perform the Lesser Banishing Ritual of the Hexagram. Return to chair and sit.

Officant 3: Move to altar, take up cup, and turning in place, sprinkle water to east, south, west, north in sequence. With each sprinkle, visualize a wave of purifying Water spreading out to the quarter. Finish by saying, "**The Temple is Purified.**" Replace cup on altar, return to chair, and sit.

Officiant 4: Move to altar, take up censer, and turning in place, cense to east, south, west, north in sequence. With each censing, visualize a wall of consecrating fire spreading out to the quarter. Finish by saying, "**The Temple is Consecrated.**" Replace censer on altar, return to chair, and sit.

General Invocation

ALL remain seated. Led by **Magus, ALL** perform 3-5 minutes of the fourfold breath, with the intention of increasing their own level of accessible magical force.

ALL RISE, and recite together this modified version of the Preliminary Invocation from *Liber Samekh*:

Thee I invoke, the Bornless One.

Thee, that didst create the Earth and the Heavens.
Thee, that didst create the Night and the Day.
Thee, that didst create the darkness and the Light.
Thou art ASAR UN-NEFER: Whom no man hath seen at any time.
Thou art IA-BESZ.
Thou art IA-APOPHRASZ.
Thou hast distinguished between the Just and the Unjust.
Thou didst make the Female and the Male.
Thou didst produce the Seeds and the Fruit.
Thou didst form Men to love one another, and to hate one another.
I am [magical motto or civil name] thy Prophet, unto Whom Thou didst commit Thy Mysteries, the Ceremonies of THELEMA.
Thou didst produce the moist and the dry, and that which nourisheth all created Life.
Hear Thou Me, for I am the Angel of HERU-RA-HA: this is Thy True Name, handed down to the Prophets of THELEMA.

OFFICIANTS remain standing. **OTHER ATTENDEES** may sit or stand as they will.

Statement of Purpose

Magus moves to stand before altar, facing east, and says: **"In the name of HERU-RA-HA, Lord of the Universe, I declare that it is our purpose to invoke the powers and spirits of Kether so that all present may benefit from an influx of the Highest Divine Light, for the performance of their own Great Work!"**

"The Temple is duly opened!" Knock on altar: *

ALL: "So mote it be!"

Magus: Returns to chair and faces East.

Specific Invocations and Bringing Down the Magical Force

ALL hold their talismans cupped between their hands, at heart level. **ALL** visualize the corresponding area of their bodies being infused with light and force, as each sephira is named and invoked by **Magus**, as follows:

Kether (Centered above the Crown of the head): **"May the One Source blaze brightly within this talisman!"**

Chokmah (Left hemisphere of the brain): **"May the Universal Will be this talisman's Force!"**

Binah (Right hemisphere of the brain): **"May the Great Mother enwomb this talisman with perfect Form!"**

Chesed (Left shoulder): **"May this talisman enjoy the bounty of Right Rulership!"**

Geburah (Right shoulder): **"May this talisman achieve its aim with Strength!"**

Tiphereth (Heart): **"May Beauty flower in the lives of all who look upon this talisman!"**

Netzach (Lower left torso): **"May this talisman find Victory in its Appointed Aim!"**

Hod (Lower right torso): **"May this talisman be a perfect receptacle of its Higher Form!"**

Yesod (Genitals): **"May this talisman stand on the stable Foundation of its Purpose!"**

Malkuth (Centered between the feet): **"May all its Force find perfect Form, as this talisman manifests its Kingdom!"**

The Completion of the Magical Link & Charging the Talisman

ALL, still holding talismans cupped in hands, visualize their entire aura infused with the colors of the Four Worlds, as they vibrate together the appropriate divine and angelic names, as given below. **The process should come to a full climax at the vibration of the Name in Assiah, as each attendee feels the force lock itself finally into their talisman.**

Atziluth (Brilliance): **"EHEIEH"**
Briah (White Brilliance): **"METATRON"**
Yetzirah (White Brilliance): **"SERAPHIM"**
Assiah (White, flecked with gold): **"RASHITH HA-GILGALIM"**

Magus: Performs the final sealing with a final repetition of the names. Knock *** ***** *** (3-5-3).

ALL: Sit peacefully and silently in the invoked atmosphere for approximately 5 minutes, feeling themselves and their talismans infused by the essence of Kether.

License to Depart and Closing

ALL keep their hands tightly cupped around their talisman, to insulate it from the banishing which is about to occur.

Magus: "In the Name of HERU-RA-HA, I now set free any spirits imprisoned by this ceremony. Depart ye in peace unto your abodes and habitations. Be there peace between us, and be ye ready to come when called. May the blessings of EHEIEH be upon you. (Pause.)

Dispensing with all further ceremony, I declare this Temple closed."

Knock * (1)

A Ritual of Tiphereth

The Temple is empty except for a black double-cube altar at the center, draped in yellow/gold cloth. Lights are dim or extinguished. Soft music of a gentle yet empowering nature may be played if desired. Hand drums are placed wherever the drummer will be seated.

The Altar: Cup of water, censer and charcoal, single lighted white or yellow taper, Tablet of Union, wine (enough for all present to have a small amount—this may be placed on a stand beside the altar)

Incense: Frankincense

The officiants and **attendees** are dressed in white robes with yellow/gold sashes or similar color charges. Alternately, a base of white street clothes with yellow/gold as the primary additional color.

The officiants are seated in a circle of chairs surrounding the altar. Other attendees sit outside this circle, as convenient.

Preliminaries

Magus: Lead attendees in Rhythmic Breathing for approximately 5 minutes, for relaxation and centering.

Banishings, Purification and Consecration

Officiant 1: Perform the Lesser Banishing Ritual of the Pentagram. Return to chair and sit.

Officiant 2: Perform the Lesser Banishing Ritual of the Hexagram. Return to chair and sit.

Officant 3: Move to altar, take up cup, and turning in place, sprinkle water to east, south, west, north in sequence. With each sprinkle, visualize a wave of purifying water spreading out to the quarter. Finish by saying, **"The Temple is Purified."** Replace cup on altar, return to chair, and sit.

Officiant 4: Move to altar, take up censer, and turning in place, cense to east, south, west, North in sequence. With each censing, visualize a wall of consecrating fire spreading out to the quarter. Finish by saying, **"The Temple is Consecrated."** Replace censer on altar, return to chair, and sit.

General Invocation

ALL remain seated.

Magus: Move to altar. Perform the First Enochian Call.

Statement of Purpose

Magus: "In the name of HERU-RA-HA, Lord of the Universe, I declare that it is our purpose to invoke the powers of Tiphereth, so that all present may be strengthened and empowered to grow in accordance with their True Will! 'For pure will, unassuaged of purpose, delivered from the lust of result, is every way perfect.'"

"The Temple is duly opened!" Knock on altar: *** *** (3-3)

ALL: "So mote it be!"

Magus: Return to chair and sit.

Specific Invocation

Officiant 5: Perform the Greater Invoking Ritual of the Hexagram of the Sun (IAO—Raphael—Melekim—Shemesh.) A fifth hexagram is drawn in the direction of the sun's placement in the heavens at the moment of the ritual. (Hexagrams are drawn in violet light on a yellow field.) Return to chair and remain standing.

Bringing Down the Magical Force

ALL: All stand, move to form a circle outside the chairs, and begin to circle the altar, clockwise. (**Drums** are played in rhythm with the chanting.) Hold hands, right palm facing down and left palm facing up. Circle deosil while chanting each of the names below in sequence. Simultanously, **all** visualize/feel the increasingly intense energies of Tiphereth filling the circle. **All** pause between names on **Magus'** lead. (Note that *IAO* is an acronym of *IHVH Eloah v'Da'ath* (אלוה וַדעת יְהוה), and may be used as the divine name of Tiphereth, as is done here.)

(for Atziluth):   **IAO**
(for Briah):   **RAPHAEL**
(for Yetzirah):   **MELEKIM**
(for Assiah):   **SHEMESH**

The Completion of the Magical Link & Charging the Eucharist

ALL: At climax of the chanting of "SHEMESH," and on **Magus'** signal, all stop moving, turn inward to face the altar (and specifically the wine), and all give the Sign of the Enterer toward the wine, feeling the raised energy flowing from the fingertips and charging the talisman. Retire in Sign of Silence, the right forefinger to the lips. Remain standing in place.

Magus: Holding hands over wine, perform final charging of the eucharist with appropriate names. Knock *** ***** *** (3-5-3)

ALL: One by one, move to the altar, take up a glass of wine, say **"May my True Will be done!"** and consume the eucharist. As each attendee finishes, he or she returns to their chair, and sits.

ALL: Sit peacefully and silently in the invoked atmosphere. **All spend 5-10 minutes scrying the astral atmosphere of the temple**, using whatever techniques they may choose (any such techniques should be accomplished silently, and without any movements that would distract other attendees). **Magus** signals quietly to bring the scrying to a close, when appropriate.

Banishing Specific Invoked Energies

Officiant 5: Perform Greater Banishing Ritual of the Hexagram of the Sun. Return to chair and sit.

License to Depart

Magus: "In the Name of HERU-RA-HA, I now set free any spirits imprisoned by this ceremony. Depart ye in peace unto your abodes and habitations. Be there peace between us, and be ye ready to come when called. May the blessings of IAO be upon you."

Knock * (1)

9

ASANA & PRANAYAMA

Asana and *pranayama* are two practices of *raja* ('royal') *yoga* that are deeply ingrained in the training system of the A∴A∴ and, of course, in other traditions around the world. Asana is posture, and pranayama is breath control. When we say breath control in this context, there's an implicit understanding that we're also speaking of control of the subtle *energy* residing in the breath and in the body. As we'll see, working with the breath through pranayama is a potent method of getting the kundalini —an integral part of our progress toward K & C of the HGA. I'm going to give you some useful tips, but for both asana and pranayama there really is no substitute for in-person supervision.

Within the A∴A∴, the aspirant will likely be experimenting with both asana and pranayama in the Probationer grade. However, there is no formal testing on these until a good bit later, in the grade of Zelator. For the test on asana, you have to be able to sit completely still in your chosen posture for a full hour. For pranayama, you must reach the second of the four stages described in the *Shiva Samhita*, which is called either 'trembling of the body,' or as Crowley sometimes refers to it, 'automatic rigidity.' This then gives way to a 'spasmodic trembling.' There are two core references in the Thelemic corpus that you'll want to use for both of these practices, *Liber E* and *Liber RV vel Spiritus*. You'll also find a good deal of additional information in *Eight Lectures on Yoga*.[16]

Asana

Within the A∴A∴ system, the purpose of asana is not to require the aspirant to master dozens of pretzel shapes. Rather, the aim is to find a posture that will allow you to sit still long enough to ignore your body. Until you can ignore your body, your mind will not be stilled; and until your mind is stilled you will not be able to master the more advanced meditation practices that are required to advance through later grades.

It is a very good idea to experiment with the different postures given in *Liber E* and elsewhere. Spend some considerable time with them. Note the differences in your results depending on which posture you choose. You're definitely going to find some postures that are more naturally suited to your body and, in contrast with what some people advise, I really don't think you need to purposely choose one that's difficult. Why frustrate yourself right from the start? You can begin with postures that are inherently easier for you.

No matter what posture you choose, you're going to have to push yourself through a good bit of discomfort and spend a good bit of time practicing before you really start to get results. This is much more likely to occur after you've extended your practice sessions beyond the half-hour mark, and with a good deal of regularity—five or six practice sessions per week at least. Until you get to that point, you're not really going to feel that asana 'lock in.' You'll know it when you feel it.

Again, the main point is to be able to forget about the body so that it's not attracting your attention. Discomfort is inevitable, but you should stop if you experience extreme pain—especially if a particular posture involves an area of existing injury or weakness. In such a case, that may not be the best posture for you. If you have bad knees or ankles, for example, the Dragon posture is not likely to be your best choice.

If you choose the God posture, one tip is to make sure that the chair height allows you to have your legs more or less at a right angle so that your upper legs are parallel to the floor. This will help you in a number of ways—it will reduce trembling in the legs, and it is also less likely to cut off circulation just behind your knees.

Of course, one of the underlying principles behind doing an asana practice is not only the stillness of the body but the forging of the self-discipline necessary for later practices, including simply sitting down and committing to doing it for a certain amount of time, and keeping regular

---

[16] Crowley, A. (1991). *Eight Lectures on Yoga.* Phoenix, AZ: New Falcon Publications.

with it in day-to-day practice. Crowley's general advice about meditation vigilance applies here: It's far better to decide you're going to meditate for 20 minutes and to spend those 20 minutes in horrible distracted meditation than to have 19 minutes of great meditation and then stop a minute early!

So, push through. Stick with it. Practice regularly. Don't be frustrated if it takes you quite a while to build up the length of time you're spending in the posture. Eventually, you'll get to that place where it locks in, and that will be a real milestone in your progress. After you break through that particular barrier, it tends to become much easier.

Pranayama

There are two core instructions here, as mentioned above. *Liber E* is basic instruction in pranayama, and when you achieve some mastery of *Liber E* you move to *Liber RV* for more advanced practices. While *Liber RV* is indeed a more advanced text, it contains so much good information on the theory and practice of pranayama, that I strongly suggest you read it carefully before you begin even the basic practices. It will help you form a more sturdy foundation for all your work.

Consult your doctor if you have any medical condition that affects the lungs, or if you have any doubts at all about the safety of these techniques. These practices are not generally dangerous unless they're performed improperly—usually by overstraining. We'll go into more detail on that a bit later.

There are a number of important benefits to be gained by practice of pranayama. For one thing, you're working to balance the energy channels in the body, the *ida* and the *pingala*—the lunar and solar currents in the spine corresponding to the two nostrils through which the breathing occurs. There are also general health benefits to proper breathing, but more subtly you're cultivating an improved ability to tolerate, contain, and direct magical force. In this case, we're speaking of the kundalini force, the life power which is resident in each of us. Through pranayama practices you forge a more stable and balanced energy system in your body so that you will be better able to direct these forces through magical ritual, willed intention, and in many other ways.

The benchmarks for pranayama results described by Crowley and the *Shiva Samhita* are in fact physically discernible Kundalini effects.[17] The four stages of this process are:

1. Fine perspiration on the body
2. Automatic rigidity, which gives way into a spasmodic trembling.

---

[17] *Shiva Samhita.* (1996). New Delhi: Munshiram Manoharlal Publishers Pvt. Ltd.

3. 'Jumping about like a frog'
4. So-called 'Levitation'

I'll leave it to your experimentation to detect what these phases actually entail. Please don't get so hung up on these traditional descriptions that you unduly front-load your experience with expectations. Proper practice and (ideally) competent supervision will teach you everything you need to know.

The practice begins as described in *Liber E*, with timed in-breaths and out-breaths. Crowley describes progressive levels for this, starting with breathing in for ten seconds through one nostril, out for twenty through the other nostril, back in for ten through that nostril, then back out for twenty through the first nostril. I always begin my practices with an in-breath through the left nostril, just as an easy way to mark where I'm starting and finishing (refer to the audio-visual materials for a video demonstration).

The photo captions in *Liber RV* are easily misconstrued. Crowley says there should be exertion, but it's very important to note that this does not mean *straining*. What is meant by exertion is that there is effort made to completely expel the air from the lungs and to completely fill the lungs on the inhalation; but the process itself is fairly serene and nearly silent, not noisy and raucous. The aim is smooth, regular breathing and fullness of in-breath and out-breath. You should never, *ever* feel short of breath. If you do, back down on your breath-times, and stay there until you can truly do it comfortably for a full hour. Only then should you move on to the next level.

The more advanced levels also include a period of holding of the breath between the inhalation and the exhalation. This pause is called *kumbakam*. There is a stillness and a silence during this pause that (with practice) potentiates some of the most advanced meditation results. Once again, I will leave it to your experimentation to show you what occurs in this place of stillness; but suffice it to say, it is a very powerful part of the process.

As you see in the old and grainy photos in *Liber RV*, the fingers, thumb, index and middle finger are used to pinch the nostrils shut. Basically, you're bracing your index and middle fingers on your forehead and then using the thumb and the ring finger to pinch alternating sides of the nose. Also, in the *Liber RV* illustrations, you'll see that Crowley is digging in the elbows into the chest in order to expel the air, and leaning back, pulling the head back and expanding the lungs during the inhalation. Again, this is a way of using the whole body to promote fullness of the breaths.

You will want to time the in-breaths and out-breaths very precisely, and I find the best method for this is to have a ticking clock nearby.

Using this method, you don't have to think about the pace of your counting or look repeatedly at a silent watch or clock. A metronome would work fine as well, as long as the sound isn't too annoying.

One thing you will *not* find in the published instructions is what to do when you've concluded the timed breathing, yet I have found that these moments can bring some of the most striking results of the whole practice. Let's say you've done 20 or 30 minutes worth of cycles in one of and concluded with the last exhalation through a single nostril. I suggest that you really savor that first breath in through both nostrils and spend the next five or ten minutes with gentle, easy, natural breathing. This can be a real 'high'—having gone through the entire pranayama session, balancing the two energy channels in alternation, you're now experiencing the effects of their conjoined action in an ecstatic and energized state. You can accentuate this experience with visualizations, and other more advanced practices taught within A∴A∴, the Temple of the Silver Star, and elsewhere. Don't miss the chance to relish the peace and stillness this moment offers.

One of the most common problems with the practice of pranayama, aside from the tendency to strain too much, is clogged nostrils. The traditional remedy for this is the *neti* pot, which is used to cleanse the nostrils with salt water. Decongestant nasal sprays are another option. You shouldn't use these chronically, but if you're having two or three stuffy days and you want to try to do pranayama, these modern conveniences can be very helpful.

One additional technique for combating stuffy-nose syndrome is to use the hand that is not being used to pinch the nostrils to hold open whichever nostril you're breathing through. It's rather awkward, but on those particularly stuffy days this may help get you through your practice session. On the other hand, there are going to be days when you're simply too sick or stuffy to do these practices. Don't beat yourself up about that, just pick a different sort of practice for that day, and return to pranayama when you're able.

As with most of the practices in the A∴A∴ curriculum, asana and pranayama are means to an end and not the end in themselves. Ultimately, success in these practices converges with the devotional exercises, the ritual magick, advanced meditation, and other tools in the outer grades of A∴A∴ to lead the aspirant right to the threshold of K & C.

Recommended Reading:

Crowley, A. (1991). *Eight Lectures on Yoga*. Phoenix, AZ: New Falcon Publications.

Crowley, A. (1992). Liber E. In I. Regardie (Ed.), *Gems from the Equinox*. Scottsdale, AZ: New Falcon Publications.

Crowley, A. (1992). Liber RV vel Spiritus. In I. Regardie (Ed.), *Gems from the Equinox*. Scottsdale, AZ: New Falcon Publications.

10

Meditation & Visualization Practices

This chapter will review the basics of meditation practice, and give some tips and troubleshooting advice. We'll also take a look at a few useful and important visualization practices relevant to the Thelemic practitioner—some from the formal A∴A∴ curriculum and some from other sources. Like many of the topics covered in this book, meditation has a huge continuum of practice. In the earliest stages, it's *really* basic; yet it's also a practice that can carry one through to the highest levels of attainment.

Typically, when we speak about meditation in the context of the curriculum of A∴A∴, we're likely to be referring to raja yoga-style meditation; but you'll see from the discussion here that there are a lot of other options open to you. Some within the traditional A∴A∴ curriculum rely on Buddhist techniques, and some are entirely unique practices designed to potentiate certain transformational processes in the system.

In the system of A∴A∴, the Probationer is likely to do quite a bit of experimentation with *dharana* (concentration) as well as *asana* and *pranayama*. In the Neophyte and Zelator grades the aspirant works with the practices known as MMM and AAA (drawn from *Liber HHH*). Essentially, these are guided imagery exercises based on the initiatory formulæ of these grades. They are undertaken as a means of deepening the aspirant's understanding of these formulæ, and accelerating their action. The Practicus works with *Liber Turris,* which is a powerful but very challenging practice in control of thought.[18] *Liber Jugorum* is a form of control over thought, word, and deed, spread out across several grades.[19] The whole process is brought to a climax—a single point of focus—at the Dominus Liminus grade. As stated on the Dominus Liminus task paper, "He shall meditate on the diverse knowledge and power that he has acquired and harmonize it perfectly." In other words, the climax of all the raja yoga that has gone before is the resultant one-pointed focus of the mind. The Great Work becomes a living meditation, throughout the day-to-day life, on the synthesis of the elemental grades and all that they represent inside the aspirant at this stage of the path.

The meditative aspects of raja yoga begin with the process of concentration, called *dharana.* When this is sustained successfully, we experience *dhyana*—the union of subject and object, ego and non-ego, the observer and the observed. In the course of improving our ability to meditate, we also obtain more control over the vacillations of the mind itself, and this is known as *pratyahara.* Finally, all these techniques may ultimately lead to the result we call *samadhi,* which is a transcendent state of consciousness beyond rational apprehension or description.

Since basic practice begins with *dharana,* that's what we're going to focus on here. It really is the bread and butter of daily practice and is likely to be so for weeks or months before other more advanced results occur. *Asana* is often used as a preparation for *dharana,* as well as being practiced simultaneously. As noted in Chapter 9, one of the main purposes of *asana* is simply to attain skill in keeping the body still, thereby allowing the mind to ignore stimuli coming from the body. When we are not distracted by the body, we can put our focus on the object of our meditation.

It is useful to have some quantitative sense of how you're doing, and that's why many teachers recommend that you count the inevitable 'breaks' of concentration that occur during your meditation. One of the easiest ways to do this is to use your fingers. You count on one hand, and as soon as you hit five breaks on that hand, you put down one finger on the other hand, and continue. When you get another five on the 'singles' hand, you put a second finger down on the 'fives' hand, so you know you've had ten breaks. Obviously, you can count up to twenty-five breaks this way, which is usually plenty. If you get past twenty-five

---

[18] Crowley, A. (1992). Liber Turris. In I. Regardie (Ed.), *Gems from the Equinox.* Scottsdale, AZ: New Falcon Publications.

[19] Crowley, A. (1992). Liber Jugorum. In I. Regardie (Ed.), *Gems from the Equinox.* Scottsdale, AZ: New Falcon Publications.

breaks, don't bother continuing with the counting. Just put it down as a bad session and try to do better the next time.

Generally speaking, you should begin each meditation session with a specific time-goal in mind. You should train your mind and body to listen to your conscious intention, and requiring them to shut up and be still for a pre-determined period of time is a major step toward developing this self-discipline. Later on, the goals shift toward more advanced results of *dhyana, pratyahara*, and *samadhi.* Yet at this beginning stage, the crucial task is to maintain vigilance and obey your own inner taskmaster—not letting your mind or body intrude, interrupt or otherwise be an obstacle to your stated will.

It is very important that your attitude during meditation is one of *allowing,* not forcing, the mind to be still; much as you can't lie in bed and force yourself to go to sleep. Initiation of sleep is not an active process, but a passive one, where you relax the mental control that keeps you vigilant and alert. Your attitude toward yourself during the practice should be gentle rather than punitive. It becomes yet another distraction from meditation if you're cursing at yourself for letting your mind wander—but your mind certainly will wander! When it happens, simply think of it as a cloud passing over the sun, and gently draw your attention back to the focus of your meditation.

Holding Mental Images
Let's take one classic meditation technique as an example: holding a single image in your mind. Classically, you might choose one of the *tattvas*, such as the red equilateral triangle (*tejas)*. Soon after you begin, you will notice that the mind will play all sorts of tricks on you. The image will jump around, change color, assume ridiculous proportions, and engage in all sorts of other mischief. Again, when this happens, rather than mentally 'clenching' on it, or being upset about it, you should *soften* around it. Allow the shape-shifting, color-changing, or whatever it may be to pass, and simply reinforce the basic image. Focus on the image for a set period of time, count your breaks, and record the other conditions of the experiment such as how much food you had in your stomach, your level of fatigue, the physical conditions of your meditation room, any psychological disturbances that might form your mental set going in to the exercise, and so on.

Mantra
Another type of meditation you might wish to try is the use of silent, rhythmic *mantra*. Choose a phrase or multi-syllabic word like "Ra-Hoor-Khuit" and repeat it in a sustained, rhythmic and unbroken fashion, i.e. "Ra – Hoor – Khuit… Ra – Hoor – Khuit … Ra – Hoor – Khuit…," and so on. Insert a pause of approximately the same length as each of the

syllables, to establish a consistent four-fold rhythm. Do this for the specified period of time, and count your breaks. Any mantram will work, but you'll probably want to choose something with which you feel a certain personal resonance.

Breath Awareness
The practice of breath awareness is another good option for meditation. This really can be as simple as focusing on your inhalations and exhalations, but I find it is more effective if you pair it with timed breaths. For example, you could use the classic 'fourfold breath' technique described by Israel Regardie—simply make each phase of the breath (in—pause—out—pause) of equal length. The key with this practice is not to make each phase too slow, otherwise you'll find yourself straining for breath.

An equally simple, but considerably more powerful, breathing-awareness technique is called *mahasatipatthana*. This practice involves observation of the passage of the breath while silently commenting on what is observed. It is not exactly a mantra, in that it should not devolve into a rote rhythm; rather, it should remain an active observation. You begin by witnessing your breath, at a natural rate and depth, and each time you breathe in, you say silently, "The breath moves in." As you breathe out, you say silently, "The breath moves out." Interestingly, as you progress with this (likely over the course of many weeks of consistent practice) your results will typically show a progressive dis-identification with your ego. For example, you might go from simply saying, "The breath is moving in; the breath is moving out," to noticing what you're actually observing is that there is a *sensation* that the breath is moving in and out. Later, this may transform into an awareness that what you're experiencing is merely a *perception* of a sensation of the cycles of the breath. This is crucial: you change what you're saying silently to yourself, based on what you're actually noticing; and if you follow this to its conclusion you'll get to some very interesting places indeed. I don't want to spoil it for you by front-loading your experience, so try it yourself. See how you experience the ego-disidentification, and what conclusions you draw from it after ample practice.

Even an advanced meditator will attest that it is quite difficult to get the mind to *cease conscious thought,* but the practices found in Crowley's *Liber Turris*, involve doing just this. Here are its core instructions:

> 0. This practice is very difficult. The student cannot hope for much success unless he have thoroughly mastered Asana, and obtained much definite success in the meditation-practices of *Liber E* and *Liber HHH.*

On the other hand, any success in this practice is of an exceedingly high character, and the student is less liable to illusion and self-deception in this than in almost any other that We make known.

1. First Point. The student should first discover for himself the apparent position of the point in his brain where thoughts arise, if there be such a point. If not, he should seek the position of the point where thoughts are judged.
2. Second Point. He must also develop in himself a Will of Destruction, even a Will of Annihilation. It may be that this shall be discovered at an immeasurable distance from his physical body. Nevertheless, this must he reach, with this must he identify himself even to the loss of himself.
3. Third Point. Let this Will then watch vigilantly the point where thoughts arise, or the point where they are judged, and let every thought be annihilated as it is perceived or judged.
4. Fourth Point. Next, let every thought be inhibited in its inception.
5. Fifth Point. Next, let even the causes or tendencies that if unchecked ultimate in thoughts be discovered and annihilated.
6. Sixth and Last Point. Let the true Cause of All be unmasked and annihilated.
7. This is that which was spoken by wise men of old time concerning the destruction of the world by fire; yea, the destruction of the world by fire.
8. Let the Student remember that each Point represents a definite achievement of great difficulty.[20]

There is much more of value to be found in this liber, but those are the basic instructions. I encourage you to try these practices when you feel you are ready.

Visualization Practices

Here we're talking about visualization in a different sense than described above. These practices are more active and complex—akin to modern 'guided imagery' exercises.

The curriculum of A∴A∴ is cleverly designed so that the Neophyte and the Zelator undertake what are essentially self-guided imagery exercises based on the initiatory formulæ of those grades. These

---

[20] Crowley, A. (1992). Liber RV vel Spiritus. In I. Regardie (Ed.), *Gems from the Equinox*. Scottsdale, AZ: New Falcon Publications.

exercises are found in *Liber HHH*, sections MMM and AAA, which correspond to the Neophyte and Zelator formulæ, respectively. I'll give you a taste of the MMM exercise here, in case you want to experiment with it. If you attempt this practice, I suggest you start by recording yourself reading the instructions, as it would obviously be distracting to try to take yourself through these visualizations while glancing at a book every few seconds. Eventually, you'll want to memorize the whole set of instructions. It will undoubtedly require multiple trials to get optimal results, and your own level of initiation will be one determinant of your level of success. Those acquainted with *Liber Pyramidos* or other expressions of the Neophyte formula will recognize a few familiar themes here. This is the core instruction:

0. Be seated in thine Asana, wearing the robe of a Neophyte, the hood drawn.
1. It is night, heavy and hot, there are no stars. Not one breath of wind stirs the surface of the sea, that is thou. No fish play in thy depths.
2. Let a Breath rise and ruffle the waters. This also thou shalt feel playing upon thy skin. It will disturb thy meditation twice or thrice, after which thou shouldst have conquered this distraction. But unless thou first feel it, that Breath hath not arisen.
3. Next, the night is riven by the lightning flash. This also shalt thou feel in thy body, which shall shiver and leap with the shock, and that also must both be suffered and overcome.
4. After the lightning flash, resteth in the zenith a minute point of light. And that light shall radiate until a right cone be established upon the sea, and it is day.
    With this thy body shall be rigid, automatically; and this shalt thou let endure, withdrawing thyself into thine heart in the form of an upright Egg of blackness; and therein shalt thou abide for a space.
5. When all this is perfectly and easily performed at will, let the aspirant figure to himself a struggle with the whole force of the Universe. In this he is only saved by his minuteness. But in the end he is overcome by Death, who covers him with a black cross.
    Let his body fall supine with arms outstretched.
6. So lying, let him aspire fervently unto the Holy Guardian Angel.
7. Now let him resume his former posture. Two and twenty times shall he figure to himself that he is bitten by a serpent, feeling even in his body the poison thereof. And let each bite be healed by an eagle or hawk, spreading its wings above his head, and dropping

84

thereupon a healing dew. But let the last bite be so terrible a pang at the nape of the neck that he seemeth to die, and let the healing dew be of such virtue that he leapeth to his feet.

8. Let there be now placed within his egg a red cross, then a green cross, then a golden cross, then a silver cross; or those things which these shadow forth. Herein is silence; for he that hath rightly performed the meditation will understand the inner meaning thereof, and it shall serve as a test of himself and his fellows.

9. Let him now remain in the Pyramid or Cone of Light, as an Egg, but no more of blackness.

10. Then let his body be in the position of the Hanged Man, and let him aspire with all his force unto the Holy Guardian Angel.

11. The grace having been granted unto him, let him partake mystically of the Eucharist of the Five Elements and let him proclaim Light in Extension; yea, let him proclaim Light in Extension.[21]

In the remainder of this chapter, I will present a few other options for visualization exercises drawn from outside the formal A∴A∴ curriculum. All of these practices should begin with preparatory relaxation and rhythmic breathing.

The Inner Teacher: Follow a path into a forest and see a figure approaching, which you conceive as the perfect inner teacher. You can think of this an aspect of the Holy Guardian Angel, a wise mentor, or anything else you like. Regardless, the key is that you have confidence in the wisdom which will be imparted to you. When the teacher approaches, ask for a symbol, a word, an action, or other instruction, with full awareness that this instruction will be of particular use to you at your stage of the Great Work.

The Inner Lover: Build in your mind and heart a sequence of visualizations of all the forms of love you have experienced. Take yourself through a series of visualizations where you try to tap in as viscerally as possible to (for example) the hug you once received from a friend or a parent, the embrace of a lover, and so on—whatever forms of love you have ever known and can recall easily. As you move through the sequence, build up the intensity and vividness of the feelings of love,

---

[21] Crowley, A. (1992). Liber HHH. In I. Regardie (Ed.), *Gems from the Equinox*. Scottsdale, AZ: New Falcon Publications.

until your entire being is subsumed with this force. Feel your vast capacity for experiencing love and *know* that in actuality, you have access to this powerhouse of force at all times, and you can generate it with no other human intervention. You may wish to conceive that the source of this love is, ultimately, the HGA itself.

The Inner Treasure: Conceive that you are going down into the recesses of your mind—deep into the unconscious. Go down stairs or down an elevator—whatever visual device works for you. There you discover an ancient chamber in which there is a treasure chest. You know that you will find three objects within. You also know that each of these objects, which may be familiar or unfamiliar to you, will convey a specific teaching relevant to your present life situation. It might be a suggestion about how to overcome an obstacle; it might be something that gives you insights into your particular stage of the Great Work. In any case, you should mindfully reach into the chest and see which objects present themselves to you. Don't try to decide in advance what you will find. Take careful note of what they are, then (either within the meditation or after) consider what these symbols might mean to you. As always, record your results in the magical diary.

Recommended Reading:

Crowley, A. (1991). *Eight Lectures on Yoga.* Phoenix, AZ: New Falcon Publications.

Crowley, A. (1992). Liber E. In I. Regardie (Ed.), *Gems from the Equinox.* Scottsdale, AZ: New Falcon Publications.

Crowley, A. (1997). *Magick: Liber ABA.* Hymenaeus Beta (Ed.). York Beach, ME: Samuel Weiser, Inc. [Note: with particular attention to Part I, Mysticism]

Crowley, A. (1992). Liber HHH. In I. Regardie (Ed.), *Gems from the Equinox.* Scottsdale, AZ: New Falcon Publications.

Crowley, A. (1992). Liber Turris. In I. Regardie (Ed.), *Gems from the Equinox.* Scottsdale, AZ: New Falcon Publications.

11

ASTRAL PROJECTION & THE CONTROL OF
THE BODY OF LIGHT

Astral projection is one of the most basic magical techniques and one of the most important to master as you progress on your path. In the system of A∴A∴, the Neophyte is thoroughly tested in the mastery of the "Body of Light", although he or she will likely have been experimenting with such things right from the outset as a Probationer. In his excellent essay, "Notes for an Astral Atlas," Aleister Crowley writes:

> The general control of the Astral Plane, the ability to find one's way about it, to penetrate such sanctuaries as are guarded from the profane, to make such relations with its inhabitants as may avail to acquire knowledge and power, or to command service; all this is a question of the general Magical attainment of the student. He must be absolutely at ease in his Body of Light, and have made it invulnerable. He must be adept in assuming all God-forms, in using all weapons, sigils, gestures, words, and signs. He must be familiar with the names and numbers pertinent to the work in

hand. He must be alert, sensitive, and ready to exert his authority; yet courteous, gracious, patient, and sympathetic.[22]

General Considerations

Much of the discussion in this chapter will be practical in nature, but I think it's important to discuss a bit of theory about the process of astral projection and the nature of the astral body itself.

One of the issues that should be clarified right at the outset is the distinction between the etheric body and the astral body. This distinction can be understood in terms of the Tree of Life. As discussed earlier in this book, the Tree of Life is a symbolic representation not only of the process of creation of the material world but of the component parts of the human psycho-spiritual constitution. Accordingly, if you look at the way the Sephiroth on the Tree successively manifest, it is evident that mind manifests before body. The collective spheres of the ruach form a template—a skeleton of sorts—for the eventual manifestation of the physical body at Malkuth. Just as the physical body of humans is built on this astral skeleton of energy, so is the physical world based on a similar astral framework. The most dense layers of this are more properly called the etheric world; accordingly, the most dense layer of our energy body —short of the physical body itself—is the etheric body. The etheric body more closely resembles the actual physical form of the body, whereas the astral body resembles mind itself. It is more rarefied, and capable of taking on a wider diversity of forms, not just those which are more closely tied to the physical forms that are built upon it (as is the case with the etheric body).

The reason I'm taking such pains to distinguish between the astral and etheric bodies is that there are distinctly different sets of practices involved in working with them when you undertake astral or etheric projection. When etherically projecting, you're going to be in a "body" that rather closely resembles your physical body, and the landscape that you're exploring will be like an energetic skeleton of your actual physical surroundings. An etheric projection experience will give you the sensation of leaving your body and walking around the room, the house, the neighborhood, and so on. An astral projection experience, on the other hand, will take you to a landscape that is completely different from your physical surroundings, and quite possibly different from any materially existing place whatsoever. Remember, this is the realm of mind itself—infinitely plastic, and able to shape itself into forms that simply don't exist in the physical world.

---

[22] Crowley, A. (1997). *Magick: Liber ABA.* Hymenaeus Beta (Ed.). York Beach, ME: Samuel Weiser, Inc.

Testing Entities and Confirming the Plane

Let's look at a few techniques and tools, so you can begin (or refine) your experiments. There are a few general procedures you should always observe. Crowley emphasizes one particular point repeatedly in his writings on this topic: the importance of testing all entities that you encounter. None of these entities are going to be offended if you don't believe them about who they are or what they say they're trying to tell you. So test them, using signs or formulæ that you may know, such as saying, "Do what thou wilt shall be the whole of the Law," to which they should respond with "Love is the law, love under will." Or use A∴A∴ grade signs, such as the Sign of the Enterer with the Sign of Silence as a response. You should ask any entities that appear for their names, and the spelling thereof. Check the gematria of the name, and the nature of the surroundings that you find yourself in, using your knowledge of magical correspondences (see *777*) to be sure you have "arrived" in the proper plane. For example, if you've invoked Jupiter and yet you find yourself in some sort of landscape that is full of orange-colored hermaphrodites, you may have taken a left turn into Mercury. (The most likely cause of such occurrences is an improperly performed invocation, or residual extraneous energies from an improperly banished space.) If you detect an error, try to discover its source and start the experiment over from the beginning.

Working Methodology

When preparing to undertake an astral or etheric projection, it is best if you are not too full of food, especially meat. Excessive fatigue is to be avoided as well. If you are in the middle of projection and you find yourself feeling fatigued, either mentally or with (what will feel like) physical fatigue, it's best to end the session then, rather than straining yourself by persisting. I also suggest you avoid orgasmic release in the day or so leading up to your projection, as it appears the life energy which would otherwise be discharged via orgasm is a useful "fuel" for astral visions.

Set aside a solid hour or so, when you won't be disturbed; choose a quiet place, preferably the temple in which you are accustomed to working. Start with a basic banishing—I suggest the LBRP or the Star Ruby for this purpose. For your first experiment, try etheric projection. Settle into a relaxed posture, do some rhythmic breathing for a few moments, and get as relaxed as you can. Then, imagine that you are exuding energy out the front of your physical body (some teachers suggest that you see this emerging from your *manipura* chakra as a silvery cord). Shape this externalized energy into a form that corresponds to your physical body. You have now formed an etheric double. Next, try to transfer your consciousness into this etheric double, and begin looking around the room you're in. Begin to see with those eyes, walk around the room, look at objects, go outside, walk around in your yard, and so on. Just explore the etheric world and see what you come up with. If you want to test yourself on this etheric level of work, you could have a friend who is in a location that you've never been to or don't know very well. Etherically project to that place and see if you can then tell your friend about details that you wouldn't have had knowledge of otherwise. Your friend can then either confirm or deny the accuracy of your description.

Now, let's talk about the tools and techniques of astral projection. It begins much the same way. You've banished, you're seated in a relaxed posture, and then you externalize the energy in front of you. Once again you shape it into a double of yourself. I think you'll find you get better results if you see yourself robed in magical garments that correspond to your grade, or the specific type of work you're doing. For example, if you want to visit a particular sephira on the Tree of Life, you might clothe yourself in the robe of the A∴A∴ grade that corresponds to that sephira. Once you've externalized the energy, shaped it the way you want, and transferred your consciousness into the astral double, then (and here's where the difference between etheric and astral work comes into play), begin to rise straight upward in your astral body.

The purpose of this technique is to trick the mind into letting go of its hold on the physical body using the imaginal device of physically rising higher. It's not necessarily that your astral body is "going" anywhere, *per se*; it's just that you need some kind of device to shake up your perceptions. So rise straight up and keep going, higher and higher, until you find yourself in some sort of landscape you can begin to explore. Once you've arrived at your desired destination, it's often useful to perform a LIRP and perhaps also a Middle Pillar ritual, to energize the astral body for the work that's ahead. Next, call for a guide and rigorously test it. Get a name, check the correspondences, test with signs and words, and so on. And then explore the region as best you can.

Once you've done all the exploration that you're going to do, thank and dismiss your guide. You can then return to your body. Move your muscles around, and really feel yourself solidly back in your body. You want to avoid so-called *astral bleeding,* where all of your energy has not come back to the body properly; so be sure that this is strongly visualized and that you feel fully reunited with your physical body. You might wish to very mindfully give the Sign of Silence, figuring yourself as Harpocrates in the egg. You may also wish to do another LBRP after you're back—just to be on the safe side, and to come out of the whole experience without any unwanted lingering influence of whatever specific region you were exploring.

Troubleshooting

If you get into trouble, such as feeling harassed or threatened by entities you encounter, try enlarging yourself into a huge towering God-form of Ra-Hoor-Khuit and powerfully send the entity away. Or you can draw a large banishing pentagram and project that toward the offending entity. Occasionally, you may go very deep into a vision of some kind and have trouble finding your way 'back' to your physical body. One thing Crowley suggests in such circumstances is to envision yourself in a giant chariot drawn by great steeds, and then command them to take you back to your body. This may sound a bit silly but it works. You will doubtless develop other techniques for getting out of trouble as you gain expertise, but these should get you started.

Testing Your Success

As you will see in the chapter on the methods and tools of A∴A∴, the work of the path of *tav* during the Neophyte grade of A∴A∴ involves the development of control of the astral body. The Superior will test the Neophyte using various techniques such as scrying a symbol that is unknown to the person being examined but well known to the examiner. The task is to see if they can detect the basic nature of the symbol through astral inspection. You can do this yourself if you have a friend who is fairly magically adept, or at least knowledgeable enough to pick a sigil or a symbol and grasp its basic meaning. They should pick a symbol with which you are completely unfamiliar. They can then give you the symbol, and you scry it by imagining it is inscribed on a large astral "door." Project through the door and see what you find. If you've done well, then what you find there—the correspondences, the tone of the place, and any information given to you by entities—will match the nature of the sigil, and your friend will be able to confirm this. Another test is to have a friend who is a competent magician invoke specific forces into a room while you are not present; you can then go in and explore the space using the procedures I've described above.

This chapter just scratches the surface of the many possible techniques you could use to explore the astral and etheric worlds, but hopefully this will be enough to get you started, and perhaps stimulate you to experiment and see what you find. As with many other magical techniques, your persistent practice will be well rewarded.

Recommended Reading:

Denning, M. & Phillips, O. (2010). *A Practical Guide to Astral Projection*. Woodbury, MN: Llewellyn Publications.
Muldoon, S. & Carrington, H. (2003). *Projection of the Astral Body*. Whitefish, MT: Kessinger Publishing, LLC.

12

DEVOTIONAL PRACTICES

In *The Book of the Law* we read, "Wisdom says: be strong! Then canst thou bear more joy." [II:70] One important tool for strengthening ourselves in accordance with this injunction is the diligent performance of devotional practices in our daily magical work. This advice is not to be taken lightly—spiritual ecstasy can overwhelm a weak or unbalanced vessel. It is crucial to train ourselves in a gradual and progressive manner, and this chapter will review some of the tools available for this course of work.

The primary technique involved can be summarized in these words: "Invoke often. Enflame thyself in prayer." While this may seem like obvious or underwhelming advice, I think what's often missed is that it is this very devotion that *fuels* much of the work of the First Order of A∴A∴ as we progress toward Knowledge and Conversation of the Holy Guardian Angel. *Liber Astarte*[23] is the primary instruction in such methods, and not surprisingly it appears on the syllabus of the Philosophus, the grade corresponding to Netzach.

As I referenced in Chapter 15, this flame of devotion, aspiration and desire is *directed,* by virtue of the training in raja yoga in the A∴A∴,

---

[23] Crowley, A. (1992). Liber Astarte. In I. Regardie (Ed.), *Gems from the Equinox*. Scottsdale, AZ: New Falcon Publications.

toward that one single aim of the First Order aspirant—the K&C. Without this training of the mind, there are too many vectors of force shooting out in different directions. On the other hand, without the enflaming of the self through devotional practices, there is spiritual dryness—the mind may be focused and sharp, but the flame of aspiration is missing. The Hod and Netzach aspects of ourselves must work together in this endeavor, as we aim ourselves forcefully and *precisely* towards Tiphereth and the HGA.

Before we explore the more formal techniques given in *Liber Astarte*, let's look at a few simple daily practices you may find useful. The first is essentially a mindfulness practice—an awareness of lovingly embracing the reality presented to us in each and every moment. This not only reminds us that every experience of life is an aspect of Nuit, and as such, a perfect expression of the All; but also it enables us, in that moment, to consciously identify with that star at our center, the *khabs*, rather than the human personality—the *khu* we have woven about it.

The wisdom teaching here, which each of us must verify for ourselves through experience, is that it is only the personality level of our being that judges, rejects, or condemns the experiences of life. It is only that outer shell that attempts to steer away from things that we deem to be offensive or repulsive, and toward those things that we find beautiful. There is indeed a deep impulse toward beauty in the human soul that can guide us toward the HGA. However, we must transcend the reflexive ego-level rejection of things that don't fit our prejudices and aesthetics, and the equally habitual and automatic acceptance of things that please our ego.

The HGA has constructed the present reality to be the perfect opportunity for your growth; to be *exactly* the lesson you need at any given moment, to hone you into the perfect vessel for its indwelling. If you push away the reality right in front of you, rejecting that aspect of Nuit manifesting in your life right at that moment, it is like you are refusing to locate yourself on a map. How can you proceed to enact your will and follow your path forward to a goal, if you refuse to acknowledge your present location as a starting place? Embrace all the universe offers you in your daily life whether your ego likes it or not. You will thereby maximize your ability to move forward in accordance with will.

Another useful daily practice is to maintain mindfulness of all aspects of love we encounter. As we'll see with our review of *Liber Astarte* later in this chapter, each form of love we encounter—whether of a partner, a parent, a friend, a child, even a kind stranger—is a glimmer of the love of the HGA. Here again, this tap into the most enlightened aspects of ruach that are symbolized by the sphere of Tiphereth, the center of the spiritually awakened ego-consciousness.

Now, let's take a look at some of the formal devotional practices available to us in the curriculum of A∴A∴. *Liber Had* and *Liber NU* are two practices I strongly recommend. These are essentially tantric instructions in the cultivation of worship of the inner energetic polarities symbolized by these two 'deities.' You identify with a particular viewpoint, either of Had or of Nu, and then aspire to attain its opposite (and complement.) The methods used in these libri have much to teach us about strengthening the muscles of devotion. You can read more about these practices in the chapter on sex magick.

Another very important daily practice is *Liber Resh*. As discussed in Chapter 4, many people undertake this as a mindfulness practice—as a way of 'tuning in' to the Thelemic current throughout the day—and certainly this is a generic benefit of *Resh*. Yet there are a few ways to deepen the devotional aspects of this practice worth mentioning. At each quarter you are adoring one manifestation of the divine principle symbolized by the sun. Accordingly, you have an opportunity at each quarter to narrow your focus of worship onto one of these particular manifestations—Ra at dawn, Ahathoor at noon, and so on. As with any invocation or adoration such as this, the more intensely you identify with the God-form, the more magical force will be available to you.

The second part of each quarterly adoration in *Liber Resh*—the part that begins with "Unity uttermost showed!"—is an opportunity to adore the single divine principle *behind* all of these multifaceted manifestations of the solar principle. We can conceive of this in several different ways. This might simply be an adoration of the physical sun in the macrocosm; or we could adore that solar, generative, life-giving aspect of self within each of us; or we can take this as an opportunity to adore our own HGA, symbolized by the sun.

The only limit here is your own creativity and 'right ingenium,' as you develop your unique inner language of devotion. This is, in fact, the central purpose of devotional practice. Through experience, we cultivate a sense of the divine; a sense of awe and reverence in our relationship to the divine; and we use that as a springboard for further attainment.

Now let's move on to our consideration of *Liber Astarte*. While it is formally assigned to the Philosophus, even the Probationer is likely to experiment with it. In this practice, beautifully described by Crowley, you pick a deity—any deity that appeals to you—and develop various methods of worship in order to strengthen the 'muscles' of devotion. It is like a trial run, if you will, of the eventual K & C working. Crowley gives fairly detailed instructions on developing invocations and other forms of worship, decorating the shrine of your deity, and so on. Importantly, he also encourages us to remember that this deity is really just one reflection of the divine. If we lose sight of this, we risk overly identifying with a partial force, rather than the one spiritual star in our sight—the HGA.

One of the key practices in *Liber Astarte* is the development of a sevenfold adoration (seven being the number of Netzach) in honor of your chosen deity. Crowley describes how the seven parts of this adoration reflect seven aspects or varieties of love, thus:

> First, an Imprecation, as of a slave unto his Lord.
> Second, an Oath, as of a vassal to his Liege.
> Third, a Memorial, as of a child to his Parent.
> Fourth, an Orison, as of a Priest unto his God.
> Fifth, a Colloquy, as of a Brother with his Brother.
> Sixth, a Conjuration, as to a Friend with his Friend.
> Seventh, a Madrigal, as of a Lover to his Mistress.
> And mark well that the first should be of awe, the second of fealty, the third of dependence, the fourth of adoration, the fifth of confidence, the sixth of comradeship, the seventh of passion.

As an example of how these instructions might translate into actual practice, let's take a look at a few excerpts from Jane Wolfe's working of *Liber Astarte*, which she began in November, 1933, at Agape Lodge of O.T.O. She chose the goddess Hera—the wife of Zeus in Greek mythology—to be the focus of her work. As Crowley recommends, there are seven stanzas in Wolfe's invocation of Hera, each of which corresponds to one of the seven aspects of love listed above. Here is the second stanza, which represents "an Oath, as of a vassal to his Liege":

> Hera, Invincible, Sovereign Goddess!
> To thee do I swear my fealty and allegiance.
> Great Goddess of Power, Majesty, and Might!
> To thee do I swear my fealty and allegiance.
> Thou that wieldest the Thunderbolt and Lightning!
> To thee do I swear my fealty and allegiance.
> Thou that causest the Earth and All that dwell therein to tremble
> To thee do I swear my fealty and allegiance.
> Great Mistress of the Wind and Storm!
> Proud-Crested Sovereign Goddess!
> To thee do I swear my fealty and allegiance.

Contrast this with the sixth stanza of the adoration, which represents "a Conjuration, as to a Friend with his Friend":

> Hera, Beloved Friend!
> Chief Protectress of Woman!
> Guardian of Childbirth and of Children!

Dispenser of Fertility and Abundance!
Lover of the Pomegranate and the Vine!
Regard me, a woman, walking in your midst.
I need Thy Guidance –
That my Mind may be open to the Influence of the
Highest;
That my Heart may be flooded with Love;
That my Soul may be purged of Selfishness;
That my Body may be Strong and Resilient,
My whole Being, Firm-Flexible!
For the Working of my Will!

Finally, consider the seventh stanza of Wolfe's adoration, "a Madrigal, as of a Lover to his Mistress," as well as the final climactic lines:

Hera, Mistress! Wife! Lover!
Thou Adored and Adoring!
Bend close to me, Thou Lover, that I may feel Thy Breath
upon my face!
Thy Dear, Delicious Perfumes in my nostrils!
At the Touch of Thy Body I am caught up in a Rapture of
Delight!
Thy Mouth swings me out over the world!
Heaven, Hell, and Starry Sky,
Time, Space, and Eternity,
Are all dissolved in Thy Blissful Embrace!
And Thy Being merged in mine carries me through Eons
of Time
Out, Out into the Great Sea of All-That-Is!

I stand among the Gods! I stand among the Gods!!
And I do my Will among the Living!!
Mistress! Wife! Beloved!
Thrice, Thrice, Thrice Beloved HERA!!!

Each of these aspects of love conveys an instruction in the relationship to the HGA. That is, each and every form of love that we perceive and experience in our lives is a foreshadowing of the love of the HGA—a hint or glimmer of that rapturous union that awaits us. Crowley addresses this idea in *Liber Astarte* when he says:

Thus do thou pass through all adventures of love, not omitting one; and to each do thou conclude: How pale a reflection is this of my love for this Deity! Yet from each shalt thou draw some knowledge of love, some intimacy with love, that shall aid thee to perfect thy love. Thus learn the humility of love from one, its obedience from another, its intensity from a third, its purity from a fourth, its peace from yet a fifth. So then thy love being made perfect, it shall be worthy of that perfect love of His.

No matter which specific practices you choose to undertake, I am sure you will find that the devotional components of your magical work are a source of beauty and power. It is my hope that these pathways of love will, one day, lead you to the embrace of your own Holy Guardian Angel.

Recommended Reading:

By Aleister Crowley:

Crowley, A. (1992). Liber Astarte vel Berylii. In I. Regardie (Ed.), *Gems from the Equinox*. Scottsdale, AZ: New Falcon Publications.
Crowley, A. (1992). Liber E. In I. Regardie (Ed.), *Gems from the Equinox*. Scottsdale, AZ: New Falcon Publications.
Crowley, A. (1992). Gnostic Mass. In I. Regardie (Ed.), *Gems from the Equinox*. Scottsdale, AZ: New Falcon Publications.
Crowley, A. (1992). Liber NU. In I. Regardie (Ed.), *Gems from the Equinox*. Scottsdale, AZ: New Falcon Publications.
Crowley, A. (1992). Liber Had. In I. Regardie (Ed.), *Gems from the Equinox*. Scottsdale, AZ: New Falcon Publications.
Crowley, A. (1992). Liber Resh vel Helios. In I. Regardie (Ed.), *Gems from the Equinox*. Scottsdale, AZ: New Falcon Publications.
Crowley, A. (1992). Liber VIII. In I. Regardie (Ed.), *Gems from the Equinox*. Scottsdale, AZ: New Falcon Publications.

By other authors:

Swami Vivekananda. (1982). *Karma-Yoga and Bhakti-Yoga.* New York, NY: Ramakrishna-Vivekananda Center.

13

LIBER SAMEKH & THE INVOCATION OF THE HOLY GUARDIAN ANGEL

A listener to my *Living Thelema* podcast once wrote to me asking, "In your episode on the HGA, you say to 'invoke often.' Is there a specific invocation ritual?" My response to him then is just as true and relevant today: the gradual movement toward the climactic invocation of the Holy Guardian Angel is so personal and individualized, there is no way anyone else could hand you a pre-made ritual which would fit you perfectly. It must be *your* ritual, and it will be customized *exactly* to reflect your inner state and your spiritual needs. All along the path toward full Knowledge and Conversation, you will be gathering tools, rituals and all manner of inner, symbolic elements—very personalized, and very unique to you. It may be difficult for the beginner to believe, but by the time you're ready for the climactic K & C working you will have a very good idea of the necessary tools. These may be based on existing documents like *Liber Samekh* and *Liber VIII*, but these will be skeletons for you to clothe with flesh; they are unlikely to be verbatim instructions maximized for your personal use.[24] Don't slavishly adhere

---

[24] Crowley, A. (1992). Liber Samekh. In I. Regardie (Ed.), *Gems from the Equinox*. Scottsdale, AZ: New Falcon Publications.

to anyone else's instructions in this, the most profoundly personal of all magical workings.

I want to begin by suggesting that you carefully re-read Chapter 2 concerning the Holy Guardian Angel. It is important to have a solid understanding of the nature of the HGA, and of the relationship between the aspirant and the HGA as it gradually develops across the First Order grades of A∴A∴, to get the most out of this present discussion.

Indeed, we must 'invoke often,' and 'enflame ourselves in prayer.' In the final analysis, this is *almost* the only essential element in terms of technique. It is the central key of any approach to Knowledge and Conversation. Any invocation of the Light of your Angel—in whatever form that takes for you, repeated with ever-intensifying love and aspiration, over a sufficient span of time—will likely meet with success. Certainly, there will be phases of your work where this will involve a formal ritual, but not always. The key is the relentless, day-to-day, moment-to-moment focus on aspiration—earnestly invoking the HGA as you may know how, and as you will be instructed.

As you may have guessed from the title of this chapter, *Liber Samekh* will be the main focus of our discussion here. Not only is the ritual itself a work of art, but Crowley's commentary on it, in particular the Scholion that accompanies it, is some of the most lucid, informative, and practical information about the real inner work of ritual magick you will find anywhere. He describes the visualizations in detail, and explains how to throw yourself into each of the component parts of the ritual. It is incredibly rich and well executed, and I strongly recommend that you study *Liber Samekh* and the commentary thoroughly and repeatedly throughout your magical career.

Liber Samekh was originally composed by Crowley for the use of Frank Bennett (Frater Progradior) in his own invocation of the HGA. Accordingly, it is an excellent example of Crowley's approach to teaching others in this matter. Here we can read some of Crowley's most cogent discussion of the nature of the HGA, and the relationship between the HGA to the aspirant, packaged for a beloved student under his supervision.

The ritual begins with an invocation adapted from the Preliminary Invocation of the *Goetia*. One of the most notable things about this invocation is the way the language changes from the first few lines to the final passages. Initially, the HGA is addressed with 'thee' and 'thou,' suggesting that the aspirant is in a dialogue with a relatively separate-feeling external entity. In contrast, the final passages make it clear that the desired goal of union with the HGA has been attained; or at least, the aspirant's full awakening to the reality of the Angel's existence, and the beginnings of conscious and willed communion.

There is an initial invocation to the Angel, and then the bulk of the ritual is a sequential but functionally simultaneous invoking of all four elements, climaxing with a crowning of all under the regency of spirit, the 'fifth element,' or quintessence. That is, these are sequential invocations of the quarters, but the net effect when the ritual is completed is that you have simultaneously invoked all four elements and crowned them with spirit.

You will recall that the whole purpose of the First Order grades of A∴A∴ is to fashion oneself into a suitable vessel for the indwelling of the HGA. Accordingly, this ritual is a recapitulation—and a full and final integration—of the work the aspirant has already accomplished in a preliminary form across the first order grades. Within the ritual, the magician goes to each of the quarters sequentially, tracing invoking pentagrams and vibrating so-called 'barbarous names' corresponding to the nature of that quarter. The real key of this stage of the ritual is to throw yourself as vividly and intensely as possible into identification with the element being invoked. This is an important general recommendation for any ritual, of course, but it is more important here than anywhere else I have encountered. Crowley discusses this in his commentaries in reference to the level of difficulty of the ritual. It can be quite challenging to maintain the concentration and intensity of focus that this ritual demands. You throw yourself into embodiment of the energies of each quarter as strongly as you possibly can. When you come back to the center, you must attempt to do the very same thing, but with the element of spirit–the aspiration to the HGA itself, and the cultivation of complete receptivity to its indwelling.

The climax of this ritual is a perfect example of the utility of juxtaposing energetic opposites in order to amplify the effect of a ritual. There is an infinite, upward, active extension of self followed a infinite, inward contraction. Crowley says this is almost like 'hiding' from the Angel within the innermost 'citadel of self.' The alternation of the magician's identification with these opposites vaults the self beyond them into an entirely different state of consciousness. This is the climactic upward surge of the 'sparks of self' that completes the ritual and affects a conscious communion with the Angel.

In his beautiful yet quite practical commentary corresponding to section F of the ritual, Crowley writes:

> The Adept now returns to the Tiphereth square of his Tau, and invokes spirit, facing toward Boleskine, by the active Pentagrams, the sigil called the Mark of the Beast, and the Signs of L.V.X. [...] He then vibrates the Names extending his will in the same way as before, but vertically upward. At the same time he expands the Source of that Will – the secret symbol of Self – both about him and below, as if to affirm that

Self, duplex as is its form, reluctant to acquiesce in its failure to coincide with the Sphere of Nuith. Let him now imagine, at the last Word, that the Head of his will, where his consciousness is fixed, opens its fissure (the Brahmarandra-Cakkra, at the junction of the cranial sutures) and exudes a drop of clear crystalline dew, and that this pearl is his Soul, a virgin offering to his Angel, pressed forth from his being by the intensity of this Aspiration.[25]

This pertains to the active extension of self. Next, we must balance this with the withdrawal of self, and the receptive phase of the climax. I will quote at length from Crowley's commentary here, because this material speaks to the very nature of the Angel itself, and the relationship between the adept and the Angel. In passages such as this, we can fully appreciate the value of Crowley's poetic talents when applied to descriptions of this subtle inner work—the language is truly transcendent. The following comments correspond to section G of the ritual:

> The Adept, though withdrawn, shall have maintained the Extension of his Symbol. He now repeats the signs as before, save that he makes the Passive Invoking Pentagram of spirit. He concentrates his consciousness within his Twin-Symbol of Self, and endeavours to send it to sleep. But if the operation be performed properly, his Angel shall have accepted the offering of Dew, and seized with fervour upon the extended symbol of Will towards Himself. This then shall He shake vehemently with vibrations of love reverberating with the Words of the Section. Even in the physical ears of the adept there shall resound an echo thereof, yet he shall not be able to describe it. It shall seem both louder than thunder, and softer than the whisper of the night-wind. It shall at once be inarticulate, and mean more than he hath ever heard.
>
> Now let him strive with all the strength of his Soul to withstand the Will of his Angel, concealing himself in the closest cell of the citadel of consciousness. Let him consecrate himself to resist the assault of the Voice and the Vibration until his consciousness faint away into Nothing. For if there abide unabsorbed even one single atom of the false Ego, that atom should stain the virginity of the True Self and profane the Oath; then that atom should be so inflamed by the approach of the Angel that is should overwhelm the rest of the mind, tyrannize over it, and become an insane despot to the total ruin of the realm.

[25] Crowley, A. (1992). Liber Samekh. In I. Regardie (Ed.), *Gems from the Equinox*. Scottsdale, AZ: New Falcon Publications.

But, all being dead to sense, who then is able to strive against the Angel? He shall intensify the stress of His Spirit so that His loyal legions of Lion-Serpents leap from the ambush, awakening the adept to witness their Will and sweep him with them in their enthusiasm, so that he consciously partakes this purpose, and sees in its simplicity the solution of all his perplexities. Thus then shall the Adept be aware that he is being swept away through the column of his Will Symbol, and that His Angel is indeed himself, with intimacy so intense as to become identity, and that not in a single Ego, but in every unconscious element that shares in that manifold uprush.

This rapture is accompanied by a tempest of brilliant light, almost always, and also in many cases by an outburst of sound, stupendous and sublime in all cases, though its character may vary within wide limits.

The spate of stars shoots from the head of the Will-Symbol, and is scattered over the sky in glittering galaxies. This dispersion destroys the concentration of the adept, whose mind cannot master such multiplicity of majesty; as a rule, he simply sinks stunned into normality, to recall nothing of his experience but a vague though vivid impression of complete release and ineffable rapture.

Repetition fortifies him to realise the nature of his attainment; and his Angel, the link once made, frequents him, and trains him subtly to be sensitive to his Holy presence, and persuasion. But it may occur, especially after repeated success, that the Adept is not flung back into his mortality by the explosion of the Star-spate, but identified with one particular 'Lion-Serpent,' continuing conscious thereof until it finds its proper place in Space, when its secret self flowers forth as a truth, which the Adept may then take back to earth with him.

This is but a side issue. The main purpose of the Ritual is to establish the relation of the subconscious self with the Angel in such a way that the Adept is aware that his Angel is the Unity which expresses the sum of the Elements of that Self, that his normal consciousness contains alien enemies introduced by the accidents of environment, and that his Knowledge and Conversation of His Holy Guardian Angel destroys all doubts and delusions, confers all blessings, teaches all truth, and contains all delights. But it is important that the Adept should not rest in mere inexpressible realization of his rapture, but rouse himself to make the relation submit to analysis, to render it in rational terms, and thereby enlighten his mind and heart in a sense as superior to fanatical enthusiasm as Beethoven's music is to West African war-drums.

Setting aside the obvious ethnocentrism of that last sentence, it seems that what Crowley is attempting to convey is that Knowledge and Conversation, once attained, is of little use if the *only* effect is to enflame the adept and inspire spiritual ecstasy. That's certainly a useful aspect of it (and an important tool for further work) but you have to *do something* with that knowledge. You have to find a way to express this ineffable experience in rational terms, so that your work in the world can be informed, enlivened and enriched by your experience. You go out into the world a changed person—a newly made adept—armed with the truth attained through Knowledge and Conversation; but you can't do that with full effectiveness if you haven't translated the ineffable into the rationally expressible.

Having reached the climax of this ritual and attained (at least momentarily) conscious communion with the Angel, the ritual proceeds to the closing, which is called the Attainment. As I noted earlier, the language is now of *identity* with the Angel, as follows:

> I am He! The Bornless Spirit! Having sight in the feet:
> Strong, and the Immortal Fire!
> I am He! The Truth!
> I am He! Who hate that evil should be wrought in the World!
> I am He, that lighteneth and thundereth!
> I am He, from whom is the Shower of the Life of Earth!
> I am He, whose mouth ever flameth!
> I am He, the Begetter and Manifester unto the Light!
> I am He, The Grace of the Worlds!
> "The Heart Girt with a Serpent" is my name!

Here is another very important practical consideration. It is clear from the instructions that this ritual is to be performed in the Body of Light; that is, it is performed in the astral body of the magician rather than simply performed physically as we might do in our routine daily rituals. In order to learn the ritual, however, you're almost certainly going to need to practice it physically—actually moving to the quarters and following through the instructions in terms of postures, pentagrams and so on. Once it has been mastered physically, however, it is very important to perform it in the Body of Light. In part, this is because the astral substance of self is intimately connected with the language of symbol through which the Angel expresses itself; but also, the magical 'muscles' you build through repeated performance of this ritual in the Body of Light will be of great use to you in a broad array of contexts.

Let's review a few practical points in terms of constructing and implementing a formal retirement for Knowledge and Conversation. In classical sources on this—such as the Abramelin materials—there is an expectation of almost complete solitude for months at a time, and a very specifically constructed temple in which to perform the working. One of Crowley's great gifts to modern magicians was an understanding that there needs to be a way to progress down the path of attainment and still function in the modern world. Most of us don't have the luxury of being independently wealthy, withdrawing from the world without having to work for months, and buying Boleskine House! If you contemplate the requirements set forth in *Liber Samekh* and *Liber VIII,* it will be fairly simple to hybridize these practices and integrate them into your daily routine—at least for a time—before moving into a full and formal retirement with an actual withdrawal into solitude.

Liber Samekh is designed to be performed over eleven months, whereas *Liber VIII* is a ninety-one day working. Hybridizing these you might, for example, have a preparatory period of several weeks or months with gradually building intensity of performance. You might go from once a day, to twice a day, to four times a day, building up gradually week to week until finally at the climax you might spend a week or more in complete retirement. With a bit of advance planning, it is quite feasible, even in today's busy and complex world.

When you get to the actual solitary retirement, it is extremely helpful to have an assistant who can bring food, handle outside emergencies, and be there to respond to any requests. Run out of candles? Your assistant is there to go fetch more! I suggest, however, that you avoid even visual contact with this assistant, in order to strictly maintain your focus on the work at hand. Communicate through written notes if necessary, and make arrangements for bathing, meals, and other necessities so that you and your assistant are never in the same place at the same time.

Naturally, a purpose-built temple is ideal for this, although few of us have that luxury. Nevertheless, you may find it quite difficult to attempt a retirement within your normal living space, with your children running around just outside a thin door. Accordingly, I urge you to find a separate dwelling place of some kind—perhaps a retreat center, a secluded rental cabin, or even a hotel room. Don't despair if you seem unable to find an ideal setting. Remember, Karl Germer attained Knowledge and Conversation while in a concentration camp, with nothing in the way of conventional magical tools or a temple, and armed only with pure aspiration. So, while all of these trappings of the invocation of the Angel, and the elaborate preparations of the space and the materials certainly enhance the work, they are ultimately merely tools. It is the *inner work* that is crucial.

If you persist in this work, invoking often and enflaming yourself in prayer to the Angel; if you listen inwardly for the communication of the tools and the ritual forms as you build toward the final working, you will succeed. Persistence is ninety-five percent of the work. I've never seen anyone persist in the system of A∴A∴ and not succeed. All the 'failures'

I've witnessed involved aspirants who quit doing the work, one way or another. They stopped doing daily practices, gave up on the path, or succumbed to their egos and didn't follow the system as it is laid out. But not once have I ever seen someone *persist* in the work and fail. Never doubt yourself in this regard. Persist, with intelligence, courage and devotion, and you will attain!

14

SEXUAL MAGICK & SEXUAL MYSTICISM

Many spiritual traditions across history have included esoteric instruction in the use of sexuality as a sacrament—as a mode of forging a link with the divine—and in the application of sexual force to magical aims. Various well-known tantric and Taoist traditions, for example, have featured these approaches, and within Thelema we have a diverse set of practices, instructions, and imagery to access in many of Crowley's explanatory writings, and in our Holy Books themselves. It is widely known that the O.T.O. teaches certain secrets of sexual magick, but I will not be discussing any secrets of O.T.O. in this chapter. What I *will* be discussing are my observations of the general formulæ of sexual magick and mysticism present in many traditions that I've studied, including (and of course, especially) Thelema. This is a vast subject and as with many magical techniques you could spend a lifetime studying only this topic and not exhaust its possibilities. We'll just scratch the surface in this chapter, but I think the discussion here will be useful as you pursue your experiments along these lines.

The word *tantra* means "to weave" or "weaving." The implication is that the tantric practices, the sexual magical and mystical practices under discussion here involve a weaving together of the experience of divine ecstasy as it occurs in and through human beings. Sexual magick and mysticism are about fully living in the world, and in our bodies. This is so quintessentially Thelemic and so pleasantly post-Christian! Gone is the dualistic view of the body as a sinful or lesser aspect of our nature. Here in our Thelemic tantra, we are not only allowed but *encouraged* to live fully in our bodies and experience ecstasy as manifestation of the divine, not as something separate from it.

Sex magick is, first and foremost, *magick*. As such, it is founded on the same definitions and processes that we associate with any other magical technique. That is, sexual magick requires the use of the proper force, applied via a suitable medium, using the most efficacious techniques, to the desired end. One useful definition of an effective magical operation is that magician "utters" the name of Tetragrammaton (*yod heh vav heh)* in all the Qabalistic Four Worlds simultaneously. The Four Worlds are, of course, *Atziluth, Briah, Yetzirah* and *Assiah*. Placed in the context of sexual working, we have *yod*—the primal force itself, that universal generative power we can symbolize by the wand or the lance; and *heh*, the vessel for that power, the higher soul of the magician, the cup or the grail. These are the Atziluthic and Briatic levels, respectively, and they are in a very real sense the force that fuels the operation. Next comes *vav,* the world of Yetzirah—the use of the mind to shape the force and the desired goal, impressing the will upon the eventual talisman. Lastly, we have the final *heh*, the world of *Assiah*, which is the talisman or eucharist into which we lock the power of all that has gone before in the operation.

I mentioned above that Thelema is particularly well suited to tantric work, and you don't have to look far to find some strong evidence of this. *The Book of the Law,* as understood via Crowley's commentaries thereon, is full of valuable instruction in sexual magick and mysticism, both in theory and in practice. We are given a specific pantheon of Thelemic deities—the polarities of Nuit and Hadit, and Ra-Hoor-Khuit as the result of their union. These deities are ripe and ready to use as living images of, and gateways into, the inner processes of sexual magick and mysticism. For example, in Chapter One, we read about "the consciousness of the continuity of existence," and this passage evokes that aspect of the tantric experience in which we weave together all of the divine ecstasy of the universe itself—the universe experiencing itself through our ecstasy—as Nuit says that her joy is to see our joy. This is just one of many examples. For additional examples and relevant discussion, I suggest you review Crowley's commentaries on Chapter One, verses 12, 51, 52, and 63; Chapter Two, verses 26 and 70; and Chapter Three, verses 55-57. The language, theory and practice of Thelemic tantra is hard-wired into our system, and has been right from the very beginning. We don't need to impose doctrines, dogmas, or divine names from any other sources, including traditional tantric systems. We already have a vital and powerful set of tools within our own Thelemic pantheon.

Prerequisites

Let's take a look at a few important prerequisites to effective use of sexual magick and mysticism techniques. First, you need to be able to control your mind—to show some mastery of raja yoga. Second, you need to have cultivated the ability to direct magical force using this mental control, in a precise manner. Third, you need an internally consistent symbol system that includes emotionally charged avatars of the universal polarities which traditionally would have been called Shiva and Shakti. In Thelema, we have Hadit and Nuit, The Beast (or Chaos) and Babalon, and so on. By "emotionally charged," I mean that you need to have a connection to the symbol sets such that you can effectively enflame yourself in ever-intensifying adoration and ecstasy as you strive to unite these opposites. You have to be able to cultivate a powerful, passionate yearning—of Hadit for Nuit, and of Nuit for Hadit—to really connect these concepts to their inner energetic counterparts; otherwise it's a dry system, mere words on paper.

Furthermore, you need to have thorough knowledge of your own sexual arousal patterns, as is probably self-evident. With this knowledge, you can obtain a certainty, through vivid experience, of the truth that the divine and the ecstatic are *one*. This gradual process is one of identifying sexual ecstasy with divinity itself and, conversely, identifying divinity with ecstasy. Ecstasy becomes accessible as a general phenomenon, independent of what we previously thought of as being merely "sexual." So, almost in a Pavlovian fashion, you gradually, progressively, increasingly, have the inner experience that God is really sexy and sex is truly holy! Eventually, these two ideas become inseparable. You find ecstasy in every phenomenon, as we are enjoined to do in *The Book of the Law*. This opens up as a reality for you when fully living out your will and fully engaging in life; you are in fact an active participant in the process of the universe experiencing itself. To find this ecstasy in everyday life is a real gift. And Thelemic sexual mysticism, as described here, opens us up to this treasure.

Another helpful prerequisite is a magical relationship with a sex partner, including a shared symbol system. It should be self-evident from the discussion above that the more the two partners are aligned in terms of the names and powers that they associate with certain energies, and their corresponding inner experiences, the more powerful the magick can be. Having an existing sexual relationship with the sex magick partner is also beneficial since you will have well-developed physical, emotional and sexual vocabulary. Finally, it is vital to have good communication with your partner about all of these things—on the magical level, on the emotional level, and on the relationship level—because if there is tension between the partners on any of these levels you compromise the effect of the working.

Stages of Training: Purification, Consecration & Initiation

Training in the techniques of Thelemic sexual magick and mysticism can be usefully divided into three stages, which I will refer to as purification, consecration, and initiation. In the first phase of *purification*, you are cleansing your relationship to the sex-force itself—the sexual, generative, life-giving principle resident in all humans. In our culture, and many other cultures across recent centuries, there has been an immense amount of shame and guilt associated with sexuality. Even those of us who consider ourselves sexually liberated Thelemites may discover that we have some residual shame and guilt complexes that need to be rooted out. Accordingly, in order to fully comprehend, experience, and express the divinity of the sexual force and the sexual impulse, we first need to wash away—to purify—those residual shards of shame and guilt that may cling to us. One approach to such purification might involve meditation sessions where you bring to mind all sorts of clearly positive and pleasant-feeling aspects of the concept of generativity: growing plants, the sun, or images drawn from mythology that are, for you, vibrantly alive, healthy and life-giving, with a tinge of the sexual intensity. Examples would be the deities Aphrodite, Pan or Priapus, and so on. Essentially, you are reprogramming those aspects of yourself that may have been unduly influenced by the shame and guilt complexes instilled by sex-negative society. You are reprogramming your associations so that sexuality can be experienced vividly as a vital, positive force in all its aspects. The real definition of a pure thing is that it is *only itself*, and is not tainted with any extraneous elements. And indeed, you want the sex-force to be purely itself so that you, the sexual magician, can be in right relationship to it.

The next phase of training involves the *consecration* of the sex-force to your desired goals. What you are actually training here is the ability to direct the sex-force to unite with specific ideas and/or entities. You're training your mind to harness the force that you have purified and direct it, under will, in very specific ways. One of the most fundamental (and strongly recommended) practices is that of devoting all of your ecstasy to Nuit; most specifically, devoting the ecstasy of orgasm to Nuit, seeing this as an offering to Her, and abiding in awareness that Her ecstasy is in yours. I have to say that over many years of practice, in myself and my students, I have found this to be one of the most powerful means available of strengthening and sharpening the will itself. You can consecrate your sex-force to other aims, of course, in much the same way as you focus the mind on the goal of any other type of magical ceremony. The power of the sex-force can be directed to unite with any other idea that relates to the goal of your operation. If you're doing an Enochian working, for example, and you want to have a more vivid and vital experiencing of the entity that you're invoking, you can devote the energy of sexual release to that aim. The key here is to "fall in love" with the object of the ritual, experience the entirety of the working as a courtship and romance, climaxing in ecstatic union with the very *idea* of the entity in question.

Here are a few practical exercises which may be helpful as you navigate the purification and consecration stages of your training. Begin by undertaking a series of meditations in which you contemplate the generative forces in nature, or symbols suggestive of these forces, such a growing tree, the endless process of the evolution of the human species, DNA, the sun, the cosmic lingam and yoni, the lance and grail— whatever inspires you along these lines. Meditate on these themes until you have cultivated an ability to create a sacred atmosphere through this imagery. When this is easily done, start bringing in sexual feelings— remembrances of past sexual experiences and feelings. Make these feelings as vivid as possible, while remaining wholly in the sacred space created by the contemplation of the previous ideas.

Continue this practice regularly over several weeks or more. Through this repeated and gradually intensifying pairing of the sacred and the ecstatic, you will come to an awareness of the fact that they are *one and the same*. It will seem almost as if the pleasure centers of the brain are being permanently altered by flooding them with sacred imagery. When this is an experiential reality for you, and not merely a metaphysical idea, you are ready to move on to the next stage: Live each day devoting all pleasure, all ecstasy, most specifically your sexual ecstasy, unto Babalon or Nuit. Do this regularly for a full month at least. Make these devotional offerings as intense and as frequent as possible. It may be helpful, during sexual climax or other ecstatic moments, to visualize a great grail into which you pour the golden liquid of your ecstasy. After several weeks of this practice, you may be ready to move to the next stage of your training.

The final phase is that of *initiation*—the full formula of sexual mysticism and magick. Ideally, this work is accomplished by two magicians who have passed through the preliminary purification and consecration stages, thereby multiplying the force generated. When both partners are trained in this way, they are better able to accomplish the task in the world of Yetzirah; that is, using the mind to channel the force in the appropriate direction to the appropriate end. Since the physical components of the eucharist—the combined sexual fluids—are designed by nature to carry forth Will in the form of the life of the species, the first matter of your working is ready-made to be a vessel of will-force. It is as if you are allowing your 'old' self to die, sending forth the will in the form of the desired ritual outcome. With the eventual consumption of the eucharist, or its use as a consecratory agent for talismans or sigils, that willed outcome is 'locked in' as a template for a new life going forward. You might even think of the magician as a computer receiving a new software program on which to base its operation; the software, of course, is the will of the 'dead' magician that has been impressed upon the Eucharist. You are merely adding the imprint of the desired magical goal, and mastering the technology of doing this is the central task in this third phase that I'm calling initiation. We'll discuss this aspect of the training in more detail later in the chapter.

Thelemic Sexual Mysticism

If you've been reading between the lines so far, I think you will not be surprised to hear me say that firm grounding in, and a real identification with, the power of Thelemic sexual mysticism is a prerequisite to fully empowered Thelemic sexual magick. That doesn't mean it's the *only* onramp to powerful sexual magick, by any means, but you will be maximally effective in your use of the sex-force only if you have consciously connected with it's inherent divinity. It then becomes one of the most potent fuels for enflaming yourself in ritual, whatever your ritual aim may be.

The body of Thelemic writings left for us by Crowley has tremendous potential—real inherent power—to tune us in to the vital and life-giving power of our sexual force. If you spend a significant amount of time immersed in Thelemic culture, and participate regularly in Thelemic rites such as the Gnostic Mass and others, you will likely develop a deeply ingrained symbolic system ripe for use in sexual mysticism and magick. You will develop emotional and energetic connections to the concepts of Nuit, Hadit and Ra-Hoor-Khuit, for example; and to the will itself as an expression of Selfhood that flows through the sex-force and other channels. You will become "hard-wired" to link certain symbols, phrases, images, and divine names to these intrapsychic experiences, and this brings true magical power.

Let's look at a few examples of the wonderful materials in the system of the A∴A∴, so you can get a feel for their utility in your work with Thelemic sexual mysticism. The first of these is section SSS from *Liber HHH*. This particular practice is assigned to the Practicus of A∴A∴. It appears at this particular stage of training in A∴A∴ to build on the work with pranayama done in the Zelator grade. Pranayama is a potent stimulator of kundalini. Here in the Practicus grade, the aspirant practices the techniques of SSS as an acceleration of that kundalini work. In SSS, Crowley places the images and energies associated with Nuit and Hadit at the opposite poles of the spine (the corresponding concepts in traditional tantric approaches would be Shakti and Shiva, respectively). He begins with a quote from *Liber VII*, Cap. I (vv. 36-40):

Thou art a beautiful thing, whiter than a woman in the column of this vibration. I shoot up vertically like an arrow, and become that Above. But it is death, and the flame of the pyre. Ascend in the flame of the pyre, O my Soul! Thy God is like the cold emptiness of the utmost heaven, into which thou radiatest thy little light. When Thou shalt know me, O empty God, my flame shall utterly expire in thy great N.O.X.

He then proceeds to describe the technique:

0. Be seated in thine Asana, preferably the Thunderbolt. It is essential that the spine be vertical.
1. In this practice the cavity of the brain is the Yoni; the spinal cord is the Lingam.
2. Concentrate thy thought of adoration in the brain.
3. Now begin to awaken the spine in this manner. Concentrate thy thought of thyself in the base of the spine, and move it gradually up a little at a time. By this means thou wilt become conscious of the spine, feeling each vertebra as a separate entity. This must be achieved most fully and perfectly before the further practice is begun.
4. Next, adore the brain as before, but figure to thyself its content as infinite. Deem it to be the womb of Isis, or the body of Nuit.
5. Next, identify thyself with the base of the spine as before, but figure to thyself its energy as infinite. Deem it to be the phallus of Osiris or the being of Hadit.
6. These two concentrations and may be pushed to the point of Samadhi. Yet lose not control of the will; let not Samadhi be thy master herein.
7. Now then, being conscious both of the brain and the spine, and unconscious of all else, do thou imagine the hunger of the one for the other; the emptiness of the brain, the ache of the spine, even as the emptiness of space and the aimlessness of Matter. And if thou hast experience of the Eucharist in both kinds, it shall aid thine imagination herein.
8. Let this agony grow until it be insupportable, resisting by will every temptation. Not until thine whole body is bathed in sweat, or it may be in sweat of blood, and until a cry of intolerable anguish is forced from thy closed lips, shalt thou proceed.
9. Now let a current of light, deep azure flecked with scarlet, pass up and down the spine, striking as it were upon thyself that art coiled at the base as a serpent. Let this be exceedingly slow and subtle; and though it be

accompanied with pleasure, resist; and though it be accompanied with pain, resist.

10. This shalt thou continue until thou art exhausted, never relaxing the control. Until thou canst perform this one section during a whole hour, proceed not. And withdraw from the meditation by an act of will, passing into a gentle Pranayama without Kumbhakham, and meditating on Harpocrates, the silent and virginal God.

11. Then at last, being well-fitted in body and mind, fixed in peace, beneath a favourable heaven of stars, at night, in calm and warm weather, mayst thou quicken the movement of the light until it be taken up by the brain and the spine, independently of thy will.

12. If in this hour thou shouldst die, is it not written, "Blessèd are the dead that die in the Lord"? Yea, Blessèd are the dead that die in the Lord![26]

These beautiful and poetic meditations and contemplations enhance the aspirant's identification with the opposites in one's self and in nature, as 'personified' by Nuit and Hadit. Ultimately of course, the goal is Knowledge and Conversation of the Holy Guardian Angel, and the belovéd with whom we unite is this HGA; but these exercises stoke the fires of the life-force itself, and aid us as we strengthen our ability to direct that force toward this spiritual goal.

Liber NU is another instruction that may be quite useful in developing your sexual mystical practice in the context of the Thelemic pantheon. While much of this instruction is not explicitly sexual, it serves to cultivate the necessary devotional and emotional connections to the pantheon; and as discussed above, this is an important prerequisite to Thelemic tantra. Here are a few relevant passages:

> Meditate upon Nuit as the Continuous One Resolved into None and Two as the phases of her being.
>
> Meditate upon the facts of Samadhi on all planes the liberation of heat in chemistry, joy in natural history, Ananda in religion, when two things join to lose themselves in a third.
>
> Let the Aspirant pay utmost reverence to the Authority of the A∴A∴ and follow Its instructions, and let him swear a great Oath of Devotion unto Nuit.

---

[26] Crowley, A. (1992). Liber HHH. In I. Regardie (Ed.), *Gems from the Equinox*. Scottsdale, AZ: New Falcon Publications.

Let the Aspirant live the Life Beautiful and Pleasant. For this freedom hath he won. But let each act, especially of love, be devoted wholly to his true mistress, Nuit.

Let the Aspirant yearn toward Nuit under the stars of Night, with a love directed by his Magical Will, not merely proceeding from the heart.

The Result of this Practice in the subsequent life of the Aspirant is to fill him with unimaginable joys: to give him certainty concerning the nature of the phenomenon called death, to give him peace unutterable, rest, and ecstasy.[27]

Thelemic Sexual Magick

Having reviewed some of the key Thelemic source texts related to sexual mysticism and kundalini work, let's move on to a more explicit discussion of sexual magick. What follows are some useful techniques I've encountered in a number of traditions, in the form of an outline of how a sexual magick ritual might be carried out. This will be applicable to solo work as well as rituals with a partner. As I said at the beginning of the chapter, much of what follows is based on principles that would be applicable to *any* effective magical working, whether sexual or otherwise.

As with any magical working, the first step is to identify the goal of the ritual. This process should include a thorough self-examination for any conscious or unconscious factors that are running counter to the purpose of the working. If you have some ambivalence about actually obtaining the result of the working, it will compromise the effectiveness of ritual. Consider whether the practical conditions are in place for the manifestation of the object of the working; as with all magick, you need to get Malkuth in order first so that the conditions are amenable. As it is said: you must prepare the temple for the indwelling of the god. You might also want to perform a divination concerning the conditions of the working and its probable outcome. Discuss any worries, resentments, or unstated emotional concerns between you and your partner. Get all this out on the table and out of the way before moving forward with the working. In any magical operation, but particularly in sexual magick, intrusive and distracting thoughts and emotions can divert the force from its intended target.

If you do decide to go forward with the working, undertake the usual preparations. As with most rituals following the western ceremonial tradition you may wish to write an invocation to the particular deity you have chosen to symbolize the forces invoked, and select sigils, talismans, mantras, colors, incenses, and similar correspondences. As usual, *777*

---

27 Crowley, A. (1992). Liber HHH. In I. Regardie (Ed.), *Gems from the Equinox*. Scottsdale, AZ: New Falcon Publications.

and the Thelemic Holy Books are good references to consult in this regard.

When you are ready to begin the ritual itself, spend a few minutes simply relaxing and connecting with your partner emotionally. This will help ensure that any personal disconnection resulting from a busy day at work, not spending much time together lately, and so on, is not an obstacle. Ritually bathe, don your magical robes mindfully, and perform the standard temple banishings such as the Lesser Banishing Ritual of the Pentagram or Hexagram, the Star Ruby, or others as appropriate. The next step is the consecration of the temple, and the turning on of the power to the temple using general invocatory rituals or other procedures, such as the Anthem from the Mass, the first Enochian Call, the Star Sapphire, pranayama, or the Middle Pillar exercise.

Next, move on to specific invocations connected to the object of the working—these could be ritualized or poetic—and then make a proclamation of the purpose of the working. Having set all this in motion, and having all things arranged in terms of your sigils or talismans and the temple space itself, put out of your mind the idea that you're doing a ritual and simply use all available erotic skills, whether solo or with a partner, to enflame yourself in the act of love.

Turn your attention to your chosen sigils, mantra, or other symbols in the room, to provide a simple mental focus on the aim of the ritual, without too much intrusion of detail. This also allows you to keep a reasonable amount of attention on your arousal patterns, and the sexual act itself, to keep that particular flame burning.

You will find it most effective if you stay engaged in coitus for at least an hour or so, before moving toward climax. When you and your partner are ready, unleash the entire power of the ecstatic climax as if it were an offering to the object of the ritual. If you have personified the object of a ritual in terms of a deity, this might be experienced as if you were making love with the deity themselves—as if you have held them as your belovéd throughout the ritual and the climax is an offering to them. Complete the formal working with the consumption of the elixir as a eucharist, or by using it to anoint sigils or talismans. You then close the ritual space, including covering any talismans or sigils to protect their charge, and perform the final banishings. As always, record the results in your magical diary as soon as possible after the conclusion of the working.

So, as you can see, there's really nothing terribly different about the *structure* of a sexual magick ritual compared to any other type of ritual that uses the classical ceremonial design elements; but the fuel for the fire, the engine for enflaming the will and powering the invocations, and the resulting spiritual union with the desired goal are all accomplished by specifically sexual means. The practice of Thelemic sexual magick and mysticism is a powerful and ecstatic path to attainment, and I strongly encourage you to explore it along the lines I have set forth in this chapter. I have great confidence that you will not resent being given this particular homework assignment!

Recommended Reading:

By Aleister Crowley:

Crowley, A. (1996). *The Law is for All*. Tempe, AZ: New Falcon Publications.

Crowley, A. (1992). Liber HHH. In I. Regardie (Ed.), *Gems from the Equinox*. Scottsdale, AZ: New Falcon Publications. [Note: particularly section SSS]

Crowley, A. *Amrita, The Elixir of Life*. Unpublished manuscript.

Crowley, A. (1992). Liber NU. In I. Regardie (Ed.), *Gems from the Equinox*. Scottsdale, AZ: New Falcon Publications.

Crowley, A. (1992). Liber Had. In I. Regardie (Ed.), *Gems from the Equinox*. Scottsdale, AZ: New Falcon Publications.

By other authors:

Avalon, A. (1974). *The Serpent Power*. New York, NY: Dover Publications.

Chia, M. & Chia, M. (2005). *Healing Love through the Tao: Cultivating Female Sexual Energy*. Rochester, VT: Destiny Books.

Chia, M. & Winn, M. (1984). *Taoist Secrets of Love: Cultivating Male Sexual Energy*. Santa Fe, NM: Aurora Press.

Feuerstein, G. (2003). *Sacred Sexuality: The Erotic Spirit in the World's Great Religions*. Rochester, VT: Inner Traditions.

Kraig, D. (1999). *Modern Sex Magick*. St. Paul, MN: Llewellyn Publications.

Mumford, J. (2002). *Ecstasy Through Tantra*. St. Paul, MN: Llewellyn Publications.

Van Lysebeth, A.(2002). *Tantra: The Cult of the Feminine*. York Beach, MA: Weiser Books.

PART TWO:

PERSPECTIVES ON THE PATH OF ATTAINMENT

15

THE METHODS AND TOOLS OF A∴A∴

But I have burnt within thee as a pure flame without oil. In the midnight I was brighter than the moon; in the daytime I exceeded utterly the sun; in the byways of thy being I flamed, and dispelled the illusion. [28]

There is no shortage of published material concerning the system of the A∴A∴, in terms of its overall approach and its training methods. This is certainly by design, as Crowley intended the methods and materials of A∴A∴ to be widely accessible and, in time, widely replicated. There is plenty of available material concerning what the system is, yet it is rare to find cogent and practical discussion of why and how the system works. Accordingly, it is my hope that by the end of this chapter, you will have a better sense of why the tasks, tools and methods of A∴A∴ are arranged the way they are, why they unfold in a certain manner across the grades of A∴A∴ and how they lead you towards the Knowledge and Conversation of the Holy Guardian Angel and beyond.

---

[28] *Liber LXV,* Cap. V, v. 9.

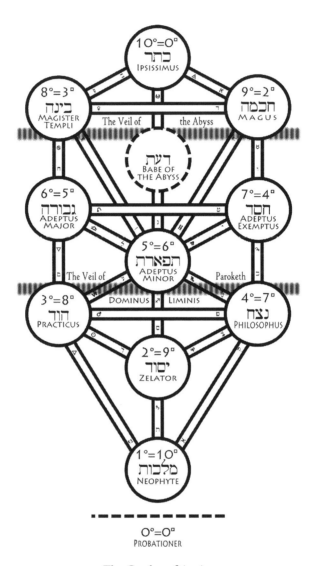

The Grades of A∴A∴

There is a specific technology here, to be sure, but it tends to be discussed in terms of a grade-by-grade analysis, such as the way the tasks and the nature of each grade are attributed to the four elements, or the corresponding sephiroth. We'll consider it from this perspective as well, but I want to get beyond that approach and shift the focus to the type of training that's occurring along the way. I have broken down the system below Tiphereth into five training 'tracks'—essentially, five different types of tools that work together to bring you to Knowledge and Conversation. These five training tracks unfold concurrently across the first order grades (Probationer through Dominus Liminis). Let me briefly outline the five tracks, and then we'll cycle through and discuss them in more detail. Obviously, I cannot discuss every task assigned in A∴A∴ in this place. Rather, I will emphasize the key practices that exemplify the five training tracks, and show how they complement each other in the unfolding path of the aspirant.

Track One: The development of magical skills and techniques.

Track Two: The training of the mind—to focus, to empty, to become and remain receptive.

Track Three: The stimulation and activation of the chakras and the raising of kundalini.

Track Four: Devotional practices.

Track Five: Balancing the psycho-magical constitution.

Before we look at these in detail, it should be emphasized that everything in the A∴A∴ system below Tiphereth—everything leading up to the $5°=6^{\square}$ grade of Adeptus Minor—is devoted solely to the accomplishment of the K & C of the HGA. It is easy to lose sight of this, due to the diverse nature of the tasks assigned, and the many traditions that are woven together in the system. Furthermore, every aspirant has their own prejudices and predispositions that lead to magical myopia. In any case, the whole point of the system is not to accumulate a grab bag of unrelated magical techniques, but to become fully yourself. You must attain the K & C of the HGA, that you may discover with certainty your True Will. Then, you must carry out that will with force and precision.

Track One is the development of magical skills and techniques. This track is actively worked from the very earliest stages of the A∴A∴—as early as Probationer.

Probationer
The Probationer is likely to be experimenting with a full spectrum of magical techniques, but by the time of the passage to Neophyte (assuming the Probationary year is successful) there will be even more specific emphasis on the traditional magical tools. It's a bit like learning an alphabet. You simply have to learn the basics, and let them form a foundation for everything you do after. The focus here is on pentagram and hexagram ritual forms (Lesser, Greater, Supreme, and so on) as well as on developing competence with the resulting elemental, planetary and zodiacal invocatory and banishing rituals.

Neophyte

The Neophyte is essentially formulating their own "astral atlas", if you like. There may also be experimentation with the Enochian system (although this is not specifically assigned until the Practicus Grade) as well as various Solomonic and Goetic techniques.

What is essentially happening here, by design, is that much of the traditional instruction that would have occurred in the old Golden Dawn *Second* Order is being handed to the Neophyte right out of the gate, with only the preparation of Probationer as a preliminary. These skills are drilled in from the very beginning of the system—but why? This is the question I'm going to be asking at each stage of the training. Why here? Why now? What's the point of training this particular skill set?

It may not be immediately obvious why the ability to correctly perform a pentagram or hexagram ritual, or any of these other techniques, is necessarily related to the path toward Knowledge and Conversation. Consider: if you can't design a ritual to effectively invoke a fundamental aspect of nature, such as a particular element or a particular planetary influence; if you can't competently design and execute a ritual such as this, and make yourself an adequate vessel for the invocation and utilization of a particular force—how can you design the ultimate ritual of invocation—that of your own HGA? The basics simply must be mastered. To be sure, learning any specific ritual form, such as a hexagram ritual, is in itself of little consequence; but as a tool for developing your capacity to invoke, safely contain, and direct magical force, it is invaluable.

The Neophyte is also trained and tested in the control of the Body of Light, and in the related techniques of scrying and so-called astral projection. The Neophyte is tested by his or her Superior in these procedures, to ensure the Neophyte has developed adequate facility with the Body of Light in order to competently explore the astral realms. This skill is important because the ability to speak the language of symbol, which is the natural language of the astral world—and of the subconscious mind—is directly related to the aspirant's growing capacity to receive consciously the various communications from the HGA. While initially in the path of the aspirant these impulses will likely be more or less subconscious—speaking through dreams and intuitive flashes of various kinds—the more consciously one can speak and understand this language the closer one is to conscious communication with the Angel. After all, conscious communication with the Angel, at will, is more-or-less the very definition of successful K & C.

Practicus

The Practicus moves on to work with divination. Why? How is the practice of divination at all connected to K & C? Keep in mind that divination is yet another method of using the conscious mind to receive subtle impressions from a set of symbols, and if you can't sit down with a set of universal symbols like the Tarot or the I Ching and get something apprehensible and useful out of them, how can you possibly begin to tune into the very, very subtle impressions that will be coming to you, at this stage of training, from the HGA? How can you build the right sort of radar, with the necessary level of sensitivity, if you can't execute something as basic as a Tarot reading?

Philosophus

The Philosophus is tasked with mastering evocation and working with talismans. How is this leading towards K & C? Think about what evocation actually is at its core: it is the ability to externalize magical force, particularized to a specific form and type of energy of your choosing. For example, the evocation of a particular spirit into a triangle requires the ability to tap into a specific energy source, and to effectively use the correct spiritual "muscles" to bring it down into manifestation. Whether you see such an act as purely psychological, or as an interaction with an actual external entity, you still have to have manifest something concrete in front of you; and by doing so you are strengthening the muscles that will allow you to interact compellingly, vibrantly and effectively with the HGA when the time comes. I do not mean to imply that the nature of K & C will be exactly the same as that of conversing with your average Goetic spirit; however, the muscles strengthened by perfecting the skills of evocation will be directly applicable to the eventual K & C working.

Similarly, the ability to create and consecrate powerful talismans is an important preparation for K & C. What is the nature of a talisman? It is a physical object imbued with a specific force as chosen by the magician. If you can competently design and consecrate a talisman such that you can a channel a specific force into a specific object, and that object can hold that power and can be of use to you—this ability will be certainly be useful as you approach K & C. After all, what are you yourself, if not a talisman of the force of your Angel? Your entire life, your very being, your physical body, indeed, every ongoing living process must be a talisman of the nature of your Angel. If you can't imbue a physical talisman with specific force as simple as, say, Mercury, how can you possibly make your entire being a conscious talisman of the influence of your Angel?

Track Two is the training of the mind to focus, to empty, and to become and remain receptive.

Here we have another set of tasks that's very likely to be approached from Probationer onward. While one can choose whatever practices one likes as a Probationer, it is very important to have some exposure to the basics of *asana* (postures) and *dharana* (concentration practices). Through these *raja yoga* practices, the aspirant is beginning to develop skill in stilling and focusing the mind, and training it to become receptive to subtle impressions. In addition, through the use of reflective meditations and study of the Holy Books, the aspirant will strengthen his or her ability to gain deeper understanding of important arcana of all sorts. Why is this important? Perhaps it is rather self-evident that if you can't get your mind to be quiet—if you can't still the flurry of everyday thought and allow your mind to become receptive to subtle impulses for something as simple as meditating on a line of text—if you can't hold your concentration on a red triangle for a few minutes—how can you possibly get your mind to be still enough, and free enough from interior chatter, for the ultimate "meditation" of the final K & C working?

These raja yoga practices continue across the First Order grades, of course, climaxing with Dominus Liminis. For example, *Liber Turris* is assigned in the Practicus and Philosophus grades to strengthen the ability to destroy thoughts at their source in the brain. *Liber Yod,* for the Dominus Liminis, serves as training in bringing the entirety of the mind to a single point of focused intensity. All of these practices, placed here just as the aspirant is "on the home stretch" coming toward Tiphereth, are entirely consistent with the aim of the Dominus Liminis to harmonize all the work done in the Order so far; to aim with one-pointedness to the Knowledge and Conversation of the Holy Guardian Angel. If you can't get your mind to focus without distraction on a single point—if you can't bring all of yourself, all that you have found yourself to be, together as a single unified vector of magical force—you will likely have great difficulty moving efficiently toward K & C.

Finally, we have the practices of *Liber Jugorum*, which develop the aspirant's control of thought, word, and deed. The Practicus attempts to control speech; the Philosophus action, and the Dominus Liminis thought. Why? If you can't control your speech in simple everyday life, how can you compose and deliver the most perfect invocation for your Angel? If you can't control action in your everyday life, how can you control your action toward creating the perfect ritual to invoke your Angel? If you can't control thought in your everyday life—if you can't keep yourself away a certain kind of thought, or draw yourself toward another kind—how can you, at that supreme moment of focus, direct all your attention one pointedly to the HGA? The control practices of *Liber Jugorum* strengthen many magical muscles necessary for ultimate success in the Great Work.

Track Three involves the stimulation and activation of the chakras, and the raising of kundalini—the divine, life-giving, regenerative force resident in every human. Through various practices, this life force can be intensified, and applied in specific, targeted ways to transformational processes in the body, in the mind, and in the subtle energy centers with which we work.

Many Probationers will be working with asana, and this practice is preliminary to more advanced kundalini work. The formal testing on asana is not required until the Zelator grade, where one must sit perfectly still in front of one's Superior for a full hour before being passed. When there is sufficient facility with asana, it is appropriate to begin working with *pranayama*—the control of breath. This also may start as early as Probationer, but formal testing does not occur until Zelator. One of the important things to note about this testing of pranayama is that the desired results (often described as "fine perspiration" and "automatic rigidity") are in fact early signs of kundalini activity. These are just the beginning stages, but it is evident that even at the level of Zelator, work is being done to initiate the flow of kundalini, and concrete results are beginning to manifest. In practice, these early results assist with the growing awareness of ecstatic energy states in the mind/body apparatus, and with the conscious direction of this energy to desired ends.

This process is greatly amplified via the practices given in Section SSS of *Liber HHH,* which is assigned to the Practicus of A∴A∴. This beautiful and powerful practice—essentially an instruction in Thelemic tantra—involves the conscious movement of energy between the base of the spine and the brain. The aspirant conceives of these opposite poles as being Nuit and Hadit, and builds up a sort of "courtship" between them. After much extended practice, typically over the course of many days or longer, the aspirant brings the work to a climax as these poles are at last allowed to unite in ecstasy. What is the utility of this practice in terms of our training? In addition to the considerable mystical benefits, any such practice where the aspirant becomes a conscious vessel of magical force, and learns to direct it in a targeted fashion, is training important magical muscles. Even magical ritual has this effect. While it might not be self-evident that any effective magical ceremony has kundalini-related effects, however subtle, I have found that this is generally the case. After all, in such rituals, you are building yourself into a battery of force—embodying it, controlling it, and directing it. And the nature of this force, broadly speaking, is identical with that which we are calling kundalini—the very essence of life-giving, creative energy. No matter how we might particularize this force in a given ritual via additional procedures, we still have to plug into the source.

As with the other training tracks, the process of raising the kundalini is of fundamental importance in the A∴A∴ system. In a very real sense, the kundalini is the fuel that potentiates all the transformations we undertake in this system. All of the willed transformations of self are given more power and more potency by virtue of this energy being raised and applied in the intended manner. Additionally, and very importantly, the ecstasy that occurs when these kundalini-related practices are brought to their conclusion is in itself transformative, healing, and evolutionary; its nature is to potentiate the transformation of the human into the more-than-human. The experience of this "divinized" ecstasy is so important in the path towards K & C that it can't be overstated. By the time we have completed this work in the First Order of A∴A∴ our consciousness of the divine nature of our own ecstasy should be so acute and so vivid that the very idea of God—the idea of our HGA—is the is the sexiest thing we can imagine. Likewise, sex is perceived as inseparable from holiness—it is, in fact, true worship. These transformations of our basic conceptions and experiences of self, life force, and sexuality as an embodiment of divine force are pivotal in the progress towards K & C (see Chapter 14 for more on this).

Track Four is the devotional practices—the *bhakti yoga* of the A∴A∴ system. While this work is especially assigned to the Philosophus grade corresponding to Netzach, the aspiration, the devotion, the fire, the passion for the path itself, and the progress toward union with the Angel are not new to the aspirant. Indeed, it is highly unlikely that an initiate would even progress to the Philosophus grade at all, without having been fueled by intense devotion and aspiration all along. I'm sure if you reflect back to what first drew you to the magical path—what made it come alive for you—you can see that there was an element of devotion and aspiration that was calling to you, no matter how you might have experienced it at the time. All of the truth and beauty that enraptures you, that unfolding mystery for which you continually reach, that siren song that calls you onward—all of these are simply one or another aspect of the Holy Guardian Angel active in your life and consciousness. When Joseph Campbell says "follow your bliss," he's not kidding around. This is a process of discovering what makes you come alive, what makes you love, what keeps you reaching for the next mystery before you.

As I noted earlier, these muscles of devotion and aspiration are cultivated most pointedly in the grade of Philosophus, which corresponds to Netzach; for it is right at this moment, when you are nearly ready to begin the formal K & C working, that you must fully light the fires of aspiration. All the muscles of devotion must be active and fully developed. The key devotional instruction formally assigned to the Philosophus is *Liber Astarte*. This is a beautifully constructed work in which one essentially creates one's own religious system devoted to the deity of choice. It is clear from the instructions in the book that the point here is to gain practice in the art of worship—to exercise and strengthen the muscles of devotion, so that in the very near future, as you undertake the K & C working, you can direct this newly strengthened ability toward your own HGA. This makes a good deal of sense, since by definition, it is unlikely that the Philosophus has full conscious contact with the HGA, and will likely need other gods, symbols, and images as "stand-ins." In practice, this need tends to diminish quickly as the aspirant nears the climactic experiences of the Dominus Liminis and Adeptus Minor grades, and the HGA increasingly instructs them in all the essentials of their true religion, as they take their rightful place as the prophet of their own Angel.

Track Five is the balancing of the psycho magical constitution. We can think of this as preparing ourselves as a grail—a grail for the indwelling of the light of the Angel. If our development is unbalanced, our grail will topple. If we have failed to build ourselves into a seamless and solid vessel, our grail will leak. Force follows form, and we must make ourselves into the perfect form that, by its design, invokes the desired force—the light of the HGA.

One way we can conceptualize the process of attaining this balanced form is the passage through the elemental grades of the First Order of A∴A∴. At each grade, the aspirant builds a symbolic weapon to symbolize and concretize the inner changes occurring in that grade. These elemental weapons correspond, of course, to the four elements of earth, air, water and fire, but we can also understand them in the context of Carl Jung's four functions of the psyche: sensation, intuition, thinking, and feeling, respectively. The pantacle (disk) is the weapon of earth, Malkuth and sensation; the dagger is the weapon of air, Yesod and intuition (spiritual intuition often first manifests through the subconscious, which is attributed to Yesod); the cup is the weapon of water, Hod and thinking; and the wand is the weapon of fire, Netzach and feeling, aspiration and desire. Additionally, at the Dominus Liminis grade the magick lamp is constructed as a symbol of the crowning of spirit over the other four elements. All of these things—the four elements, the four functions of the psyche, the four weapons—are representative of the balanced development of the psycho-magical constitution. By traversing these grades in a stepwise and balanced manner, we can indeed fashion ourselves into a perfect grail for the light of the HGA, for the god will not indwell a temple improperly prepared.

In closing, let me offer a final image for your consideration, to illustrate the overarching process of the First Order grades: that of the magick lamp itself, already discussed above in the context of the Dominus Liminis grade. With asana and pranayama, we begin the endeavor of transforming the physical body—the physical design of the lamp. The more advanced kundalini practices, and the divinized ecstasy we have cultivated, comprise the oil that is the fuel for the lamp.

Through the right use of our intellect, we have chosen the correct patterns, symbolic decorations, and dimensions for the proper functioning of the lamp. Our devotion and aspiration serve as the spark that finally ignites the lamp. All of these components must be in place, and functioning properly, for the whole of the lamp to fulfill its purpose. Just so, all of the training tracks of the First Order grades must be duly mastered. With these tasks properly executed, we await the Angel's indwelling with love and devotion, and with the flame of True Will burning brightly in our hearts. For "to await Thee is the end, not the beginning."[29]

Getting Started with A∴A∴

Wherefore by their fruits ye shall know them.[30]

Since the death of Karl Germer (Crowley's successor as the Head of the Order) in 1962, there has been no *universally acknowledged* governance of A∴A∴. After Germer's death, multiple claimants arose, each with its own purported leaders and its own (sometimes rather tangled) history. You will note my use of the term 'claimant group' in this discussion. The term 'lineage,' which would be an obvious choice in other analogous spiritual traditions, has become so politicized that it is now, in some circles, synonymous with illegitimacy. However, it is abundantly clear that there are various groups claiming to be A∴A∴, hence the term 'claimant groups.'

The only manifestation of A∴A∴ I can *personally* vouch for in terms of its historical legitimacy, the competence of its leaders, and the linkage of its administrative Triad to the spiritual roots of the Order (the so-called 'Secret Chiefs') is the one whose contact information appears below. Please note, however, that I am *not* condemning the work of other groups claiming to represent A∴A∴. I have good friends within several of these groups, and it is clear that they are earnest seekers doing effective and important work. The most important thing to me, by far, is simply that the *system* of A∴A∴ is readily available for aspirants who are called to the path.

There has been some confusion regarding the relationship between the modern O.T.O. and the various claimant groups of A∴A∴. Since the early days of the modern O.T.O. in the mid-1970s, there have been

---

[29] *Liber LXV*, Cap. II, v. 62.

[30] *Matthew* 7:15–20.

initiates from multiple A∴A∴ claimant groups active within O.T.O. A few years ago, *some* in the administration of O.T.O. openly aligned themselves with one particular claimant group, and began to advertise its contact address. This is their right, and I honor their choice as an act of personal conscience. However, the simple fact is that there are a great many initiates of other A∴A∴ claimant groups active in O.T.O. at the present time, at all levels of O.T.O. membership and leadership. It is important to understand this, because in recent years some statements have been made (by individuals, not by O.T.O. *per se*) which might confuse those aspiring to join A∴A∴, causing them to believe that the claimant group actively promoted by O.T.O. is the only viable option for those who also happen to be O.T.O. initiates. This is simply inconsistent with the actual facts of the situation. Please note that my presentation of these facts in no way reflects a criticism of those administering O.T.O.—they have the authority to govern O.T.O. as they see fit, and I have much respect for their work in this regard.

If you are called to the work of A∴A∴, I encourage you to do your own research and come to your own conclusions about which particular path is best for you. Ultimately, your personal spiritual attainment—the fruits of your own work—will be the best indicator of the wisdom of your choice.

A∴A∴
P.O. Box 215483
Sacramento, CA 95821
www.onestarinsight.org

16

Tarot & the Path of Initiation

Probably the most common misunderstanding about the Tarot is that it is merely a tool for divination. What is often missed is that the *reason* it is such a magnificent system for divination is that it is a *complete symbolic map* of all the transformative processes in the universe, and in every individual walking the path of spiritual attainment. When you think about it, it is easy to see that it would be impossible for any system to be ideal for divination unless it embodied all of these laws of nature. After all, if you have a question in mind, but there are certain aspects of life and consciousness that are simply inaccessible or inexpressible in a divination system, that system will not be broad enough in scope to provide you with a complete answer.

My purpose here, however, is not to review the use of Tarot as a divination tool (although I present a suggested layout and interpretive strategy at the end of this chapter). Rather, it is to examine the ways in which the Tarot functions as a symbolic map of the transformations occurring in *you* as you walk the path of attainment. Most particularly, I will discuss the unfolding transformative processes represented in the trumps of the Thoth Tarot corresponding to the paths on the Tree of Life leading up to the Knowledge and Conversation of the Holy Guardian Angel. I won't go into too much detail about the specific images on the cards, however, so I suggest you have your Thoth deck handy as you read this chapter.

As you may know, the entirety of the Tarot can be mapped out onto the Tree of Life. The sephiroth depict static states of consciousness and are attributed to the small cards and court cards of the Tarot, whereas the paths are referred to the trumps, and show the transformative processes related to the interplay of the sephiroth they connect. Much of our discussion in this chapter will focus on the trumps' role as 'mediators' between their adjacent sephiroth, the corresponding transformations occurring in initiates of A∴A∴. The A∴A∴ system of attainment is, of course, also based on the Tree of Life, with each sephira corresponding to an initiatory grade, and both the sephira *and* the connecting paths showing the relevant tasks of that grade. In each grade, the initiate undertakes tasks corresponding to that specific sephira as well as the paths that lead to the *next* grade. For example, as a Neophyte, your tasks will reflect the nature of Malkuth as well as the path of *tav* that connects forward to the next grade of Zelator, at Yesod. Keep this scheme in mind as you read about the various processes discussed here.

As with any discussion of the Qabalah and the Path of Return, it is important to keep in mind that you will feel the influence of these processes at many points across your lifetime. For example, consider the sphere of Geburah, which corresponds to Mars, force and will. You will have many 'Geburan' moments woven throughout your life—times of intense energy and power, or (less constructively) aggression and anger. But our focus here is on the unfolding of the A∴A∴ path, where your spiritual 'location' can be mapped out to a single, specific sephira at any given point in your life, corresponding to your grade in the order.

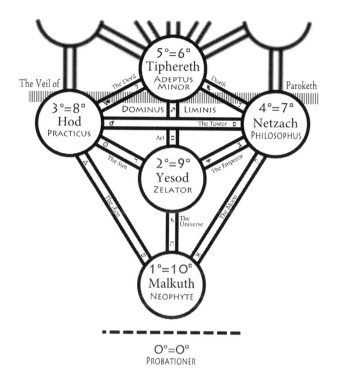

The Tarot Trumps and A∴A∴grades below Tiphereth

Let's review briefly the nature of the sephiroth below Tiphereth; that is, the sephiroth through which you will pass in your progress through the A∴A∴ grades of Neophyte to Dominus Liminis, and on to Adeptus Minor and the K & C of the HGA. Malkuth is attributed to the grade of Neophyte, the element of earth, the physical body and the material universe. Yesod is attributed to the grade of Zelator, and corresponds to subconscious, autonomic processes in the mind and body, and to the generative, sexual power resident within every human. Hod, which corresponds to the grade of Practicus, is essentially the human intellect. Netzach, corresponding to the grade of Philosophus, is associated with emotion, aspiration, and desire. The Veil of Paroketh, beneath Tiphereth, represents the actual psychological and spiritual 'veil' which wards the entrance to the Second Order of A∴A∴, and corresponds to the grade of Dominus Liminis ("Lord of the Threshold").

135

Neophyte: Malkuth, and the Path of Tav

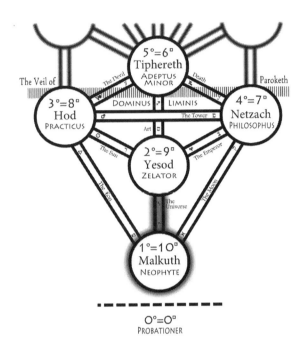

The nature of the Neophyte's task corresponds to the sphere of Malkuth and to the path of *tav*—the Universe card. As noted above, the symbolism of Malkuth is that of the material world, and Yesod the subconscious mind (which is our initial perceptual mechanism for the astral world). The Neophyte must work to increase his or her perception of the subtle forces interpenetrating the material world and truly *experience* that these same forces are the substrate of material existence.

The Path of Tav (The Universe)
The path of *tav* and the Universe trump corresponds to the muladhara chakra and accordingly, we see depicted on the trump the coiled kundalini. Universal mind is indeed a *force*—it is the creative power of the universe itself, and this force manifests in *form*. Form is a concept related to Saturn as well as earth, both of which are attributed to the Universe card. Here, we awaken our senses to the perception of mind as living force. These are the realities of the formative world of Yetzirah, which are opening up to us as we walk the path of *tav*. It is often in this phase that initiates begin to describe increased perception of astral forms, and indeed this ability to control the 'Body of Light' is one specific faculty being trained and tested in the Neophyte grade.

The central figure on the Universe card has her legs in the form of a cross, and as you may recall, 'cross' is the meaning of the Hebrew letter *tav*, which also alludes to the four elements. She is partly veiled—this is the veil we must peer through in order to see past the material forms around us and perceive the astral substrate beneath them. This is the veil of nature itself—that barrier formed by conditioned habits of looking at the material universe—preventing us from seeing the deeper reality behind it. This is not a dualistic doctrine wherein the physical world is 'evil' and the spirit 'good.' Rather, the material world is seen as a veil whose shape may reveal to us deeper truths, and thus the world is seen as a true manifestation of the divine. As noted above, the kundalini serpent is depicted on this trump, attributed to the muladhara chakra, and the Neophyte is beginning to undertake the activation of muladhara and the awakening of kundalini through various meditative and magical practices (see Chapter 15). We will see how this serpent force develops as we review the other trumps leading to the K & C of the HGA.

Zelator: Yesod, and the Paths of Shin and Resh

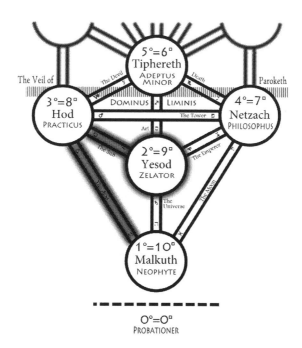

In keeping with the overall training scheme of A∴A∴, the Zelator's work will be intimately connected to the principles embodied by Yesod, but also relate to the paths leading to Hod and the Practicus degree—*shin*

(the Aeon) and *resh* (the Sun). You will recall that Yesod corresponds to subconsciousness, sexual generativity, and autonomic processes. In Yesod, the nature and function of the personal unconscious—truly the 'foundation' of the psyche—is clarified. The Zelator begins conscious, willed movement of subtle forces through pranayama and related practices. The voice of the HGA is increasingly heard, attended to and comprehended, in symbolic language if not yet directly and consciously. The initiate gradually is becoming more aware of the connection between the subconscious mind and this spiritual intuition. Dreams and intuitive flashes become important symbol sets, and the initiate attains to a state of consciousness traditionally known as the 'Vision of the Machinery of the Universe.' While this may sound a bit grandiose for a mere Zelator, this vision is truly the opening up of the initiate's ability to *feel* universal mind in action, as it flows up like an underground spring into our individual consciousness. That is not a mere intellectual understanding that all consciousness is an interconnected whole. Many aspirants are able to grasp the concept from the very beginning. Rather, what we are talking about here is an experiential awareness, a definite *knowing*, that universal mind is operative in subtle yet powerful ways in individual life and consciousness.

The Path of Shin (The Aeon)

The Aeon trump corresponds to the path of *shin* and connects Malkuth, the sphere of the elements, the senses, and the physical world, with Hod, the sphere of the intellect. Looking at the card, you will immediately notice is that it is a virtual hieroglyph of the concepts embodied by the Stele of Revealing, and thus also of the core cosmology of the Aeon of Horus. Nuit, Hadit, and Heru-Ra-Ha are all symbolized on the card. Nuit arched above; Hadit as the winged globe; and Heru-Ra-Ha in the twin forms, active and passive, corresponding to Ra-Hoor-Khuit and Hoor-Paar-Kraat. This card depicts the force of the new aeon flooding the world, its people, and its culture. The path of *shin* within each person is that channel of transformative force which revolutionizes the structures of the individual, just as it does the world as a whole. This is the Aeonic force flowing into you—your internal Hod and Malkuth. It brings *you* into the new Aeon, dissolving the outworn forms and limiting structures within your mind and body.

This card is attributed to fire, and indeed it behaves accordingly. Fire transforms, restructures, and revolutionizes everything it touches. Older versions of the card had an angel calling the dead to awaken—perhaps the old aeon's best attempt at depicting the influence of the HGA—but in the new aeon we have a clearer vision of the situation. We know that we don't need to be 'redeemed' from death, or be obsessively focused on the apparently catastrophic nature of death, as it would have been perceived in the old aeon. Instead, we find life-affirming symbols of regeneration and transformation that are accessible to us at every moment in our lives. The initiate of Yesod, aspiring to the sphere of Hod and the grade of Practicus, must come to terms with these transformations in him- or herself.

The Path of Resh (The Sun)

The Sun card corresponds to the path of *resh*, which connects Yesod and Hod. As we noted with the Aeon card, the Sun trump also has both a macrocosmic and microcosmic import. The physical sun is light- and life-giving, and brings vision and clarity to the physical world. Just so, the sun within us shines forth in our own intellect; our rational mental capacity (Hod) can help us cut through the obscurity, the confusion and the clouds of illusion that can dwell in our subconscious. One of the things human beings must confront in the new aeon is the impact of several thousand years of cultural conditioning rooted in dualistic, sin-based religions. Each of us must overturn this conditioning by allowing the inner sun to shine forth into our subconscious mind, bringing the light of the HGA to free and liberate us. This is reflected in the imagery of the card—the sun itself, and the children dancing on the green earth— all beautiful images of a true inner freedom. They are shameless and joyous. This is a depiction of the freedom of consciousness that is attainable for each of us when we have successfully passed through the ordeal of this path.

The Sun card is also attributed to the Anahata chakra at the heart center; and the opening of the Anahata chakra allows true *agape*, free love, and acceptance of the unity of beings to emerge. We are no longer living in the restriction, fear and shame that so many who have gone before us have had to contend with. Only a Zelator who has attained to this consciousness is truly fitted to pass to Practicus.

139

Practicus: Hod, and the Paths of Qoph, Tzaddi and Peh

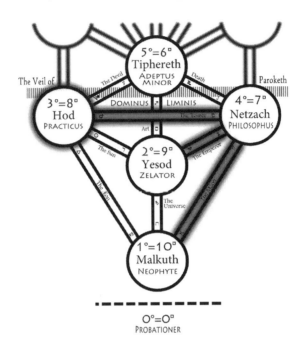

The Practicus grade corresponds to the sphere of Hod, and in this present discussion, the most important key-symbols of Hod are those of a cup and the water it contains. You will note that the weapon of the Practicus is the magick cup, and the element to which the sphere of Hod is attributed is water. The initiate of Hod is coming into a deeper recognition that the *individual* mind is a vessel for *universal* force. The individual mind is a form-giving vessel *and* a reflective mirror of the macrocosm, just as the surface of water in a cup reflects the forms above it. The initiate of Hod, through various practices, is beginning to master the conscious direction of this universal force toward specific magical aims. If you understand that the mind and the human constitution is a microcosm, then you will begin to see why this is a necessary step towards being able to truly control and direct magical force. When we develop a functional working relationship between aspects of self and the corresponding aspects of the (so-called) outer world, we have a greater ability to manipulate those forces in the outer world, according to our will.

The Path of Qoph (The Moon)

Aside from working with the forces embodied by Hod, the Practicus must also traverse the paths that lead to Netzach. The first of these is the path of *qoph*, attributed to the Moon trump, which connects the sphere of Malkuth (the physical world and body) with the sphere of Netzach (desire, emotion, and aspiration). This path represents the transition between the secure, familiar, and relatively concrete realities of our physical lives and the irrational, fiery, emotional reality symbolized by Netzach. This potentially unsettling psychological state is in evidence in the depiction on the Moon card itself. It is a night passage through the dark, the unknown, the vague and cloudy—the fearsome aspects of the unknown parts of ourselves—the unconscious world. The Hebrew letter *qoph* refers to the 'back of the head' and sure enough that is where primal, reactive brain functions are localized. The Practicus must master the fear residing in that animalistic aspect of the mind in order to proceed on the path towards Knowledge and Conversation. The HGA is a harbinger of the life beyond the physical world, but facing this new life forces us to venture into the darkness of unknown aspects of ourselves.

The Path of Tzaddi (The Emperor)

Next is the path of *tzaddi*, corresponding to the Emperor trump, which connects the sphere of Yesod (instinct, generativity) and the sphere of Netzach (desire, aspiration). The work of this path involves channeling the forces resident in Yesod towards the spiritual aim of K & C. The Hebrew letter *tzaddi* means 'fish hook' (see *Liber Tzaddi* for much wisdom on the role of the initiator in this regard). The Emperor on the card is that force within us—that inner initiator—that raises the instinctual energies of Yesod and directs them towards our spiritual goals. *Tzaddi* (as a verb) means 'to contemplate' and one of the methods of mastering this transformational process is the contemplative path of raja yoga, which is deeply imbedded in the work of the Practicus of A∴A∴.

The Path of Peh (The Tower)

The third and final path of relevance to the Practicus is that of *peh*, the Tower trump. One of the greatest obstacles to spiritual progress is the calcification of old, outworn forms and ideas of self. We must be psychologically flexible and changeable enough to allow our own evolution to take place. The path of *peh* connects Hod (intellect) with Netzach (desire, aspiration). Fittingly, the Tower trump shows the fire of Netzach blasting in and destroying, reshaping and transforming the old and outworn ideas that have become calcified in Hod. The overturned ideas of self tumble out of the tower as geometrical figures. The path of *peh* is also attributed to the svadisthana chakra. You will recall that the

141

muladhara chakra was activated with the Universe trump, and the anahata chakra activated with the Sun trump. The activation of the svadisthana chakra with the Tower completes an important triad: the life force is unleashed from its root (muladhara), and put under the regency of *agape* (anahata). Only then is it safe to amplify the force further by virtue of the sexual potencies of svadisthana.

Philosophus and Dominus Liminis: Netzach, the Veil of Paroketh, and the Paths of Ayin, Nun and Samekh

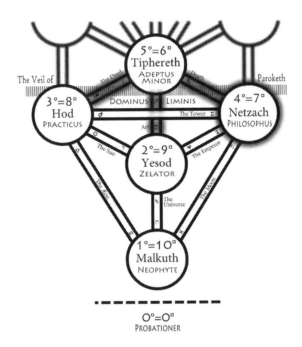

The aspirant must next attain to the grade of Philosophus, corresponding to Netzach, followed by the "portal" grade of Dominus Liminis, corresponding to the veil of Paroketh that hangs below Tiphereth. The work at this stage also pertains to the final three paths in the approach to Tiphereth and K & C of the HGA: the paths of *a'ayin* (the Devil), *nun* (Death), and *samekh* (Art).

Let's begin with a consideration of the work of Netzach. Netzach represents desire and aspiration. It is the fire and force of emotion that is the complement of the form-giving intellect of Hod. Accordingly, the work of the Philosophus involves the right use of this aspirational and devotional force. This is a supremely important phase of the work. Liber Astarte, which is the central bhakti yoga practice of the Philosophus, serves to fire up the aspirational 'engine' and strengthen the muscles of devotion. At this point, we bridge into the Dominus Liminis grade, where everything that has gone before is harmonized, synthesized and directed with fierce and one-pointed intensity towards Knowledge and Conversation.

This is a perfect opportunity for our aspiration to waver. When we have challenged ourselves to maintain a constant and vigilant aspiration, the ego has some games to play with us, and it will test us in insidiously effective ways. One of the ways that it does this is by crumbling in on itself. We begin to doubt our own ability to succeed; we get bogged down and depressed. The best piece of advice I can offer on this point is straightforward, but not easy: just don't stop *moving*. Don't stop working. As it turns out, the opposite of being stuck is…going somewhere! If you are continuing to move, you are continuing to progress.

The Path of A'ayin (The Devil)
One of the fascinating ways that this stagnation may tend to manifest itself is symbolized by the Devil trump. The Devil represents those aspects of life that seem ugly, threatening and evil; and the task of working with the transformative energy of the Devil involves seeing past the *appearance* of evil. That is, we must train ourselves to truly *know* that the apparently hideous reality in front of us (from the ego's perspective) is in fact a lesson from the HGA. We must learn to perceive that such abhorrent aspects of life have manifested for us to grapple with and learn from. If we get distracted by the ego's knee-jerk response to such things, we tend to believe that anything the ego doesn't like is bad and anything that the ego does like is good. The lesson of the Devil card is, therefore, to perceive the presence of that inner initiator, the HGA, in all manifest reality. We can see this truth in the nature of the path of *ayin*, which connects the intellect of Hod with the spiritually awakened center of consciousness at Tiphereth. It depicts the tension between what the mind is habitually pushing us to perceive, and what the *real* center of the spiritual self is attempting to teach us. The aspirant must internalize this lesson before attainment of K & C is possible.

The Path of Nun (Death)
Next, let's turn out attention to the Death trump. It corresponds to the path of *nun*, connecting Netzach, the sphere of emotion, desire and aspiration, with Tiphereth, the enlightened spiritual center. On the surface, this path (and indeed the trump itself) appears negative because in the pre-adept stage, most humans perceive death as a catastrophic end. The nature of the transformative process of the path of *nun* is that the ego lets go of the idea of catastrophic death. Just as it did in working the path

of the Devil, the ego lets go of the idea of evil and transforms it into something spiritually useful. The real mystery of the Death trump is that physical death is not an ending, but a transformation of form. As a verb, Nun means 'to sprout.' The relevance here is obvious: every change and every apparent catastrophe of destruction is a mystery of regeneration and new growth, as old forms fall away to make way for new ones. All life is constantly being transformed, and if we identify with solid calcified form, we perceive it as catastrophic death; but if we identify with the transformative process *itself*—if we identify with the eternal unfolding evolution of all things—then there is majesty, wonder and beauty in this process. This particular form of ego-transcendence is yet another essential element in the progress toward K & C.

The Path of Samekh (Art)

The final trump to consider in our discussion here is the Art card, corresponding to the path of *samekh*. *Samekh* connects Yesod, the generative, sexual, instinctual, subconscious center, and Tiphereth, the awakened spiritual self. The Hebrew word *samekh* means 'a prop' or 'a support' and corresponds to Sagittarius, the arrow. This path between Yesod and Tiphereth is deeply embedded with symbols that all relate to the uplifting of self—the firing of the arrow of aspiration toward Tiphereth. Interestingly, we do not approach Tiphereth from the sephira corresponding to the previous elemental grade (Netzach); rather, we shoot right up the middle pillar of the Tree. As Yesod is attributed to the Moon, and Tiphereth to the Sun, one of the mysteries encoded here is that the K & C is in one respect a union of the Sun and the Moon within us. That is, the receptive and reflective lunar consciousness of Yesod is wedded to the spiritually awakened solar radiance of Tiphereth, opening our minds at both conscious and unconscious levels to the influence of the HGA. Another important symbolic process relevant here is represented by the name "VITRIOL" on the Art card. This translates roughly as, "Visit the interior of the earth, and by rectification thou shalt find the hidden stone." That hidden stone is the stone of True Will and true Selfhood attained by virtue of the K & C. It is the Quintessence, the Stone of the Philosophers, and the Summum Bonum.

May these trumps of the holy Tarot be beacons to light your path toward the Holy Guardian Angel.

Sample Divination Method
(Adapted from the principles of Jungian psychology)

1. Shuffle the cards thoroughly. All cards should be facing the same direction (that is, when eventually laid out, no cards will be appear upside down).

2. Formulate a question about a situation in your own life, or the life of the person for whom you are performing the divination. The person for whom the reading is being done, whether you or another person, is called the *querent.*
3. Have the querent hold the question firmly in mind, and cut the cards into three stacks, and then reassemble them into one stack.
4. Next, draw a series of six cards from the top of the deck. Each card will correspond to a particular aspect of the querent's consciousness, or to external forces affecting the question at hand. Lay out the cards, as they are drawn, as described below. The cards and their meanings are as follows:

The Ego: The everyday personality and conscious awareness of the querent. (In traditional divination layouts, this card is called the *Significator.*) This card will indicate the nature of the querent's view of the situation, or their personality traits that are brought to bear on the matter. Place in front of you, at the far left.

The Obstacle: The basic nature of the primary obstacle in the situation. That is, the main *external* force negatively impinging on the question at hand. Place to the right of the ego card.

The Conscious Solution: A suggestion of something the querent may decide to try, or an attitude to adopt, in addressing the question. Place to the right of the Obstacle card.

The Influence of the Self: Deep, spiritually-informed influences on the querent, reflecting his or her true nature. This influence shows what the querent, *at his or her core*, is really trying to accomplish. Often, these influences are less driven by egoic wants and needs, and reflect an inner drive toward wholeness, healing, or balance in the psyche. Place above the Conscious Solution card.

Shadow Influences: Influences on the situation based on unconscious tendencies or drives in the querent. These will generally be viewed as negative or undesirable qualities in the person, but in actuality they may hold important keys to resolving the situation. Place below the Conscious Solution card.

The Outcome: A suggestion of the final result of the situation, based on the current influences visible in the layout. Place to the right of the Conscious Solution card.

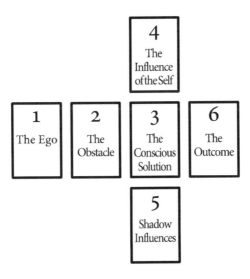

5. Use the various books listed above, or other interpretive resources, to contemplate the meaning of each card. Attempt to weave together a "story" based on all of these meanings. Don't worry if it is difficult at first. You will find your ability to derive useful interpretations will increase with repeated practice.
6. Keep in mind that all divinations are merely suggestive of solutions and outcomes, and you always have the power to make a difference by your actions and attitudes.

Recommended Reading:

By Aleister Crowley:

Crowley, A. (1993). *The Book of Thoth*. Stamford, CT: U.S. Game Systems, Inc.

By other authors:

Case, P. (1989). *The Book of Tokens*. Los Angeles, CA: Builders of the Adytum, Ltd.

DuQuette, L. (2003). *Understanding Aleister Crowley's Thoth Tarot*. York Beach, MA: Weiser Books.

Nichols, S. (1980). Jung *and Tarot*. York Beach, MA: Weiser Books.

Seckler, P. (2012). *The Kabbalah, Magick, and Thelema. Selected Writings Volume II.* D. Shoemaker, G. Peters & R. Johnson (Eds.) York Beach, ME: The Teitan Press.

Seckler, P. (2010). *The Thoth Tarot, Astrology, & Other Selected Writings.* D. Shoemaker, G. Peters & R. Johnson (Eds.) York Beach, ME: The Teitan Press.

Wang, R. (1983). *Qabalistic Tarot: A Textbook of Mystical Philosophy.* York Beach, MA: Weiser Books.

17

Initiation & Tetragrammaton

Any magical operation will likely fail unless the magician has harnessed the powers of the entire chain of creation—from the highest ineffable light down to the physical world itself. This is equally true of the process of initiation, where the candidate is in many senses the talisman of the working, and the forces in play must be mobilized in all Four Worlds in order to properly charge this talisman. In this chapter, I will discuss the application of the formula of Tetragrammaton (the divine name Yod-Heh-Vav-Heh) to the proper execution of magical ritual, and especially the process of initiation itself.

In keeping with Crowley's theses in the preface to *Magick in Theory and Practice*, we may define initiation as the process of applying an appropriate force (the ritual itself) to an 'inert' object (the candidate) to give it a specific magical trajectory (a stimulus to move toward higher consciousness, generally, or toward some other intended magical goal). In one fundamental sense, initiation is defined by its results. Given a potent and unbroken chain of power through the Four Worlds (the 'pronunciation' of the Tetragrammaton), these results *will* occur, for this chain is predicated on its harmony with the laws of nature.

Yet, as stated above, this magical force must have a suitable vehicle for its manifestation. In terms of personal initiation this vehicle is, of course, the candidate. How do we ensure that we are prepared for this influx of force? To answer this question, let us take as an example the ultimate magical initiation, that of the Knowledge and Conversation of the Holy Guardian Angel. In the Qabalistic model which forms the foundation of the system of the A∴A∴ (see Chapters 15 and 17) the aspirant must fashion him or herself into a true "grail"—a balanced and sound vessel capable of giving form to, and withstanding the intensity of, the light of the HGA. This grail is forged from the balanced attainment of the elemental grades, corresponding to the four sephiroth below Tiphereth. Crowned by the experience of the HGA at Tiphereth, the microcosmic pentagram is complete. Paradoxically, upon attainment of the K & C, the adept then takes up the task of aspiration unto the true and ultimate grail, the supernal Cup of Babalon. Keep this idea of the grail in mind as you read what follows.

We often think of initiation in terms of formal ritual processes, yet further reflection reveals that in fact, initiation occurs in many forms, day to day, through our life experiences themselves. I've constructed a model of the initiatory process based on the formula of Tetragrammaton. This model includes both formal and "informal" initiatory stages, and I will trace each stage below.

Stage 1: Yod/Atziluth

Stage One corresponds to the world of Atziluth. Before any true initiation can occur, the link to the highest spiritual sources must be forged. In an absolute sense, of course, this link is always there—every human exists as a manifestation of that spiritual seed—yet if we are to fully extend the influence of the highest into our initiatory work, we must consciously link ourselves to Atziluthic power, and bring it down through the other three worlds.

Formally, this link is forged by the magician's designing and carrying out the ritual; that is, the ritual officers themselves. There should be some form of general invocation of the highest spiritual powers, or at least of the Atziluthic powers relevant to the ritual context. In a ritual context, this would consist of those portions of the ceremonial opening which call upon such forces: general invocations such as the preliminary invocation of the Goetia (the "Bornless" invocation), a Middle Pillar-type exercise, or similar invocations. Regardless of the specific procedures involved, the result is the same: a link is forged to Atziluth, the "Secret Chiefs," the "Third Order," and so on. The names are far less important than the powers they embody.

As alluded to above, the *informal* linkage to Atziluth is the eternal presence of the star within each initiate—the yechidah of Qabalah, the Self of Jungian psychology, the Holy Guardian Angel of Thelemic tradition. Whether or not the initiate is conscious of this linkage, it is a prerequisite to his or her very life, and is therefore certainly essential to any given initiatory process.

Stage 2: Heh/Briah

Once the Atziluthic link has been consciously forged, we move from the general to the specific. That is, we activate the specific powers and energies unique to the purpose of the working. In formal ritual, this includes specific elemental, planetary, and similar forces, invoked through any number of combinations of procedures, such as pentagram and hexagram rituals, dramatic enactments, sigils, incenses, poetry, and the like. In essence, we have particularized the Atziluthic power source to the Briatic level of the candidate's psyche. Since Briatic consciousness, in any given individual, is theoretically synonymous with the influence of the HGA, we are essentially enlisting the explicit aid of the candidate's HGA in the work at hand. Ritually, this is accomplished through the Magical Oath. Even if the candidate has no *conscious* linkage to their HGA, by aligning themselves with the contents of the Oath, they bring their whole being into accord with the purpose of the initiation ritual, under the auspices of their HGA.

The Briatic world is the level of the universal will, chiah, reflected into, and informed by, the spiritual intuition of neshamah. It is this truest form of instruction, the neshamah, that descends into the candidate's consciousness in the "person" of the HGA. Any time we allow this force to break through into our conscious action, aligning our personal will with the universal will, we are indeed initiating ourselves into a new path of service. This is the *heh* stage of life's *informal* initiations—the action and presence of the HGA in our every thought, word and deed.

Stage 3: Vav/Yetzirah

In order to comprehend *consciously* this spiritually informed intuition, we must learn to speak its language, and that language is the world of symbol and metaphor. The *vav* stage of initiation involves the translation of this symbolic language into symbols comprehensible by the ordinary human intellect. The more the candidate works to develop an inner language of symbol, the easier it will be to benefit from the influx of these energies during and after initiation. This is not to say that initiations must be understood intellectually to be effective. The seeds planted unconsciously through initiatory processes take root regardless of our apprehension of them. Yet, the more we can consciously integrate what we are taught by the neshamah, the more we can live our lives in accordance with that truest will. When Abramelin describes the Angel writing in "dew" upon a "silver plate" (Yesod/Yetzirah), we may understand this to mean the reflective, receptive capacity of our own subconscious mind. Initially, in the pre-adept stages, these communications may come in the form of dreams, intuitive "flashes", creative works, and the more subtle beginnings of chakra activation. As the aspirant approaches adepthood, his or her ability to "decode" these communications from the HGA becomes progressively stronger. When these perceptive abilities are *just strong enough,* the door to full, conscious communion with the HGA opens (though the new adept might spend the rest of his or her life strengthening the relationship).

All of the above comments apply to the "informal" life initiations under discussion here. In terms of formal initiation ritual, the *vav* stage involves explicit use of visible symbols, movements, light changes, sounds, speeches, poetry, music and any number of other means to activate and make receptive the candidate's unconscious mind, and impress the object of the working upon it. If you have any experience of formal initiatory work you will immediately recall the symbols used. Upon further reflection, you will likely observe that the specific symbols used did indeed embody the translation of the object of the working into this language of the unconscious. Beyond any actual physical symbols used, a trained initiation team may be able to use their own powers of visualization and inner symbol-making to channel actual Yetziratic force in service of the initiatory goal. That is, the collective "mind" of the initiation team creates a psychic environment optimized for the candidate's apprehension of the goals of the operation. The "thicker" this psychic atmosphere, the more likely it is to truly charge and impact the talisman of the working—the candidate—assuming the foregoing procedures have made him or her suitably receptive.

Stage 4: Heh-final/Assiah

The crystallization of all the above stages in the world of Assiah is simultaneously the most concrete, yet also the most subtle stage of the whole process. Essentially, this is the stage where we lock all the foregoing changes into the physical vehicle, and externalize our inner experience into daily life. Thought precedes word, and word precedes deed. If Aztiluth and Briah represent the thought, and Yetzirah exemplifies the symbolic word issuing forth from that thought, then Assiah is the inevitable deed that results from this process. Exactly *how* this deed will be enacted is left to the subtle art of the magician. Who can say how a given individual will apply her newfound creative genius to the external world, or how a candidate in a specific initiation will actualize the teachings found within? These are the fruits of life's informal initiations.

In formal ritual, this Assiatic stage is enacted through various means, including physical stimulation of chakras, administration of eucharists, application of robes or regalia to the candidate, and so on. Suitably trained initiators are able to use the force of their own visualizations and other inner work to assist in this 'locking-in' of the effects in the physical body of the candidate. After all, the effective consecration of a talisman explicitly requires the magician to have the ability to bring this power down to the Assiatic level—and in this present example, the candidate *is* that talisman.

EXERCISE

This exercise is designed to have a priming effect on the psyche, much like fertilizing soil for seeds to be planted. Conscientious use of this exercise may help you build the necessary bridges across the Four Worlds in order to actualize a specific personal or magical goal. It utilizes imagery and energies that may allow you to activate consciously those aspects of the psyche (and beyond) that correspond to the Tetragrammaton. You will note some similarity with the traditional Middle Pillar exercise. The present exercise could certainly be augmented and intensified by vibrating the appropriate divine names at each of the centers. If you include these vibrations, it is strongly recommended that you conclude with one of the "circulations" described by Regardie and others (one such circulation involves seeing the energy moving down the front of the aura on the exhalation, and up the back of the aura on the inhalation).

You may wish to record yourself describing these steps out loud, for later use as a self-guided imagery exercise.

Step One: Choose a transformative goal, whether conceived as personal/psychological or magical. Next, choose a vivid and specific symbol to represent it—essentially an inner talisman. The image of the grail is recommended in this context, as our purpose here is primarily that of fashioning ourselves into a perfect vehicle for the divine. Alternative symbols include the Ankh, the Star of Babalon, the Unicursal Hexagram, images from the Stele, and so on. Let your own imagination and personal symbol system guide you in this. Set aside one or more periods of meditation upon this symbol, while simultaneously visualizing the desired goal. You should include as much visual and emotional detail as possible, so that the symbol becomes increasingly charged with the innate power and necessity of the desired outcome. *Feel* yourself living the new reality, pouring this intention into the symbol.

Step Two: Set aside about thirty minutes when you can be uninterrupted. Sit in your favorite *asana*. Begin gentle, rhythmic breathing. Continue for 5-10 minutes until you are very relaxed and still, inwardly and outwardly.

Step Three: YOD. Visualize a star in the heavens, the brightest in the sky. See it become your own crown center. Intensify this visualization as you aspire to the highest and most exalted conception of divinity you can imagine. As you do this, the crown center glows brighter and brighter with white brilliance. You are linking yourself to the universal will, the primal fire, the *yod* of YHVH.

Step Four: HEH. See the light pour down a shaft from the crown, filling the throat center with a slightly less brilliant white. If you have established conscious relations with your HGA, use whatever formulae the HGA has taught you to request aid in this endeavor. If you are not yet consciously in communication with your HGA, simply know that you are asking the Angel for assistance.

Step Five: VAV. Now visualize the grail or other symbol at the heart center. See the white light descend from the throat center to the grail at the heart, infusing the heart center, and the symbol itself, with yellow-gold light. Then, see this golden light-infused symbol descent to the genital center, where it changes to a lush violet color. Conceive that it is "locked in" in the subconscious. It may even feel like a "click" of sorts, at the back of the head in the region of the brain stem.

Step Six: HEH-FINAL. Feel the symbol dissolve into golden-white sparks of charged light which, in a single cycle of breath, circulate throughout the body. Every cell is filled with the light as the whole process is locked in in Assiah—anchored at the physical level.

Step Seven: Remain in stillness as you renew the vivid visualizations described at the beginning of this exercise. When ready, gradually bring yourself back to normal awareness. Record the results in your magical diary. Repeat as appropriate—I recommend at least once per week for several weeks.

Conclusion

It is my hope that the present discussion and exercises will prompt you toward further exploration and development of your own inner symbol system. Meditation on the formula of Tetragrammaton, and its correspondence to your own experiences during ritual in general, and initiation in particular, will indeed assist you in becoming that grail of which we speak—a true and fitting vessel for the light.

18

THE CHAKRAS

Given the ancient origins of the doctrine of the chakras, and its considerable influence on a wide variety of traditions, it is no surprise that there are innumerable ways to contemplate the chakra system in the context of personal transformation. Accordingly, we will limit ourselves to a certain vantage point in our discussion of the chakras in this chapter. Essentially, we will explore the chakras as a means of understanding the stages of personal transformation in the Thelemic magical path, rather than as energy centers in the body *per se*. In my opinion, there is so much focus placed on the 'energy center' idea in popular discussion that we miss out on the larger significance of the transformative model discussed here. We will be using sephirothic attributions based on those given in Crowley's *777* (column 118) with a few of my own adaptations. Also, we'll draw heavily on the work of Joseph Campbell, who has much of value to add to our understanding of the system.

The stages of transformation under discussion here apply (when considered on a grand scale) to the unfolding of the Great Work and the system of A∴A∴ from Probationer to Ipsissimus; and I will review the attributions of the chakras to specific sephiroth. It is important to note, however, that when I say that a chakra is related to a particular sephira, I'm not implying that an awakening of this chakra is synonymous with the attainment of the corresponding A∴A∴ grade. Rather, I'm describing the degree to which, in a given moment of consciousness, the 'circuit' is sufficiently complete for us to have glimpses of levels of expanded awareness and consciousness. We don't generally stay in that state for very long. As we move along in the path of return, we manage to stay in these states longer and longer; but especially in the early stages of the work, we quickly drop back 'down' into the lower chakras as we deal with the ins and outs of daily life. I can say with virtual certainty that there's not an adept in the world who doesn't sometimes regress to a reactive/animalistic state of mind in response to mundane daily stresses. That's simply the human body engaging its fight-or-flight response, impinging on consciousness, and it's going to happen no matter how high you've climbed on the mountain of attainment.

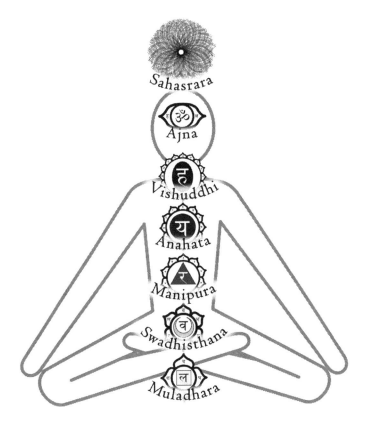

The Chakras

As many of you know, in the O.T.O. system of initiation there are certain attributions of the degrees to the chakras and, for obvious reasons, I'm not going to discuss the specifics of O.T.O. degrees here.

O.T.O. initiates may wish to review the diagram in *The Equinox*, Volume III, Number 10, which gives the correspondences between the chakras and the degrees in the Man of Earth triad, as an additional symbolic overlay on our discussion in this chapter.

Muladhara

We begin, of course, with the *muladhara* chakra, which means "root base." This is Malkuth. The psyche is essentially inert. The basic nature of this consciousness is of a binding force—the binding force of matter and of the illusion of purely material existence. The obstacles for growth here are a desire for physical security, a clinging to the illusion of physical security or safety. We are guided primarily by fear responses. This is the animalistic brain with its primal survival instinct. To transcend this state, we have to disidentify with the survival impulse as the primary center of our focus. Compare this to the A∴A∴ Neophyte's task to control the body of light. In accomplishing this task, which corresponds to the path of *tav*, we expand our consciousness to transcend the limiting belief that we *are* our physical bodies. You can readily see how this relates to the ordeal of the muladhara described above.

Joseph Campbell gives a compelling image for this struggle, drawn from the various myths relating to dragons. As you know, in many such myths the dragon is guarding a hoard of some kind, and typically this involves a woman, and/or a treasure of some kind. Consider that the virgin corresponds to Yesod, the sexual life, the vitality, the divine force within us; and the gold to Anahata, the Tiphereth center, the gold of awakened spiritual selfhood. What a compelling image! The dragon, symbolizing absorption in matter and a clinging to material things, is preventing us from accessing the regenerative power of Yesod and the light-giving adepthood of Tiphereth.

Svadisthana

Next, we have the *svadisthana* chakra. This translates roughly as "her favorite resort," or "her favorite standing place," and I attribute this to Yesod. The level of functioning here is still primarily self-serving. While muladhara-consciousness is self-serving in its focus on physical survival, at svadisthana we have broadened our concern to include survival via perpetuation of our progeny through sexual reproduction. Of course, at the animal level of awareness, we're oblivious to the will of our DNA to survive and perpetuate itself. As human animals in this unawakened state, we're mostly just aware of wanting sex for pleasure, or to produce offspring to ensure family survival, to fulfill societal or identity expectations, and so on.

The typical obstacle here is an excessive obsession with sex. Freud's libido theory was, of course, concerned with psychopathological manifestations at this level of consciousness. To transcend it, we must 'unclench' the muscles of sexual repression/obsession, and allow the sex force to seek its higher aim—the transformation of the psyche in its higher aspects. In other words, we have to perceive that the real aim of this force within us, this regenerative power, is to transform us from animals into fully-realized humans and eventually, into gods.

Rightly understood, svadisthana-consciousness can be our first glimpse of the divine power in life . We don't yet recognize it as being *within us* necessarily, but it is our first psychologically significant encounter with divinity. In the corresponding Yesod grade of A∴A∴, the Zelator works to intensify the awareness and flow of the sex force/life force via the beginning practices of pranayama.

Manipura

Next is the *manipura* chakra, which means "city of jewels." I attribute this to both Hod and Netzach together. Whereas svadhisthana as being reflective of that stage of consciousness focused on the drive toward sex, at manipura we are focused on the drive to possess *power.* This is still self-serving, but the focus is personal power within a *social* context. It takes into account the existence of a community, but the aim is still personal power, dominance over the herd, being the alpha animal in the pack. Campbell even refers to this state of mind as the 'yoga of war.' When rightly developed, it serves a more evolved purpose related to the vishuddhi chakra (more on this later), but for most humans, most of the time, this is simply a drive to control our social environment.

I noted that manipura is attributed to Hod and Netzach. It is perhaps significant that the path connecting these sephiroth is the path of *peh* (the Tower), where we go to war with our own limiting conceptions and outworn forms of consciousness in order to rebuild them into something more healthy and functional. To transcend this state, we must find a way to be centered in our own power without the need to control or dominate others to survive; to get past the illusion of others as entities that must be subjugated. In other words, we move upward toward the awakening of the *anahata* chakra.

Anahata

We should pause here to note that the three chakras we've discussed so far—muladhara, svadhisthana, and manipura—all represent essentially primal and animalistic levels of consciousness. Up to this point, a person who is living predominantly out of these stages of awareness is barely exceeding the functioning of a lower animal. The transformations that occur from this point onward allow us to become truly human and, eventually, superhuman.

Anahata means 'not hit' or 'unstruck.' And when is something 'not hit'? When there is *only one thing.* The awakening of the anahata chakra brings the awareness of the unity of human experience and consciousness. *Agape.* Anahata represents that awakened consciousness of the spiritual interconnectedness of all beings. This is the consciousness behind the 'namaste' greeting, in which those exchanging the words recognize the common divinity in each other. At this stage, however, it is still experienced in relation to other people who are perceived as external and separate beings. We have not yet evolved to the place where there is a full *experience* of the unity of consciousness—but at least we have become aware of the concept! The traditional word of the anahata chakra is AUM, signifying that all other words are merely fragments of this one Great Word, just as all manifest forms are but fragments of the One.

In the system of A∴A∴, the Knowledge and Conversation of the Holy Guardian Angel at Tiphereth brings us into awareness of our relationship to the Holy Guardian Angel; but even the Adeptus Minor is not fully and permanently conscious of the union with the Holy Guardian Angel. This takes much additional work—the work of the other sephiroth attributed to anahata in our scheme here, Chesed and Geburah, as well as the supernal triad of Kether, Chokmah and Binah.

Yet the adept of Tiphereth has nonetheless entered into a real conscious relationship with the beloved, the Angel. He or she is 'face to face' with the Angel, as in a marriage, yet it is still *perceived* as a self-and-other relationship.

Vishuddhi

Next we have the *vishuddhi* chakra, which means "purgation." This is essentially a purging of the ruach obsessions, which is essential for attainment of supernal consciousness; that is, for the crossing of the Abyss, and the transcendence of the limitations of human life and human consciousness. When the vishuddhi chakra is 'closed,' we might attribute it to Da'ath—the false 'knowledge' which is still bound up in ego-consciousness, as opposed to transcendent awareness. The opening of vishuddhi corresponds to the crossing of the Abyss and the resulting attainment of Binah.

Something very interesting is happening here with the energy of manipura. You will recall that manipura has previously been essentially facing 'outward' into the world, using its energy to conquer and gain power over others. But now, rightly understood and rightly applied, this energy—this conquering energy, this yoga of war—is turned inward and brought to bear on the transformation of the self. This is the inner war, traditionally called the 'turning about of the Shakti.' We move away from the erroneous conception that our destructive force should be used against others for our own power purposes, and arrive at the enlightened awareness that the *primary* war to be fought is against our own limiting conceptions of self. This represents full attainment of vishuddhi consciousness.

Ajna
The next chakra is *ajna,* which means 'command' or 'summoning.' Ajna is attributed to the sphere of Chokmah. Campbell says this is like seeing God, but through a pane of glass. The human soul is finally face-to-face with divinity, but there is still a separation. From this vantage point, we are uniquely positioned to experience all the ego we have built, developed, and lived in, yet we can also glimpse the worlds beyond it. In this threshold state, we have one foot in ego-consciousness and the other in the divine world.

At Chokmah, the grade of the Magus in the A∴A∴ system, we gain consciousness of our word (*logos*) – the one formula of our existence which is our unique link to universal will. But we're still one step removed from complete identity with oneness. After all, in order to have a logos that you deliver to the world, you still have to posit a distinction between the thing delivering the word and the thing that receives it. This is still not quite the level of unity we will see in our examination of the *sahasrara* chakra below.

One final note regarding ajna: Just as the force of manipura is elevated to impinge on vishuddhi, so that inner development takes the place of undue outward aggression; so here, the force of svadhisthana—the outward expression of the life force as physical sex—is introverted as ecstatic devotion to the divine within. So, here again, we have elevated an aspect of one of the 'animalistic' chakras and applied it to a higher center.

Sahasrara
Sahasrara means 'thousand-petaled.' Here, we attain to complete union with the beloved, the HGA, the All, God (fill in the blank with your favorite term). There is no separation; this is the Kether point. Here we are released from the bondage of matter, and the corpse of Malkuth is rightly seen as the deathlessness of the pure spirit. As it is said, Kether is in Malkuth. Interestingly, some depictions of the sahasrara chakra feature the bodies of *shava*—which means corpse—back-to-back with Shiva—who is, of course, the deity. We can understand this to be a statement about the close relationship of death and immortality.

The ninth century Sufi master Mansur al-Hallaj has a story that beautifully illustrates the nature of this transition from ajna to sahasrara, where we move from seeing God through a pane of glass to being God.

There was once a moth that was drawn each night toward a flame burning in a lantern enclosed by panes of glass. Night after night, the moth pounded its body against the glass in desperate longing—seeing the object of its devotion right there, but unable to reach it. Then one day the door of the lantern happened to be left open, and the moth was able to fly into the flame, where it was annihilated in ecstasy. And in that moment of annihilation—which is from our human ego-bound perspective, the moment of its death—it actually achieved its goal of union with the flame. It *became* the flame, became God.

There is a teaching that after the attainment of sahasrara the initiate returns to anahata, to abide in love in that place where we perceive divinity in relationship to the world, partaking of both divine and human consciousness simultaneously. Recall the hero's journey, where the hero has gone out to slay the dragon and obtained the reward or treasure. The hero doesn't simply wander off with the gold and the girl to settle down and enjoy the treasure just for himself. The hero comes back to society and *shares the treasure*. Just so, the overarching path of the Great Work is characterized by this service to humanity. Crowley talks about this in comparable terms when he says that the Magister crosses the Abyss, attains to supernal consciousness, and is then cast out into the sphere of his or her work in the world—the sphere best suited to his or her manifest gifts. Thus, the path of individual attainment is ultimately identical to the path of service to all humanity. What appears initially to be a hero's journey for the sake of individual development has revealed its deeper purpose: It the path towards immersion in the consciousness of the All and the devotion of everything we are to the service of that consciousness.

19

THE ROLE OF THE EGO IN THE GREAT WORK

The human ego is, by design and of necessity, an essential working tool of every magician. Before going further in our exploration of the ego's role in the Great Work, it is extremely important to understand that when I use the term ego here, I am using it in the sense adopted by Carl Jung. It is not used in a pejorative sense, as when we say someone has "a lot of ego" or that they are "egotistical." The ego, as discussed here, is simply the everyday self, the primary center of consciousness that you carry with you in everyday activities. Ego simply means 'I'. It is the 'I' that goes to the store, that goes to work, that likes and dislikes things, that consciously perceives beauty, fear and pain, and so on.

In the stages of the Great Work prior to full adepthood—that is, before Knowledge and Conversation of the Holy Guardian Angel—the characteristic state of consciousness is one of primarily identifying with the ego as the center of self. This perspective is gradually overturned across the First Order grades of A∴A∴, but most magicians in the pre-adept phase, most of the time, primarily identify themselves with the ego, whether they realize it or not.

In contrast, we have what Jung called the Self (I will capitalize this term to distinguish it from 'self' when used as a casual, general reference to oneself). This is the real center of our being. In the pre-adept phase, we're mostly unconscious; but through insight-oriented work in psychotherapy, and certainly via the magical and mystical path when rightly pursued, we open up conscious awareness of this Self. The opening of this awareness in a secular, psychotherapeutic context might include working with dream symbols, development of intuition, tracing a symbolic narrative by watching the synchronicities that occur in our lives, and similar processes. Within our esoteric work, the Qabalah and the other symbol systems form a vital framework for our interactions with our own unconscious, and they therefore open the pathway to connection with the Self.

The forging of this conscious connection between ego and Self is the central goal of the work in the Jungian psychoanalytical tradition, but it is also one way of looking at the path of the Great Work—a mode of transformation that magicians pursue in a deeper way than your average analysand (the technical term for person undergoing psychoanalysis.) In any case, it is the forging of this so-called "ego-Self axis" which informs much of our discussion here.

In this chapter, I will be using not only the terminology from the Jungian model of the psyche–'ego', 'Self' and 'shadow' and the like— but also the analogous language of Qabalistic psychology. For our purposes here, ego=ruach and Self=neshamah. These are not perfect analogies, but they are close enough for our discussion here (see figures below).

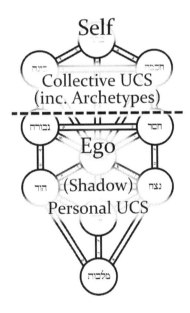

The Jungian Model of the Psyche on the Tree of Life

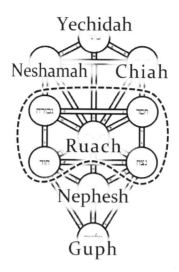

The Qabalistic 'Parts of the Soul' on the Tree of Life

Let's begin with a look at the everyday functioning of the ego. What purpose does it serve? How does it help us, and how can it hurt us? The most important fundamental here is to understand that the ego is the perceptual mechanism by which we interact constructively with the outer world. It's completely necessary to this interaction; without it, we are impotent to exert our will upon the physical reality that surrounds us. Accordingly, at no point does the magician truly engage in a permanent "destruction of the ego." Rather, through the Great Work, we come to understand the proper role and function of the ego. We put it in the proper relationship with the Self, and ultimately, we are able to *identify* with that deepest Self, the real center of who we are—the star or *khabs*.

The ego is the lens through which we perceive the outer world. It is necessarily individualized and, therefore, limited in its vision. The information we gain by the useful illusion of viewing ourselves as a separate being—the illusion of an inner and an outer world—allows us to function in that outer world. We would be unable to lead a constructive life if we were always immersed in undifferentiated cosmic consciousness. Just imagine trying to do your grocery shopping in *that* state of mind!

One of the important mechanisms of the ego's functioning—that is, one of the ways that it actually serves as a lens to look at the world—is via the psychological projections that we indulge in every day. In one sense, all perception is a psychological projection, in that we are imposing symbol sets, categories and other labels onto the mass of perceptions that come to us; it will always be filtered and interpreted by the ego. Yet we can do some very important work to grow our

165

understanding of our ego and its role in the Great Work by taking a closer look at these psychological projections—especially when we project onto *other people*.

In a negative projection, the ego protects itself by judging the faults of others rather than undergoing the painful introspection necessary for its own real growth. In a positive projection – such as idealizing a loved one—the ego yearns for union with something it perceives as external to itself and thereby misses the opportunity to recognize the soul's inherent completeness. So, in both cases, we're trapped in the self-other dichotomy. In one case it is a negative judging energy, and in the other case it is disowning an aspect of our own divinity—a part of our own wholeness. We fall into the trap of believing that we need to unite with something exterior in order to be whole and healthy. In either case, we are confronting the shadow.

The shadow, in Jungian terms, is almost literally like a shadow cast by the ego—the silhouette formed by those areas where the light of self-knowledge does *not* shine. It is all those things we do not accept as ourselves—all those unacknowledged or rejected aspects of the self, both positive and negative. Crowley provides some interesting commentary on this phenomenon in *Liber Aleph*. Here are a few key passages from the chapters titled "On Certain Diseases of Disciples" and "On Watching for Faults in the House," which flow together into a single thread of discussion.

> ...We become that which obsesseth us, either through extreme Hate or Extreme Love. Knowest thou not how the one is a Symbol of the other? For this Reason, since Love is the Formula of Life, we are under Bond to assimilate (in the End) that which we fear or hate. So then we shall be wise to mould all Things within ourselves in Quietness and Modulation. But above all must we use all to our own End, adapting with Adroitness even our Weakness to the Work. [...]

> Therefore, watch heedfully the Fault of another, that thou mayst correct it in thyself. For if it were not in thee, thou couldst not perceive it or understand it...[31]

At this point in our discussion (and from your existing understanding of the nature of the True Will) it should be fairly obvious the wants and the desires of the ego are often (especially in the pre-adept stage) quite divorced from the True Will of the real Self. And once again, our Great Work consists of forging that link between ego and Self, consciously

---

[31] Crowley, A. (1991). *Liber Aleph*. York Beach, ME: Weiser Books.

aligning our ego with the full power of the real trajectory of our soul—the True Will.

To use a technological metaphor: the state of the ego/ruach is like the bandwidth we have available for the influx of spiritual force. If the bandwidth is narrowed—if we have narrowed *ourselves* via egoic obsessions, projections, or imbalances—we have actually reduced our capacity to be a channel of this divine force. Understood in this fashion, one can easily see the importance of the self-analysis of the personality that is built into any competently executed magical training.

The ego is the part of you that feels pain, anger, joy; but *you are much more than this*. The real Self is far more expansive than this limited set of functions; although most of us, most of the time, operate day-to-day as if we are no more than a 'thinking and feeling machine.' That's one of the inherent limitations of our ego. Accordingly, one of the greatest traps in life is to believe what the ego is telling us as if it is the *only* truth. When we are in a depression, when we are overwhelmingly anxious, when we are hurt or angry, we must strive to step back from the ego's limited perspective, and remember that the part of us experiencing the distress is not the whole of us, and certainly not the core of who we really are.

The Self—that *khabs*-star at our spiritual center—is not worried about paying the bills. The Self is not worried about what so-and-so said that hurt our feelings. That's simply the ego. If we can view the ego more like a pet and less like who we really are, we can get some degree of distance on life's troubles. That doesn't mean we reject them. That doesn't mean we belittle them. That doesn't mean we pretend that we don't have these feelings and responses. As I said before, it's the ego that is our information-gathering mechanism in the world. Accordingly, attending to these perceptions and experiences of Ego is actually a doorway into deeper work.

Our goddess Nuit represents the infinite realm of all possibilities of experience presented to us. If we feel an emotion we don't like—if we reject it and try to run away from it or suppress it—we are essentially saying, 'I reject this aspect of Nuit.' I think you will agree that this is not going to be a productive way of living in the long run. We may temporarily avoid some degree of ego-based discomfort, but in the process we alienate ourselves from the perfection of the reality being presented to us. This condition is very much like having a roadmap, but refusing to acknowledge where we are on it, simply because we don't like the scenery. Instead, we must accept where we are and then decide where we want to go.

As I said earlier, the disidentification with the ruach-ego and the identification with neshamah-Self as the real center of who we are is the overarching goal; but there are dangers of doing this prematurely. These dangers fall under the broad category of ego inflation – when the ego gets a little too full of itself. This is more or less the baseline functioning of all humans from time to time. An example of this, all too common in magical communities, is a young magician who has prematurely identified with their idealized adept Self, imagining that some early successes in magick are proof of full attainment. They thereby attempt to make an end-run around the ego development which is actually a prerequisite to truly *becoming* an adept. There are no short cuts.

Some people are – by karma, by birth, by genetics, or other factors— rather precocious in their ego development (and I mean that in a good sense) in that that they seem to be on the fast track to spiritual development without falling into some of the pitfalls—the neuroses— associated with the ego. But for the most part, we all have a long and winding road to follow as we ferret out those shadowy elements of ourselves, developing our self-understanding gradually and not always comfortably.

The proper method of pursuing this work (and by 'proper' I mean gradual and balanced) is built into the First Order grades of A∴A∴, and it begins by finding Kether in Malkuth. The observing ego at Tiphereth sees the light of Kether in the natural world of Malkuth—since that is its role as a perceptual tool. The ego also (occasionally) peers into the subconscious realm of Yesod—the nephesh ('animal soul')—the personal unconscious in Jung's model.

What is *not* happening in the pre-adept stage is direct conscious perception of Kether. Rather, the initiate at this stage is looking at the reflection of that divinity in the outer world and seeing that as a pathway inward. The perception of this pathway grows in accuracy across the first order grades. Later, at Tiphereth, we open up to the path of *gimel* (Briatic consciousness) impinging directly and consciously on our spiritual perception in Tiphereth. This is the characteristic psycho-spiritual state associated with the Knowledge and Conversation of the HGA. Only a balanced Ego will be a proper vessel for this conscious communion. In the chapter on methods and tools of A∴A∴, I likened this prepared ego to a properly formed and balanced cup, ready to contain the light of the Angel.

The greater the attainment, the greater the danger of ego inflation. It would be nice if Knowledge and Conversation wiped out all of the ego's neuroses and made the adept a nice person to be around all the time. But unfortunately, every attainment has its shadow side and every adept, *however advanced,* must deal with the shadow side of their station on the path. The shadow side of Tiphereth (which in its fullness signifies spiritual enlightenment) is spiritual vanity. "Wow, I'm so cool now that I've arrived here! I've got a Holy Guardian Angel and now I'm even more powerful!" Every newly minted adept of Tiphereth will fight their own version of this battle. Ideally, it will be caught early in the process, and transcended with good-humored humility.

By virtue of persistent self-exploration, analysis of projections, and the balancing tasks of the first order, the ego has found its right place in relationship to the Angel and to the deeper Self—the link between ruach and neshamah has been forged and stabilized. Yet it is precisely at this point of apparent stability where the ego comes up against the greatest challenge it will ever encounter. It must come to terms with the futility of holding on to its sense of individual existence. As stated above, it is not that the ego must actually be destroyed—the adept will still need it in order to function in the outer world; rather, the adept must be *willing* to destroy it—to lose all sense of identity at the level of the individual personality. Why? Because only a fully developed ego/ruach that is also willing to abandon itself is a suitable offering to the grail of Babalon, and only such a full offering will entitle the adept to cross the Abyss and attain to mastery.

For further insights into this material, you might wish to refer to Robert Moore's book, *King, Warrior, Magician, Lover.*[32] He explores these four archetypes both in their fullness and in their shadow sides. He discusses the magician archetype as one of inner power—secret, subtle, and non-physical. This is obviously an important tool for living; but on the shadow side, it represents a clinging control and manipulativeness—a debased and insecure lust for personal power. This calls to mind the polarity of the Adeptus Exemptus in his or her fullness, willing to move on and abandon ego conceptions, versus the Black Brother in his towers of ego—a fortress he refuses to abandon for fear of losing personal power. In the *Parsifal* story, this is the dichotomy between *Parsifal* (in his final attainment as the Grail King) versus the wizard Klingsor, who has simply stolen the sacred spear and locked himself in his tower, ever fearful of losing the trappings of power—an epitome of the tragic heights of ego inflation.

Conclusion

All parts of the soul are sacred, and no element of the human constitution is 'evil.' The ego is an integral part of effective life as a human being, and we must strive to understand its functioning and allow it to serve in its rightful role. If you approach this task with courage, honesty, and humility, your attainment will be accelerated and enriched immeasurably.

---

[32]   Moore, R. and D. Gillette. (1991). *King, Warrior, Magician, Lover: Rediscovering the Archetypes of the Mature Masculine.* San Francisco: Harper SanFrancisco.

20

THE FORMULAS OF L.V.X. AND N.O.X.

The magical 'formulas' of L.V.X. and N.O.X. are frequently discussed in the context of the Thelemic magical path. As you may know, these terms translate as "light" and "night", respectively. There has been quite a bit of misunderstanding, or at least misplaced emphasis, when it comes to these terms. This chapter will attempt to clarify the picture. The opinions I am offering here are based on my own experience, and that of my colleagues and students over the years. Nothing here should be taken as doctrine, but merely as the considered opinions of someone who has walked the path. I encourage your skepticism and your own personal research, as always.

It is, in some ways, easier to explain and to understand L.V.X. and N.O.X. by starting at the end-point of the path of attainment, and working backwards toward the beginning. Let's start by asking ourselves, what is the ultimate goal of the path? Most of us will likely agree that it is union with God, union with the All, immersion in the infinite, the attainment of supernal cosmic consciousness, or some similar concept. In the system of A∴A∴, one of the symbolic frameworks that most vibrantly and viscerally conveys the essence of this attainment is the dissolution of oneself into the grail of Babalon—the great holy grail of the sphere of Binah. This dissolution constitutes the adept's attainment to the $8°=3^{\square}$ grade of A∴A∴, known as Magister Templi.

Now, if we are going to offer all of ourselves, our entire sense of identity and consciousness, into the grail, it follows that we have to know ourselves *completely*. It is a prerequisite to this attainment that we have *fully actualized* who we are, otherwise the offering is meaningless. As is written in *Liber Cheth*, "Thou shalt mingle thy life with the universal life. Thou shalt keep not back one drop." For this self-understanding to be complete, we must have attained the sphere of Chesed and the Adeptus Exemptus 7°=4□ grade in A∴A∴. This grade signifies the fully realized, maximally functioning ruach.

Now, still moving backwards: to actualize this perfected ruach/ego, we must have attained K & C of the HGA, thereby catching a glimpse of that star at our center, and gaining knowledge of the True Will. The K & C begins the process of deepening our relationship to the Angel, in order that we may fully realize our lives as an outward expression of our True Will (Adeptus Major 6°=5□) and thereby eventually attain to Adeptus Exemptus.

And moving even further backwards: in order to attain K & C of the HGA, we must have previously equilibrated ourselves in terms of the elements of our being, by virtue of passing through the elemental grades and the corresponding balancing ordeals of the First Order of A∴A∴. We must have moved through Malkuth, Yesod, Hod, Netzach to the grade of Dominus Liminis, affecting a synthesis and harmonization of all these elements into a suitable vessel for the light of the Holy Guardian Angel.

So we've moved from the supreme attainment of supernal consciousness backwards to the very beginning of the path. Now let's reverse direction, starting at the beginning, and discuss how we are likely to experience these transformative stages as we move through them, beginning with the formula of L.V.X.

You've probably heard about L.V.X. mostly in the context of the old Hermetic Order of the Golden Dawn, where this is a formula of their Tiphereth attainment. If you review the original 'Analysis of the Keyword,' which is a part of the Lesser Ritual of the Hexagram as published in *Liber O* and elsewhere, you'll see that the formula of L.V.X. is intertwined with the so-called 'dying god' formula that for the most part has been associated with the old aeon of Osiris. In the original Golden Dawn, the L.V.X. formula was connected with Tiphereth and was the symbol of the crowning achievement of their First Order. It symbolized a certain awakening consciousness in the new adept, but it by no means reflected the full attainment of the K & C of the HGA as understood in the system of the A∴A∴. I'll say more about this important distinction later in the chapter.

In the A∴A∴, the formula of L.V.X. is the process of seeking the light of the Holy Guardian Angel—an entirely valid formula that was overlaid with the formula of the dying god in its old aeonic manifestation, but isn't *necessarily* identical with it. That 'one star in sight' from the beginning of the path, the light of the Angel, is the L.V.X. we seek, along with the resulting self-knowledge and self-empowerment. As we move through the First Order grades of A∴A∴ the L.V.X. formula manifests itself as a process akin to the alchemical formula of *solve et coagula*, which is the dissolution of each of our component parts, and then later synthesizing them. Accordingly, the day-to-day experience of an initiate of these grades is often necessarily one of partial consciousness, corresponding to their particular stage of growth. For example, at Malkuth in the grade of Neophyte there is a great deal of emphasis on the physical body and the material universe. Later at the Zelator/Yesod we see a focus on the subconscious processes; at the grade of Hod we work extensively with the intellect; and at the grade of Netzach with our desire, emotion and aspiration. These are all simply *parts* of the one holistic self, of course, but it is sometimes useful to view ourselves in terms of our component parts, for the sake of purifying and consecrating these aspects of self to be increasingly in accord with our True Will, thereby reformulating the *entirety* the self to be a vessel for the Angel.

When we are in a particular grade, and are therefore focused on these *partial* realities, we may feel somewhat unbalanced, especially when diverging from the middle pillar grades. Yet this temporary imbalance is a necessary part of the eventual harmonization. If we merely work to enhance those things that make us most feel comfortable and balanced, we leave large portions of ourselves undeveloped both psychologically and magically. Crowley addresses this with his various warnings about the dangers of simply pandering to one's preferences, as opposed to developing those aspects of self that are more shadowy—disowned or disliked. We must compensate for these prejudices by training these less developed and less desirable aspects of self.

You will recall our metaphor from an earlier chapter, that we construct ourselves as a grail for the light of the HGA. You will also recall the potential pitfalls of this process—a grail that has a hole in it will leak; a grail that is lopsided will topple; a grail that is made out of the wrong material may be dissolved by the light or contaminate it. Eventually, when this grail is completed through the passage of the elemental grades, we offer ourselves in a receptive state to the light of the Angel. As we read in *Liber LXV*, "to await Thee is the end, not the beginning." Indeed, the formula of L.V.X. is central to the passage through the elemental grades and is intimately connected with the attainment of the K & C of the HGA.

If the First Order grades are a courtship, and the K & C is the wedding, then the grades of Adeptus Major ($6°=5^□$) and Adeptus Exemptus ($7°=4^□$) embody the task of strengthening and deepening the marital relationship. Here, the adept's intimacy with the HGA is solidified, and his or her life is conformed to be an ever more perfect vessel of the True Will. Beginning at this stage, there is a gradual transition of focus onto the N.O.X. formula, although the L.V.X. formula remains in force as well; after all, it is the formula of the Tiphereth attainment, and the newly minted adept is fresh from the K & C. The transition from $5°=6□$ to $6°=5□$ requires a transformation of the outer life of the adept into a vessel for the True Will. Relationships, career, and potentially everything else in the outer life as well as the personalities as we know it is the field of operation of the light of the Angel; and we'll find much of this reconfigured, reconstructed, and sometimes blasted apart and put back together in uniquely interesting ways as we proceed.

At this stage there tends to be an increasing awareness of an endpoint to this personal development; that is, the individual consciousness we are continuing to build, enhance and balance—the ruach-consciousness that is interacting with the Angel—is only finitely expandable. To go beyond the limitations of the ruach there is, literally, nothing left for the adept besides the transition to the N.O.X. formula.

The attainment to $7°=4□$ signifies this fully realized ruach consciousness—the human psyche (as normally understood) in its most exalted manifestation. It is only at this stage, when we have finally and fully come to know ourselves in all our aspects, that we are finally able to *offer* all of ourselves into the grail. How could we possibly have done this before? It would have been a partial offering. It would be like cutting off one of our fingers and offering it into the grail saying, "Here, Babalon, I give you everything!" when in fact we have hardly even begun to know *how* to offer all of ourselves.

Furthermore, the attainment of the Night of Pan, the All, the dissolution in the grail, requires us to recognize ourselves as nothing *but* a vessel for universal will. This is one reason for the association of the name Nemo ('No Man') with the grade of Magister Templi at Binah. There is no place for a human being in that place, because *all that one is* has been given up. It should be noted that we *can't* know what is 'beyond ourselves' at this stage. We simply know that we are a finite being that must be offered up. Therefore, any consciousness (i.e. 'light') beyond this will appear dark to us. So in one sense, N.O.X. is light that is too bright or too refined to be perceived by the ruach in its normal state. This darkness is not in fact absence of light but a qualitative difference in the *nature* of the light as we perceive it. The name Pan, meaning 'all,' enumerates to 210, which is also the valuation of the letters N.O.X. So, the Night of Pan is the night of All, and the All is the transrational and transpersonal, the starry night beyond the sun (i.e. our attainment of Tiphereth.) The perception of our own interior star has evolved; the star that has been in our sight from the beginning is now seen as simply *one*

174

star in the company of stars in the heavens, and we offer it freely and joyously into the grail.

I mentioned earlier in the chapter that there is often misplaced emphasis in the interpretation of L.V.X. and N.O.X. The first of these misconceptions is the idea that L.V.X. is a path of 'good' and other-serving, whereas N.O.X. is 'evil' or self-serving—basically the traditional dualistic attributions of light and darkness as good and evil. If you consider everything I've said so far about these formulas and the way they fold into the path of attainment, it should be clear that we're not talking about good and evil here. We're talking about stages of attainment and the specific formulas that unlock those stages of attainment.

Another misconception I encounter fairly frequently is the conflation of the L.V.X. formula with the old aeon formula of the dying god. The L.V.X. formula simply involves seeking the light within us. In the old aeon, this process was projected on to the idea of an external redeemer, the god who dies for us and embodies (by projection) the Neshamah or superconsciousness. In the new aeon, however, we can now understand this as an extension of self. There is no reason why the L.V.X. formula must be linked to the dying god myth in its old aeonic form. In the new aeon, we see that we can redeem *ourselves*, with each moment a death of the old and a rebirth into the new. We are as a child born anew into each moment, via transformation of our consciousness. The redemption here is not from sin, but from the delusion of mortality. It is redemption from the absorption in the physical world and the apparent finality of death; an awareness of deathlessness, the principal of immortality resident in each of us; that solar divine being in our core – our star or *khabs*. It is a redemption that allows us to have an increasing ability to identify with the star within as the center of our being rather than the limited ego-personality in which we have imprisoned ourselves through our lack of full self-awareness. It enables us consciously to place the neshamah on its throne as the rightful ruler of both ruach and nephesh, with no need for 'external' divine aid.

The L.V.X. formula still holds immense power when understood and employed in light of these new aeon truths. For example, there are several Thelema-based, Golden Dawn-patterned orders (including the Temple of the Silver Star) that have revamped their presentation of the old Adeptus Minor ritual from the Golden Dawn to reflect these new aeon realities, with very powerful results. In some such adaptations, the symbolic lesson is that we are not bound to an old aeon cross of passive self-sacrifice but to the cross of the elements, showing our mastery of the formula of the pentagram. Furthermore, I think it's important to emphasize that the L.V.X. formula reaches its climax in the attainment of Tiphereth, yet it does so without denigrating the importance of the further attainment of Binah. It simply recognizes Tiphereth as the pinnacle of one stage of development.

In closing, it is very important to note that in the A∴A∴, the L.V.X. formula functions on a different level than that in Golden Dawn-based outer orders. In these systems, the attainment of Tiphereth is in the world of Yetzirah, signified by incrementally deepened knowledge of the True Will, and a more vibrant connection with that solar center at our core, but there's still much work to do. This is not equivalent to Knowledge and Conversation of the Holy Guardian Angel, which is the nature of the Tiphereth attainment in the A∴A∴. In the A∴A∴, the K & C actualizes the attainment of Tiphereth in the world of Briah, and this marks the beginning of willed and fully conscious connection between the Briatic and Yetziratic worlds. Here the adept consciously experiences the supernal spiritual reality impinging itself on the ruach. This is in marked contrast to the pre-adept stage where superconsciousness communicates chiefly though the nephesh—through intuitions, dreams and other symbolic content, filtered through the personal unconscious. Likewise, the further attainment of Binah represents our ascension to the consciousness of Binah of Atziluth. There is an inward and upward progress through the four worlds as well as the sephiroth on the Tree of Life.

I recognize that much of the material in this chapter has been heavier on theory than much of the rest of the book. It is my hope, however, that you will be able to use the theory here to inform your own practice. Most importantly, I have attempted to give you a glimpse of the nature of the changes in consciousness that await you along the path toward mastery. To that end, I will close with a brief guided meditation that summarizes these transformations of consciousness.

EXERCISE:

Perform preliminary relaxation practices, and regularize the breath. Then allow the following phrases to arise in your mind, and spend a few moments meditating on the doctrine of each sephiroth before moving on to the next. You may wish to record yourself reading these phrases, and perform the meditation while playing back your recording; or simply refer to the version I recorded as a part of the *Living Thelema* podcast segment called "Advice from the Tree of Life."

Malkuth
I live in the physical world. I have a body with which I may experience this world and all its sensory wonders and pleasures. My senses are the eyes and ears of the Universe, and through my life, the Universe witnesses and experiences itself. Yet, I am not my body.

Yesod

I see past the veil of matter to perceive the astral patterns underlying the physical world. The life power flows through me, as the force of my Will expressing itself in the boundless and ever-changing patterns of the unconscious Mind. I wield the life power in service of my own evolution, and in service to the evolution of humanity. Yet, I am not my Mind; and I am not my astral body.

Hod

I possess an intellect with which I build conscious thoughts as Cups of Form, to give shape to the liquid of magical Force. I use reason and mental discipline to organize myself and my life in service of the Will. Yet, I am not my Intellect.

Netzach

I possess emotions as a fuel for aspiration and a medium for love. My soul yearns for the Divine, and I enflame myself in prayer as I aspire to Union with That which is beyond. Yet, I am not my emotions; and I am not my aspiration.

Tiphareth

The Light of the Holy Guardian Angel shines on the center of my being, from which I instruct and direct all the parts of myself toward their Right Function. This Center of Consciousness serves as the Prophet of the Holy Guardian Angel, whose Voice is the True Will. Yet, I am more than this Center of Consciousness.

Geburah

My Will is an extension of Universal Will, and I construct my inner and outer life to be a perfect Form for its expression. The Power of all Life is available to me in every moment. Yet, I am more than my Will.

Chesed

I have consciousness of the path of my soul, in the many lives I have lived before this one, and I govern my consciousness in the light of this knowledge. I strive, in all things, to live fully as an expression of the Highest Light. Yet, I am more than this.

Binah

I have full consciousness of the Grail of Holy Blood, into which the droplets of my individual lives have fallen, for I am that Grail. I have mingled my individual life with the Universal Life, and let go of all attachments of the small ego. I tend to the garden of my lower self, with love and care. I receive the Word and give it birth. Yet, I am beyond the Grail.

Chokmah
I bear the Word—the primal impulse of all the life of humanity. I am the Universal Will, all-powerful and infallible—the Lance that is plunged into the Grail of All. Yet, I am beyond the Lance and beyond the Word.

Kether
I am the One Source, from which all things proceed, and to which all return. I am No-Thing, yet in me is the potential for All Things that can exist. I am the Primal Point that Sees every possibility, yet Knows the Unity of All. I AM.

21

THE RIGHT USE OF MAGICAL POWER[33]

The magical path is inherently a path to power. The nature of this power, its potencies and its dangers, has been the subject of much debate and discussion, yet I believe at least one principle is fundamental: the effective, constructive and humane application of this power requires a balanced magician. The aspiring magician is confronted with conflicting, and potentially derailing, notions of power from the start. The magical path itself challenges the aspirant to harmonize these power drives with an ever-increasing conscience, rooted in will; a conscience which guides the magician toward the right use of his or her power. Without detracting from the correct view of the Great Work as the union of microcosm with macrocosm, we can alternately express its '5 united with 6' as a union of power (5, the pentagram, the Mars force, Geburah), with the central emblem of harmony and beauty (6, the hexagram, the divinely-inspired ruach, Tiphereth).

In this chapter, I will explore the keys to the use of this magical power. In particular, I will focus on the training that leads the aspirant to the attainment of Tiphereth, and the subsequent work of the newly made adept as he or she works the paths above Tiphereth, establishing the balance of beauty and strength so essential to the execution of the True Will.

---

[33] Originally published in *Cheth,* Vol. II.

{N.B.: My discussion of the sephiroth and paths refers primarily to the progress of an aspirant of A∴A∴, but would be equally applicable, at a different level of intensity, to those working the corresponding degrees of the Temple of the Silver Star or similar orders patterned on the Tree of Life, or even an entirely solitary path formulated along these lines.}

Any discussion of magical power is likely to draw our attention to the energy often called the 'Mars force,' also known as kundalini, the life-power, and various other names in analogous traditions. On the Tree of Life, the Mars force is primarily represented by the sephira Geburah. This sephira is the fifth in sequence from Kether, thus formulating the pentagram, itself a symbol of magical power. In addition to its attribution to Mars, Geburah is the seat of the personal will, and a linkage point to that universal will impinging upon it from the supernals, specifically Chokmah. In contemplating the Tree of Life, this is the most easily visible key to the source and right use of magical power: The entirety of the personal will, that aspect of the ruach the magician has (rightly) deemed to be individual and unique, is merely an individualized expression of the universal will which it **serves**. With this truth in mind, we can examine the aspiring magician's approach to Geburah from the sephiroth below.

> Verily destruction is the foundation of existence,
> And the tearing-down thou seest
> Is but the assembling of material
> For a grander structure.
>   (*The Book of Tokens*, from "The Meditation on Peh")

> Break down the fortress of thine Individual Self,
> that thy Truth may spring free from the ruins.
>   (*The Book of Thoth*, from the discussion of the Tower Atu)

Long before the magician attains to the full magical power of Geburah, s/he must face the trials of the sephiroth and paths beneath Tiphereth, balancing the four elements within him or herself. The keystone of this pre-Tiphereth training, in terms of the relationship to magical power, is the work of the path of *peh*. Here the magician's first encounter with the force of planetary Mars is also his or her first crossing of a "reciprocal" path on the Tree, as the path of *peh* connects the intellect of Hod with the desire and aspiration of Netzach. Another implication of this arrangement is that the intellect is consciously applied in order to choose and define the object of the Desire of Netzach. The right use of aspiration and pure desire (Netzach) is achieved by the intellectual apprehension (Hod) of the appropriate goal. The completed work of Malkuth, Yesod, and their related paths is now balanced by *peh*, just as the magical force is simultaneously "stepped up" a notch with the increased activity of the Svadisthana chakra, to which *peh* is attributed. Indeed, the magician's growing power is automatically held in check by the balance inherent in the Tree. Even at this early stage of development, balance is the key to power.

Furthermore, the passage of the path of *peh* is a safeguard against the power drive taking a predominant role in the advance toward Tiphereth. One who quests after the Angel with the main goal of increasing his personal egoic power is blocked from true mastery of this path. For the nature of the path itself (seen in the Tower Atu) is the overturning of such ideas, which bind, confuse and otherwise subvert direct apprehension of the true order of the universe. The passage of the path of *peh* thus purifies and consecrates the aspirant's magical power at the microcosmic level, preparing him or her for the eventual attainment of increased power at Tiphereth in a safe and constructive manner. The many examples of tyrannical behavior seen in socio-political history and in our present times would seem to be evidence of the dangers of misperceived and misapplied personal power. In these cases, we see that the power drive is used as an exercise of personal dominance, or alternately, the aggressive and destructive impulses are projected onto the "other" (person, country, racial/ethnic group, "enemy"), as a rationalization for our own intolerance and aggression.

The ordeal of the path of *peh* being accomplished, the magician strives onward toward Tiphereth, the one visible goal at this stage of the work. The approach to Tiphereth is guarded by two additional paths, both Mars-related, which impinge on the development of magical power in the aspirant: *ayin* (The Devil) and *nun* (Death). The ordeal of the path of *ayin* (Capricorn, in which Mars is exalted) includes the development of the consciousness of the transcendent, divine realities behind the appearance of 'evil.' As long as we continue to project the dualistic ideas of good and evil onto the world, we are unable to develop the tools for **responsible** use of our own power. These tools include the ability to refine our conscience, in accordance with the True Will, such that our exercise of power is truly in service to the world around us. Knee-jerk judgments of others, and the resulting dualistic thought and behavior patterns, tend to steer us toward one-sided use of power, typically to diminish our egoic discomfort with those things we have labeled as evil!

The ordeal of the path of *nun* (Scorpio, ruled by Mars) requires a similarly uncomfortable task, from the perspective of the ego-personality: the surrender to a 'higher' authority, and letting go of the illusion of ego-mastery. In other words, we face the death of the 'I' we have worked so hard to cultivate throughout our lives up to this point. Here again are keys to the right use of power—as long as we cling to the ego, our actions are driven by the fear (*pachad*, a name of Geburah/

Mars) of losing our identity and autonomy. We attack those things which threaten us in this way, expending valuable energy in the process.

Upon the full attainment of Tiphereth with the Knowledge and Conversation of the Holy Guardian Angel, the adept is centered and balanced in this higher illumination—the King is bathed in the light descending from the crown. The relationship between adept and Angel has just begun, however, and takes effort and time to grow. The central tasks of the new adept are to strive to deepen the communion with the Angel, to further refine his or her ability to receive and interpret its instructions, and to effect a right balance in the psyche between the human ego and its new superconscious contact-point. That is, the Adept must adapt his or her ruach to operate in a fluid fashion given the breakthrough of the Briatic consciousness (neshamah). Fortunately, this trail has already been blazed for us: the methods are clearly spelled out in the tasks of the paths of *mem* and *lamed*, and they lead the way to the full attainment of magical power at Geburah.

> For even as He abideth in the thick darkness and in the blinding light, in the elements, in the planets, and in the mighty circle of the Heavens, even so shall I abide...
> (*Liber Siloam sub figura CDLI*)

> Absorb thyself in this Great Sea of the Waters of Life.
> Dive deep in it until thou hast lost thyself.
> And having lost thyself,
> Then shalt thou find thyself again,
> And shalt be one with me,
> Thy Lord and King.
> Thus shalt thou learn the secret
> Of the restoration of the King unto his throne.
> (*The Book of Tokens*, from "The Meditation on Mem")

The path of *mem* represents the influx of the strength of Geburah into the reflective waters of the human intellect of Hod. While the aspiring magician encountered the **influence** of this path at Hod, it is only after the attainment of Tiphereth that the path is worked in full. In the A∴A∴ curriculum, the task of this path is the attainment of the state known as the 'Sleep of Siloam'—a blissful, peaceful union of adept and Angel. This attainment reinforces the central lesson of the path of *mem*: the adept now knows, without a doubt, that his or her true master is the Holy Guardian Angel. His ego is now positioned as the figure in the Hanged Man Atu—overturned, and receptive to the direct influence of the master's light. It seems appropriately paradoxical that this first path leading directly unto the power of Geburah from "below" is one of ego-

182

humility and receptivity—the very traits that will allow the adept to wield his newfound power with deep conscience and vision. That is, these newly discovered potencies will serve the universal will, particularized as the consciously realized True Will of the Adept, rather than nepheshic drives or the whims of the small ego.

> This is again a hieroglyph of "Love is the law, love under will". Every form of energy must be directed, must be applied with integrity, to the full satisfaction of its destiny.
> (*The Book of Thoth*, from the discussion of the Adjustment Atu)

> I am the power of equilibration
> Which holdeth Ruach in balance
> Between formation and destruction,
> As a drive with his goad
> Keepeth his ox from straying off the highway.
> Yet is this directive power inherent in Ruach itself,
> For I myself am that great Breath of Life...

> 'Have I not free will?' saith the fool;
> But the wise know that in all the chains of worlds
> There is no creature
> that hath any will apart from my One Will

> My Will is free indeed,
> And he who knoweth it as the wellspring of his willing
> Remaineth free from error.
> (*The Book of Tokens*, from "The Meditation on Lamed")

The path of *lamed*, attributed to Libra and symbolized in the Tarot as the Adjustment Atu, is the second and last of the two paths traversed as the adept moves from Tiphereth to Geburah. This path reflects a truth with which the adept of Tiphereth is doubtlessly growing very familiar: his or her every thought, word and deed exact precise and unremitting consequences. It is an oft-noted dictum of the Great Work that the further the aspirant travels along the path, the less "elasticity" s/he finds when inadvertently deviating from it. In Malkuth, the aspirant might never even notice such deviations, but further progress in the work brings more immediate (and sharp!) reminders from the universe whenever there is a sidestep. It is an arguable point whether this feedback mechanism is due to some universal principle (so-called 'karma' et al.), increased sensitivity to inner promptings, or some combination of both.

In any case, the path of *lamed*, in the form of the Adjustment Atu portrays these karmic laws in action. This path, the direct linkage between the power of Geburah and the beauty and harmony of Tiphereth, displays the balance of these potencies which is necessary for their right use. This right use is then, by definition, in accord with the laws of nature, and with the True Will of the adept, given voice by his or her Angel.

> Remember that unbalanced force is evil; that unbalanced severity is but cruelty and oppression; but that also unbalanced mercy is but weakness which would allow and abet Evil.
> (*Liber Librae sub figura XXX*)

Recommended Reading:

Case, P. (1934). The *Book of Tokens: Tarot Meditations.* Los Angeles, CA: Builders of the Adytum, Ltd.

Crowley, A. (1992). Liber Librae. In I. Regardie (Ed.), *Gems from the Equinox.* Scottsdale, AZ: New Falcon Publications.

Crowley, A. *Liber Siloam sub figura CDLI.*

Crowley, A. (1993). *The Book of Thoth. A Short Essay on the Tarot of the Egyptians.* York Beach, ME: Weiser Books.

22

21ST CENTURY ALCHEMY: THE SCIENCE & ART OF MYSTERY[34]

Fundamental questions are guideposts; they stimulate people. One of the most creative qualities a research scientist can have is the ability to ask the right questions. Science's greatest advances occur on the frontiers, at the interface between ignorance and knowledge, where the most profound questions are posed. There's no better way to assess the current condition of science than listing the questions that science cannot answer. Science is shaped by ignorance.

—David Gross, 2004 Nobel laureate in physics[35]

Introduction

Alchemy. The word conjures images of medieval sages, laboring in dark laboratories filled with arcane scientific apparati, striving to

---

[34] Originally published in *Neshamah*, Vol. I, No. 3. (2010).

[35] Quoted in "125 Questions: What We Don't Know," *Science*, Vol. 309. (2005). p.76.

transform lead into gold. Medieval alchemical literature discusses procedures for separation and combination; the application of heat and distillation; the principles of decay and regeneration. In many cases, these texts appear purely practical in nature, expanding the boundaries of what was the cutting-edge science of the time. Yet, from the standpoint of modern depth psychology, we can see the transformation of physical substances as a metaphor for a process of inner change. Simple contemplation of such a physical change process brings us in sympathy with it, even if its *apparent* object is entirely outside ourselves. Accordingly, we may conclude that the medieval alchemists were themselves the *prima material* of the working.

The metallurgical and chemical experiments of the medieval alchemists were on the frontiers of intellectual exploration in Europe at that time; at the fertile boundary between the light of knowledge and the dark mystery of the unknown. At this crossroads all things seem possible, and the mind is made open to what is otherwise hidden or disguised. The great questions and quests of humankind are projected upon the infinite expanse of possibility at this meeting place of the known and the unknown. They are framed in the language of the science which has brought them to that point.

Let us, then, propose a more specific definition of alchemy: alchemy is the Science and Art of transforming consciousness. Its vocabulary is born out of the cutting-edge theories and unanswered questions on the frontiers of science. Its central method is the extraction of meaning from mystery, through the lens of psychological projection.

Science has moved on since medieval times, for better or for worse. The purification, transformation, and production of metals are now performed on a vast scale in thousands of factories and mills. Science now fronts against the unknown in a multitude of modern fields, including physics, biology, computer science and psychology. If we accept that ancient alchemists were performing inner transformations using contemporary, state-of-the-art tools as a metaphorical projection screen, doesn't it follow that true *modern* alchemists would do the same? If so, we must look to the frontiers of *today's* science for these modern alchemical tools. If alchemy is truly the science and art of extracting meaning from mystery, by way of psychological projections, only the mysteries of today's unanswered questions will present us with a projection screen of sufficient size.

Lawrence M. Principe is a chemist and historian of science at Johns Hopkins University. Some years ago, he was a co-organizer of a conference at the Chemical Heritage Foundation in Philadelphia, which collects archival material related to alchemy and other chemical sciences. He remarked:

What do chemists do? They like to make stuff. Most chemists
are interested not so much in theory as in making substances
with particular properties. The emphasis on products was the
same with some alchemists in the 17th century.[36]

Accordingly, we may imagine that the ancient alchemists were
fascinated by the creative and transformative act itself. Humanity was on
the threshold of discovering the underlying principles of matter, the facts
of its nature, and the laws of its combination and action. And yet, while
on the quest for this factual knowledge, they touched on many governing
principles of the mind and the soul. Just as humanity was coming to
terms with its ability to create and define reality, its divine birthright,
these truths were echoed in the frontiers of its science.

My propositions in this present discussion apply to humanity as a
whole. It has always been the case, across the course of human evolution,
that mystics and other extraordinary seekers are the droplets on the crest
of the wave of progress, and reach their conclusions long before the
critical mass of humanity. What I'm discussing here, on the contrary, is a
much broader process. It is the evolution of collective human
consciousness, played out on the field of psychological projections onto
the frontiers of scientific inquiry. The unanswered mysteries of
contemporary science become the hooks on which our society (usually
unconsciously) hangs its aspirations, ideals and fears, its questions about
the mysteries of life, and its strivings for meaning and understanding.
By this definition, we are all alchemists.

The Nature of Psychological Projections

Let's begin with a discussion of the projection process itself. The
Jungian model of consciousness is fundamentally a psychology of
dynamic energy. The human psyche is composed of interweaving energy
patterns, which tend to cluster around certain basic thought-forms. These
include the concepts of "self," "God," "other," "I" (the ego), and so on.
The ability of the psyche to move and discharge energy between these
constituent parts is essential to its health. The ego tends to be a
stumbling block to the free flow of this energy, however. It seeks to
maintain the illusion of autonomy and sovereignty, and accordingly,
certain ideas, images, and emotions become repressed or otherwise
restricted, forming what is known as the shadow. Unacceptable ideas are
diverted into forms which are less threatening to the ego. For example:
Some aspect of our deep conscience observes that we are often cruel to

---

[36] "Transforming the Alchemists," *The New York Times*. August 1, 2006.

others. Yet, this fact is unacceptable to the ego—it doesn't want to be challenged on its bad behavior. This "judging" aspect of ourselves—this channel of energy—still needs to *flow somewhere.* The target of this flow often turns out to be *another person* who is observed behaving cruelly. The "judge" gets to proclaim guilt, and the ego gets to pretend it is just a bystander in the trial, taking satisfaction in the condemnation of the evildoer.

Such negative emotions are not the only candidates for projection, however. Jung pointedly and repeatedly emphasized that there is "gold" in the shadow. We also project our deepest loves, our dearest hopes, our most exquisite ideas of beauty and transcendence, onto the world around us, because we are often unable to accept these qualities as aspects of ourselves. All that is required is the impulse toward energy flow, and a suitable object for the projection. If we are alienated from our own strength, we project it onto a movie hero. If we feel incomplete, we project the idea of a perfect partner onto a desired romantic interest. And....*if we cannot accept our own divinity,* and we feel lost on the path to finding ourselves, we project the entirety of the spiritual journey, and its destination, onto a *myth.*

Some of these myths are now known to us *as such,* because to a great extent, we have evolved past the need for them, or their particular symbols have lost their hold on us. For example, we can look back at the great Greek myths of Hercules and without too much struggle, we see it as a myth created by a society struggling to come to terms with its own strength, and mastery of its environment. These myths are more perceptible to us precisely because we have a distanced perspective on them—the distance of aeons of time, and corresponding cultural evolution. On the other hand, we rarely perceive the myths we are currently living. We tend to be conscious only of the myths that have completed their transformative work upon us. Accordingly, if we want to understand our current transformational patterns, we must try to discover the living myths of today's world—*the things we actually believe in*—and the gods we truly worship. These alone have the *numinosity*—the spiritual power—required for our alchemy. For medieval alchemists, the tools and methodologies of the physical sciences had this power. That is, they projected their path of transformation onto this particular screen—a myth about the power of certain tools and processes to create miraculous changes in matter. This projection "worked" because there was enough ambiguity about the actual *answers* to their questions to fire their creative imagination—to keep them reaching for the next mystery.

The Mystery Projection

> The invisible world can be a dangerous place if approached improperly, without the necessary preparation and commitment to the process. Those who embark on this quest will be tested to see if they have the necessary fortitude to pull away the veil between the visible and the invisible. Striving toward this goal will bring about some surprising consequences, not the least of which is the recognition that the *process* by which we come to this level of consciousness is far more important than any specific knowledge we may have gained along the way. –June Singer, from *Seeing Through the Visible World*[37]

The process to which Singer refers involves, among other things, the act of psychological projection. We can become conscious of these projections, but more often we engage in them blindly, because we have found no better language with which to address our inner problem. The next stage of our inner evolution doesn't yet have a frame, a language, a science of its own. It needs a "hook" on which it can hang in order to know itself. I call this the *mystery projection.*

For our purposes here, it doesn't matter whether the medieval alchemists knew the true nature of their work. Perhaps some did; probably many did not. Those who did not understand the true nature of their work unconsciously developed a language of transformation accessible to others. Those few who did understand were simply a few steps ahead—they realized the psycho-spiritual value of the language and continued to use it as a veil for the deeper meaning they had discovered.

The equivalent situation in the modern scientific world, for example, would be on the one hand the quantum physicist whose conscious interest is exploring the patterns of probability of light passing through tiny slits in a plate, or on the other hand his colleague, who goes home at night to ponder the significance of probability waves as an existential question. If we are locked into a materialist, reductionist viewpoint, we are simply "doing physical science." If, on the other hand, we are ready for a deeper relationship with the process, it *will* present itself as such.

Ilya Prigogine, a 1977 Nobel laureate, writes:

> The basis of the vision of classical physics was the conviction that the future is determined by the present, and therefore a careful study of the present permits an unveiling of

---

[37] Singer, J. (1990). *Seeing Through the Visible World: Jung, Gnosis and Chaos.* San Francisco, CA: Harper San Francisco.

the future. At no time, however, was this more than a theoretical possibility. Yet in some sense this unlimited predictability was an essential element of the scientific picture of the physical world. We may perhaps even call it the FOUNDING MYTH of classical science. The situation has greatly changed today...[38]

So, it seems our present task is to discover *today's* founding myths— the mythologized set of assumptions that characterize our current state of scientific understanding and also, according to my thesis, the current state of our spiritual and psychological evolution. Myths are the dreams of a culture, and these myths are the field onto which we project our quests for understanding, our strivings for spiritual insight, and our deepest fears of the unknown.

Founding Myths and Mystery Projections in Modern Science

I was assisted in my research for this article by *Science* magazine's 125th anniversary series entitled, "125 questions: What we don't know." This series surveyed the current frontiers of scientific knowledge in a number of fields, and highlighted the unanswered questions driving cutting-edge research. My research was admittedly (and intentionally) a superficial survey on my part of the scientific disciplines discussed in *Science*. While I was conducting my initial research for this article, a friend of mine remarked that my research might require in-depth knowledge of a great number of diverse scientific fields. I replied that I would use my *naïveté* in service of the project, since the projection process itself requires just such an attitude. That is, we are confronted with the unknown, and we attempt to fill in the gaps. The gaps then become the projective canvas for the psyche (individual and collective) to reveal itself. A sophisticated practitioner of any of these sciences would, quite obviously, have important insights into these matters. However, our present avenue of inquiry requires a more distanced "layperson" to perceive the patterns at work. A microscope would give us details about the flecks of paint on a work of Picasso, but we don't really *see* the painting until we stand back a few paces. What is missing from the microscope's minutely detailed "expertise" is *naïvely creative imagination*. An adult looks to the sky and sees clusters of white water vapor, whereas a child sees dragons.

---

[38] Prigogine, I. (1980). *From Being to Becoming.* New York: W.H. Freeman and Co., p. 214.

Working along similar lines, musician Brian Eno uses intentional limitation, chance, and technical *naïveté* to encourage a certain innocence to enter his music. These factors may force us to take a novel approach to situations. We're off guard, uncertain, and unable to rely on habit and routine. In other words: we are alive and alert, thinking and feeling our way through a problem, a maze or a mystery. I attempted to maintain this sort of mindset as I researched and wrote this article, and I encourage the reader to do the same while contemplating its content.

Let us, then, examine a variety of modern scientific disciplines in light of the theses described above. For each science, I will attempt to determine the "founding myths" implied by the state of the frontiers of the particular science, and extract the mystery projection operative within the context of the myths. When I was reviewing the material from these various disciplines, I often used a set of "mystery questions" to stimulate and identify my own projections. For example:

• "I wish we knew the answer to this question, because then we could…"
• "If only we could discover X, then…"
• "That fact (a scientific discovery) is amazing, because…."
• "I never thought humans would be able to…"
• "We shouldn't mess with X. It's dangerous because…."

You may wish to do the same as you read the following sections, to stimulate your own projection process.

It is important to note that this brief survey is purely speculative. That is, I do not assert that the scientific findings described here are valid because they reflect esoteric doctrines, nor am I attempting to validate esoteric doctrines by virtue of scientific discoveries. My aim is merely to elucidate the projection process which is active in any culture exploring its scientific frontiers. So, let us stand back a bit, de-focus our eyes, and maybe, just maybe, we can perceive the mystery behind the science, and behold the dragons instead of the clouds.

Biology/Genetics

One of the simplest and best known examples of a projection onto biological mysteries is the evolving theory of human illness. Any study of history or anthropology will reveal various cultures' priest-shaman-physicians, and their belief that demons or other evil spirits were the cause of illness. Today, of course, we place the blame on bacteria and viruses. The thresholds of knowledge are different, as are the tools of science used, and the language employed, but the mystery projection is the same: invisible forces are at work. They attack us, and attempt to kill us. We need specialized help to rid ourselves of them. What are these forces? How can we stop them? To whom do I appeal for aid?

Many of the great modern biological questions revolve around of the potency of DNA as creator, transformer, preserver of who and what we are as humans. Though still *consciously* conceived of as a biological question regarding a physical substance (i.e. the founding myth of modern genetics), the mystery projection reveals a deeper level of meaning. Through our projections of transformative power onto the physical substance of DNA, we contemplate and investigate our own divine, creative power, and by extension, our role in the transformation of humanity itself.

Our growing understanding of the genetic determinants underlying our existence inevitably reveals the mystery projection-questions: What forces shape and change us? What in our lives can we consciously control? What are the limits of our personal power in affecting our circumstances? What is fated and immutable? Clearly, though we sought to understand the influence of the physical building blocks of life, we have stumbled into a contemplation of destiny vs. free will.

In examining our relationship to other animals, modern genetic research is investigating the question of what makes us uniquely human. Here, our projections carry us toward the contemplation of the central existential mystery of what it means to be human and, by extension, of the meaning of life itself. Carl Jung once remarked that we will never know what is unique about human consciousness until we encounter non-human consciousness.[39] He was referring to the possibility of eventual contact with extra-terrestrial intelligence, but the logic can certainly be applied to the comparative genetic research already underway.

In addition to the burgeoning field of genetics, modern biology is pursuing fascinating questions concerning the biological basis of consciousness. In our attempt to discover the "seat of the soul" within our physical brain, we come face to face with the mystery of the mind. The mystery projection here: What's behind the veil of matter? It is not uncommon, in our daily lives, to note that there seems to be more to "us" than a mere collection of cells and organs. But now, with the advent of modern biological research techniques, we appear to be on the threshold of actually discovering the physical basis of such experiences. The astute reader will likely note that similar 'discovery thresholds' have always characterized scientific progress—and that is precisely my point! The feeling of being *almost there*—that sense of the mystery being just *barely* out of reach—is the fundamental fuel for the fires of projection. It is the anticipated ecstasy of discovery that keeps the quest alive, regardless of the scientific methodologies employed. Medieval

---

[39] *Jung on Film* (videotaped interview). (2000). Homevision.

alchemists sought the "soul" of a substance in a purified distillate or a powdered residue. Today, we seek the soul in tiny neuronal webs. These are indeed "merely" projections—but projections which are alive with the promise of magic and meaning.

Some scientists seem to straddle the apparent abyss between science and mysticism quite openly. Biologist Rupert Sheldrake, for example, has put forth his theory of "morphogenetic fields." This theory includes something akin to a "radio transmitter" model of species development over time—no less than a biological construct explaining the transmission of archetypes. Sheldrake posits that a species develops not only due to its current environment and physically transmitted DNA encoding, but also due to the traces of past experience. As an illustration, he notes that if we were ignorant of the electro-mechanical principles of a radio, we would hear it and conclude that nothing is added to it when it is playing music—the music doesn't make it heavier—yet it *is* in fact receiving something, and that *something* defines its behavior and its nature at any given moment. In this line of thought, Sheldrake is reaching for facts and language to express the mystery of the archetypes of consciousness. The physiological truth of this theory is not our concern here. Instead, we are interested in the theoretical gymnastics Sheldrake undertakes in his attempt to navigate the mystery threshold—in other words, his alchemy. His work is a projection onto the mysteries of our origins, and the question of why any given person takes the form they do. It also parallels the theories of quantum physics positing that non-proximal objects affect each other across space-time—the principle of non-locality.

A final example of modern alchemy being conducted in the biological fields is the science of aging. Researchers in this field consciously explore the founding myth that the body is a machine that breaks down over time—a process that can perhaps be slowed, stopped, or even reversed. Clearly, these researchers are the modern equivalent of the ancient explorers who sought the fountain of youth—a projection of the deeper search for transcendence of bodily limitations and physical human life. This particular example is instructive in that it shows us how the same mystery projection can be applied to different sciences in different eras—only the tools have changed. In the Era of Exploration, the projection was onto the idea of a physical source of the powers of immortality, for the process of geographical discovery was capturing the world's imagination. Now, in the era of DNA and nanotechnology, the projection finds a new home in these very different, but equally exciting tools and methods.

Physics

> We now know that every particle has an antiparticle, with which it can annihilate. There could be whole antiworlds and antipeople made out of antiparticles. However, if you meet your antiself, don't shake hands! You would both vanish in a great flash of light.
> –Stephen Hawking[40]

The field of theoretical physics is perhaps the scientific domain where our investigative questioning bears the most immediate fruit. The questions posed by modern physics, especially since the advent of quantum theory, simply beg for esoteric interpretation. Admittedly, this has been tiresomely overdone in New Age publishing circles in recent decades. Nevertheless, some of the more subtle mystery projections may have been overlooked, as they lie beneath the surface of the overt questions being investigated.

The quote from Hawking above may serve as a suitable starting place for our discussion. In his theory, we can see physicists striving to comprehend the very nature of matter and existence. It implies a (+1) and a (-1) inherent in all things, as well as the energy released by their rapturous union. This is no less than a scientific re-statement of the 0=2 formula, yet it also reveals a mystery projection concerning the nature of truth and reality: *Everything that is, implies its opposite.* We are immediately reminded of Crowley's comments regarding the nature of Truth and Falsehood, and the energy which becomes available to us as we slam these philosophical poles together, burning them up in the crucible of our minds.

Unification Theory and the 'Big Bang'

The quest for the so-called "unification theory" in physics reveals a similarly cosmic mystery projection. Such a unification theory, when devised, will explain all universal phenomenon, from the subatomic level all the way to the behavior of huge bodies in space. This, quite explicitly, is a science-based search for the same basic truths of life which all mystery schools and religions have sought. As Qabalists, we ponder a theory of creation which explains the origins of the world from ancient, infinite nothingness right down to the details of the manifest physical realities that surround us. The Tree of Life is our Qabalistic unification theory. Society at large, however, largely lacking a language which simultaneously describes cosmic creation and its linkage to the

---

[40] Hawking, S. (1988). A *Brief History of Time*. New York: Bantam Dell.

transformation of consciousness, projects this onto the concept of a unification theory based on physics, which concerns itself with the material universe alone.

The theories of Newtonian physics, relativity and quantum mechanics all break down when investigating the first moment of the universe's existence. Science has been able to explain these processes back to a certain point in time, but as they approach the actual moment of origin, all theories fail. The mysteries of the so-called "big bang" form a perfect field for projections, in that they tease us with unanswered questions about our ultimate origins. Here we find a mystery projection reminiscent of the Qabalistic *ain*: genesis out of nothingness, and an *absolute* which is insensible and unknowable. The Qabalah conceives of this trans-supernal point of origin as being beyond rationality–a truth beyond reason. It seems entirely possible that any eventual unification theory will require its conceiver to attain a state of consciousness which encompasses both conventional intellectual conceptions as well as a supernal-like transrationality. Indeed, such speculations seem to point us in the direction of our further evolution as a species. Perhaps the great scientists of humanity's future will need to be great mystics as well. This overlap of science and mysticism is hardly unprecedented in our *past*, but its objects of study and its frontiers will have to continually evolve, as will the human mind itself.

Consider also how popular descriptions of "God" vary with the terminology and scientific conceptions available in the contemporary science of any era of humanity's evolution. During the last Aeon, God was mostly seen as a paternal, lever-pulling deity ruling a mechanistic universe. This matched the Newtonian view of the functioning of all forces and objects in the known world. The last century, in contrast, has seen God increasingly described as "energy," "light," and an immanent, connecting "force," even in non-mystical popular culture. These conceptions, of course, mirror the current state of scientific inquiry into the origins and functioning of the universe.

Absolute Space

Physicist Lee Smolin, commenting on Newton's theories, remarks, "For Newton, the universe lived in an infinite and featureless space. There was no boundary, and no possibility of conceiving anything outside of it. This was no problem for God, as he was everywhere. For Newton, space was the 'sensorium' of God–the medium of his presence in and attachment to the world. The infinity of space was then a necessary reflection of the infinite capacity of God."[41] If any scientific frontier begs for a mystery projection, it is this one. The study of the mysteries of space throws the mind into an exalted state. To contemplate with awe the enormity, the power, the expanse, the complexity of our universe, is virtually a jnana yoga practice (compare this with Crowley's *Liber Batrachophrenobookosmomachia*, assigned to the Practicus of A∴A∴, which endeavors to accomplish this very task through detailed visualization of the physical cosmos).

The Nature of Light

One of the most heated debates in the field of quantum physics has concerned the nature of light. Specifically, physicists have sought to determine whether light is a wave or a particle. Compellingly, they have concluded that it sometimes behaves as a wave, and sometimes as a particle, depending on the specific circumstances of investigation. The mystery projection here concerns the nature of *human consciousness* as an individual or collective phenomenon; that is, we sometimes behave as if we have individual existence and independent will. At other times, we seem to be just a droplet in a wave of mass mind. As physicists turn their observing eyes to ever more microscopic subjects, their alchemy contemplates the nature of mind itself.

Black Holes

The phenomenon of so-called "black holes" is a wonderful screen for mystery projections. Consider their apparent nature: infinitely small and dense, and so potent in their gravitational pull that not even light can escape them. The mystery projection: our mind tries to grapple with the concept of the power of *nothingness*. Infinite smallness. The dimensionless point of Kether, and its infinite power.

Dark Matter

Author Charles Seife notes: "Cosmologists now conclude that the gravitational forces exerted by...dark matter, made of an as-yet undiscovered type of particle, must be sculpting...vast cosmic structures. They estimate that this 'exotic dark matter' makes up about 25% of the

---

[41] Smolin, L. (1997). The *Life of the Cosmos*. New York: Oxford University Press., p. 91.

stuff in the universe—five times as much as ordinary matter."[42] Furthermore, scientists tell us that so-called "dark energy," an antigravity force, makes up the remaining 70% of all the substance of the universe. The implications of this are striking, even on a purely physical level. Ordinary matter as we know it comprises only 5% of the known universe. The mystery projection is profound as well: there is much more to the world, and to the very nature of who we are, than we have ever perceived or imagined. Unseen and insensible forces are everywhere, and there is much more we have yet to discover about reality.

Uncertainty Principles

Various principles involving uncertainty and probability in physical phenomena, prominent in quantum physics, have become fairly well known to the lay public in recent years. Essentially, these principles assert that we cannot measure something at the subatomic level without affecting its properties, and that it is impossible to precisely measure a subatomic particle's momentum *and* its location simultaneously. The mystery projection: mind inevitably affects the universe. Our own consciousness is always a filter through which we perceive the world. Interestingly, however, new research suggests that it may be possible to measure something without affecting it *if* the measurement technique is relatively "weak," or unobtrusive. Paul Davies, a physicist at Arizona State University, comments that "weak measurements let you lift the *veil* of secrecy imposed by the uncertainty principle."[43] One potential implication of this, and another key mystery projection here, is well-known to mystics: our perceptions of the universe are more accurate when we still the mind, and impose less of our individual consciousness on the phenomenon observed.

Multiple Realities

The superstring theory of physics, as described by Brian Greene and others, posits a universe filled with multiple dimensions (eleven, to be exact), and myriad realities comprised of alternate paths for our lives. Again, the implications are staggering even on the physical plane, but in this theory we see a profound mystery projection: *The mind itself exists in multiple realities constantly.* We are simultaneously in the past, present and future, remembering past achievements or regrets, dreaming of

---

[42] Seife, Charles. In '125 Questions: What We Don't Know,' *Science*, Vol. 309. (2005). p. 78.

[43] Quoted in 'Putting Time in a (Leaky) Bottle.' *Newsweek*, July 30, 2007.

future goals, wondering about the various outcomes our everyday choices may bring. Human consciousness is undoubtedly non-linear, and thought and memory predictably discontinuous, leaving us with the very real sense of living in multiple realities within and without.

Space Exploration and the Possibility of Intelligent Extraterrestrial Life

In his final book, *The Inner Reaches of Outer Space,* Joseph Campbell asserts that our modern focus on space, and space exploration, is no less than the inner search for Selfhood and knowledge, projected outward onto the physical universe. Furthermore, it seems that we project the basic "solitude" of our individual ego onto the potential that intelligent life will be found elsewhere in the universe. That is, the outer reality—"us" looking for "them"—is a projection of our *inner* existential state – as the "I" strives to know that which is outside itself. The mystery of the nature of individual, self-conscious existence is projected onto the concept of "other worlds." Furthermore, you will recall Jung's opinion, referenced above, that we will never fully understand the nature of the human mind until we have made contact with an intelligent, non-human mind.

Computer Science

Computer science, with its emphasis on creating intelligent, complex, self-regulating thinking machines, offers us a receptive screen for mystery projections. The mere existence of computer science requires us to postulate models of "consciousness" as they might be applied to the world of silicon. In doing so, we find ourselves in much the same role as the Qabalistic *neshamah* (superconsciousness), building little ego-like (*ruach*) structures with our divine creative power. This identification with the *source* of creative power is not unlike the mystery projection previously discussed in reference to DNA.

Furthermore, it reveals what I believe is one of the central shifts in consciousness from the time of the ancient alchemists to our own era. The ancient alchemists were on the cusp of the discovery of the full power of the *ruach*, prefiguring the vibrant fruition of the arts and sciences in the centuries to follow. We, however, are poised for the next step—to bring the *ruach* into conscious relationship with the *neshamah* as a baseline state for the majority of humanity, and come into our birthright as Gods upon earth. We are finally becoming aware that we need not limit ourselves to the role of a servant, subjugated to the will of an overseeing "God" in the sky. While the ancient alchemists couched their quest in the language of *ruach*-identified worshippers, we modern alchemists can see ourselves as divine beings, capable of incredible feats of self-directed creation, and our alchemical language has progressed accordingly. Presuming that we have the fortitude to undertake the requisite inner development, we can now identify with the *neshamah*. We are the masters of our own wills, directing the *ruach* from that secret throne—the divinity of inmost Self.

Conclusion

Just as ancient alchemy was systematized within the chemical sciences from which it drew its inspiration, so is 21st century alchemy systematized, to a greater or lesser extent, in each of the scientific disciplines discussed here. Certainly, one central task of any modern aspiring alchemist must be to interlace the truths available to us in these disparate fields, and weave them together into a potent, internally consistent "mystery system." Of course, as soon as such a system is in place, new discoveries and new questions will expand scientific frontiers once more, and our alchemy will again be transformed.

As modern alchemists and magicians, we have the great advantage of several centuries of further development of our mystery schools, plus the relatively new field of psychological science, to aid us in our understanding of these inner change processes. We've learned a great deal about ourselves since Paracelsus last fired up his athanor. But we have a new problem. While medieval alchemists found their vocabulary in the (then) cutting edge processes of controlled chemical combination, distillation, and so on, and benefited from their inevitable *naiveté* with these new sciences, we in the modern era have integrated these sciences into our conscious understanding of how the world works. They have lost their mystery, and their former frontiers are now well-trod terrain. They seem self-evident, especially to those of us who devote our lives to the path of self-transformation. Even society at large has substantially integrated both the physical sciences comprising ancient alchemy, and their psychological counterparts, as simple facts of life. We need a new language—the language of modern science, empowered by the freedom and energy of the New Æon.

Yet, the language of alchemy, broadly understood, is *itself* a veil—an attempt by its practitioners, consciously or not, to reveal something of the nature of the mystery. This veil is woven by our attempts to communicate about the mystery—attempts which may, on the surface, seem unsuccessful. Yet, any apparent failure in this endeavor is in fact a success if it inspires us to the quest, and impels us to lift the veil, that we might catch a glimpse of that truth which lies eternally behind it.

Works Cited

Campbell, J. (2002). *The Inner Reaches of Outer Space: Metaphor as Myth and as Religion.* 3rd (revised) edition. Novato, CA: New World Library.

Crowley, A. (1913). *"Liber Batrachophrenobookosmomachia" In* The Equinox.

Gleick, J. (1988). Chaos: *The Making of a New Science.* New York, NY: Penguin Books.

Greene, B. (2000). The *Elegant Universe: Superstrings, Hidden Dimensions, and the Quest for the Ultimate Theory.* London, UK: Vintage Books.

Greene, B. (2005). The *Fabric of the Cosmos: Space, Time, and the Texture of Reality.* London, UK: Vintage Books.

Hawking, S. (1988). A *Brief History of Time.* New York, NY: Bantam Dell.

Jung, C. (2000). *"Jung on Film"* (videotaped interview). Homevision.

Prigogine, I. (1980). *From Being to Becoming.* New York: W.H. Freeman and Co.

Sheldrake, R. (1995). *A New Science of Life.* Rochester, Vermont: Park Street Press.

Sheldrake, R. (1995). *The Presence of the Past.* Rochester, Vermont: Park Street Press.

Singer, J. (1990). *Seeing Through the Visible World: Jung, Gnosis and Chaos.* San Francisco, CA: Harper San Francisco.

Smolin, L. (1997). *The Life of the Cosmos.* New York: Oxford University Press. 'Putting Time in a (Leaky) Bottle'. *Newsweek*, July 30, 2007.

'Transforming the Alchemists', *The New York Times.* August 1, 2006.

Various authors. (2005) '125 Questions: What We Don't Know', *Science*, Vol. 309.

23

PRACTICAL APPLICATIONS OF ALCHEMICAL SYMBOLISM

In the last chapter, we reviewed some of the broader psychological implications of alchemy, both historically and in terms of our present scientific understanding. Let us now turn our attention to a more practical matter: How might the magician use the concepts of alchemy to understand and enrich his or her personal work? The field of alchemy is so rich with symbolic content, entire books could be (and have been) written on its practical application. We will need to narrow our exploration to three specific symbolic 'templates' to address our present purposes:

1. The *solve et coagula* formula
2. The transformative processes known as the Black Work, the White Work and the Red Work
3. The doctrine, 'to make Gold thou must have Gold'

For the most part, we will discuss these templates in terms of the path toward the Knowledge and Conversation of the Holy Guardian Angel which, as I have emphasized many times in this book, is the one goal toward which all aspirants must strive from the beginning of their work in A∴A∴.

The processes under discussion here are exceedingly subtle, encompassing gradual, long-term changes in your thoughts, emotions, behaviors, and inner symbolic life. You will definitely be at an advantage if your daily magical diary is thorough and detailed. While you can plan ahead and chart a course based on these frameworks, to some degree, one of the most effective ways to detect these patterns is retrospectively, as you reflect on the practices and results noted in the diary. The more you have integrated the self-analysis and the monitoring of your physical body, your psyche, your emotions and so on, the more data will be available for you to understand your progress when viewed through the lens of these alchemical frameworks. For each of these templates, I will first discuss its basic nature, and then I will give a few practical suggestions on how to monitor or implement it in your daily life and your overall magical path.

Solve et Coagula

Solve et coagula roughly translates as "dissolve and coagulate." It refers to the process of breaking something apart into its individual elements, in order to understand and transform them before reassembling them into a newly perfected whole. One of the clearest examples of this in A∴A∴ is the progression through the elemental grades from Neophyte to Adeptus Minor. Essentially, you are looking at yourself in terms of the individual components of which you are composed, based on the symbolism of the elements and the sephiroth (see Chapters 15 and 16). Viewed from the perspective of the highest levels of attainment, human beings are not a collection of parts, but an undivided whole; yet in the First Order work of A∴A∴ you act *as if* you are composed of such parts for the sake of thorough self-analysis. At each step, you focus on one particular element, and attempt to come into a deeper relationship with that part of yourself. You must first purify it—that is, to cleanse it of any accretions that are not in accord with its basic nature. For example, the Neophyte of Malkuth must purify the physical body, casting aside any habits that might impede progress in the Great Work. Once the element has been cleansed, it must be consecrated; that is, it must be put mindfully in service to the spiritual path.

Eventually, after you pass through the four elemental grades and arrive at Dominus Liminis, these 'components' are reassembled into a perfect microcosm and offered to the HGA. You have reconstructed your very being in keeping with the pattern of the Tree of Life, and therefore with the structure of the universe itself. As I have stated elsewhere, the proper force is only drawn to the proper form, and in this case the mere existence of the proper form—yourself as a perfected microcosm—is a powerful invocation of the HGA. Ideally, your entire life becomes a *continuous, living invocation* perfectly suited to the indwelling of the Angel. Be the lightning rod, and the lightning will strike! The quintessential method of pursuing this result is, of course, the formal work of A∴A∴, but you will find the conscientious use of the daily elemental monitoring discussed Chapter 4 is a useful preliminary discipline.

The Black Work, the White Work and the Red Work
As above, we will map this out across the sephiroth and paths below Tiphereth. The Black Work relates primarily to Malkuth and the path of *tav*. Here you must differentiate the fine from the gross—to discover the reality of spirit and self that is veiled by matter. You explore the relationship between the body and the psyche, and strengthen your vision into the astral worlds by increasing your sensitivity to its subtle impressions. In practice, you accomplish this via monitoring diet, exercise, and physical health overall. Yoga practices further strengthen your physical vehicle, and astral explorations such as those in *Liber O*, bring mastery of the body of light (see Chapter 11).

Once you have seen past the veil of matter and begun to peer into the realms of spirit by strengthening your astral vision, you are ready to move into the White Work, attributed to the sephiroth Yesod, Hod, and Netzach. Broadly speaking, this is a stage of intense psychological self-exploration. Here, you survey the world of Yetzirah in its various forms —the emotional, intellectual, and intuitive faculties resident in the human personality—and reformulate them to operate with maximum efficiency and cooperation.

How does this look in practice? In Yesod, you accomplish more advanced astral work, undertake kundalini-stirring pranayama practices, and work intensely to unearth the drives, hidden agendas, and energy-blocking obstacles of your unconscious mind. Monitoring psychological projections to understand how you see the world through the lens of your own mind is an essential step, and formal psychotherapy is often a useful adjunct. In Hod, you bolster your intellectual acumen through the study of the Qabalah—this is essentially *jnana yoga*, the yoga of knowledge. A sharp mind, honed through the development of critical thinking skills, skepticism, and the mental calisthenics of the Qabalah, is a vital element to put in service of your Great Work. Finally, in Netzach, you strengthen your understanding and ability to control the forces of your desire and aspiration through bhakti yoga and related devotional practices.

Having thus completed the White Work, you stand at the threshold of the Red Work—the Veil of Paroketh (Dominus Liminis) and the eventual attainment of Tiphereth itself (Adeptus Minor). Here, the task is the confection of the alchemical stone—the solar gold at the center of the fully realized Self. It is similar in many ways to the *coagula* phase described above—the task is to bring all of your prior work to a climax. Having arrived at a place of balance and integration, you aspire to the HGA and await its light. At this stage you are very much 'stewing in your own juices,' spiritually and psychologically. The rest is not about external effort so much as awaiting the transformative work of the HGA itself. Much of whatever else needs to happen at this stage will be beyond the conscious efforts of the aspirant.

This particular stage is, quite frankly, one of the most mysterious and wondrous things to behold in all of the Great Work. It never ceases to amaze me how every aspirant seems to get exactly what they need, exactly when they need it—not too much or too little, and not a moment too soon or too late. There is something uniquely powerful about building yourself up to this stage, and then offering yourself up to the HGA freely and without egoic clinging for further transformation. The HGA inevitably responds with the force necessary to forge you, via this climatic Red Work, into an adept. Having attained this Knowledge and Conversation and its accompanying awareness of True Will, you are then prepared to go forth and enact the will in your life.

"...to make Gold thou must have Gold..."

Consider Crowley's words in *Liber Aleph,* Cap. 159, "On the Balance in which the Four Virtues have Equal Power":

> By Gñana Yoga cometh thy Man to Knowledge; by Karma Yoga thy Bull to Will; by Raja Yoga is thy Lion brought to his Light; and to make perfect thy Dragon, thou hast Bhakti Yoga for the Eagle therein, and Hatha Yoga for the Serpent. Yet mark thou well how all these interfuse, so that thou mayst accomplish no one of the Works separately. As to make Gold thou must have Gold (it is the Word of the Alchemists), so to become the Sphinx thou must first be a Sphinx. For naught may grow save to the Norm of its own Nature, and in the Law of its own Law, or it is but Artifice, and endureth not. So therefore is it Folly, and a Rape wrought upon Truth to aim at aught but the Fulfilment of thine own True Nature. Order then thy Workings in Accord with thy Knowledge of that Norm as best thou mayst, not heeding the Importunity of them that prate of the Ideal. For this Rule, this Uniformity, is proper only to a Prison, and a Man Liveth by Elasticity, nor endureth Rigor save in Death. But whoso groweth bodily by a Law foreign to his own Nature, he hath a Cancer, and his whole Œconomy shall be destroyed by that small Disobedience.[44]

---

[44] Crowley, A. (1991). *Liber Aleph.* York Beach, ME: Weiser Books.

In this passage, Crowley touches on a number of the doctrines and concepts presented elsewhere in this book, such as the idea of being balanced in the four elements, the importance of living in accord with the True Will; yet our focus here is on the idea that it takes gold to make gold. As Crowley describes, this relates to the adoption of transformative goals that are in line with our true nature, but it also applies to the larger body of aspirants to the Great Work and their interactions. You can probably call to mind a few examples of outstanding people you have met in your life—people who seem to shine in their selfhood—who live willfully and powerfully, yet also exhibit grace and dignity in all they do. These are a few of the characteristics we can recognize as signs of a true adept, whatever their particular spiritual path may be. Their very energy is contagious in a most wonderful way, and being around them is an inspiring lesson in living a vigorous life of will. The 'gold' of their attainment is recognized by some corresponding seed of gold within us, and it begins to resonate in sympathy, calling us *in our own unique way* to the path of attainment.

As a practical application of this principle, I suggest you seek out several people that inspire you in this way. Ask them about their path: How did they get where they are? What called to them or inspired them? What do they consider their best choices and their worst failures? Naturally, their path won't be *your* path, but you might be surprised to discover how many of the tools they used will be valuable to you along your way. Much as in the system of A∴A∴ itself, we can never know the particular twists and turns that any aspirant's path will take, but it is possible to set up signposts for those who follow. As we read in *Liber Causæ*:

> Every man must overcome his own obstacles, expose his own illusions. Yet others may assist him to do both, and they may enable him altogether to avoid many of the false paths, leading no whither, which tempt the weary feet of the uninitiated pilgrim.[45]

May *your* life shine as the gold of the alchemists, inspiring all those who behold it!

---

[45] Crowley, A. (1992). Liber Causae. In I. Regardie (Ed.), *Gems from the Equinox*. Scottsdale, AZ: New Falcon Publications.

PART THREE:
LIFE OUTSIDE THE TEMPLE

24

PATTERNS & CYCLES IN MAGICAL PRACTICE

"I feel so disconnected from the Great Work."
"I'm just not feeling the energy like I used to."
"Some days I feel like I just don't want to do it anymore."

Statements like these are probably some of the most common complaints I hear in my various teaching roles. This is not surprising, as these pitfalls are more-or-less inevitable along the path of attainment. There is just no question that, no matter who you are or what course of training you undertake, you will come up against such obstacles. And inevitably, you'll encounter patterns and cycles in your magical work, including dry spells, ecstatic peaks where you feel connected and vibrantly aligned with the work, and everything in between.

One of the real keys to persistence, and sustained motivation and connection with the work, is having some understanding that these cycles are inevitable—not beating yourself up when they occur, and not letting yourself slip into despondency when things aren't going like you planned or expected. In this chapter we'll examine a few different angles on this, including ways to understand and conceptualize the cycles, and how to break yourself out of dry spells when they occur.

The IAO Formula

Let's start with a discussion of how to understand these cycles—that is, how to give them a conceptual framework so that you can make sense of them and even use them to your advantage. Crowley touches on some of these topics in *Magick in Theory and Practice* when he discusses the various magical 'formulas'. One important example is called the IAO formula.

The IAO formula, understood in this present context, is a three-stage cycle applicable to any endeavor, whether magical work or something else entirely. The three stages correspond to the deities of Isis, Apophis, and Osiris. The Isis stage ('I') is characterized by an innocence—a freshness of experience—that you bring to the undertaking. For example, say you've taken on a new ritual procedure, and you're beginning to experiment with it. You're excited about it, and you're experiencing it as a stimulating new direction in your life. You approach it with a good deal of passion and commitment.

Eventually, you move into what we call the Apophis phase ('A') where you get disillusioned, you start to feel a little bit lazy, and you start to get disappointed that perhaps it's not going as well as you expected. You begin to question whether it was the right choice. You get tired of doing the same thing over and over again. Let's say you've decided, "Okay, I'm really going to work on asana now. I'm going to sit in that posture and lengthen my time." And then about the second week of doing this every day the boredom sets in, you start getting distracted, and you begin to yearn for something different. You get the idea.

And then you reach the Osiris stage ('O') in which (much like the archetype of Osiris as the arisen god who has been reformed anew) you get new insights and perspectives on the blockages you've just come through. You emerge from that miserable blackness—the 'A' phase—with a newfound clarity about the whole process.

What is essential here is to understand that you can't get to a mature understanding of any process *without* going through that middle phase. The Great Work is not all about innocence and perfection, newness and excitement, leading directly to enlightenment. It requires you to move through the frustrating, even painful disillusionment and questioning that occurs in the middle phase in order to really grasp what it's all about and integrate it.

I encourage you to keep the IAO formula in mind when you're undertaking a new task—a new course of training, for example. Let it help you avoid getting bogged down, disillusioned, and above all else, let it help you *persist* through the 'A' phase—through that Apophis darkness —and emerge on the other side so that you can attain to true mastery of the task at hand.

Solve et Coagula

Another useful conceptual model applicable to these magical cycles is our old friend, *solve et coagula.* You will recall that this consists of the *solve* phase, in which things are intentionally broken apart, analyzed, and fragmented, followed by the *coagula* phase, where things are brought together, re-integrated, and synthesized in a more refined form. Through this process, one attains a deeper understanding of the basic nature of each of the components analyzed, and the interconnectedness between them. The whole becomes truly more than the sum of its parts.

When you're in the middle of one of these stages – when your focus is so drawn to just one aspect of yourself—there will be a tendency toward dryness. Or alternately, you will be so immersed in that one point of view that it's hard to see outside your current conceptual framework. Either way, the danger is one of losing sight of the overall pattern. For example, the Neophyte may forget that all her work on *asana* is simply addressing the basic task of getting her body to be still – and is only one stage in the ongoing *solve* process; or the Practicus (immersed in the intellectual sphere of Hod) may become preoccupied with book learning, and neglect to keep the fires of aspiration burning.

More distressingly, the *solve* end of the equation (the analysis and the fragmentation phase of the work) can be very disillusioning. It can lead us to feel that there are just too many aspects drawing our attention—a multiplicity of individual life-threads that we can't weave into a coherent whole, or usefully comprehend. It can be quite overwhelming.

What's the remedy to all this frustration? When you feel this way, remember that you're simply on one end of the cycle. You're in a phase of the path where it's *supposed* to feel that way, until you get to the next phase—the *coagula* phase of synthesis. So try not to lose heart at those moments. To be slightly cliché about this, things have to fall apart before they can fall back together; and when they fall back together, it will be in a refined and perfected pattern, by virtue of the falling apart and the self-knowledge it has engendered.

The Upward Spiral

Here's another general principle you may find useful. When you get to a stuck place, a dry spell, or an obstacle that feels like an blockage in your work, one of the greatest gifts you can give yourself is to see it as an upward spiral rather than a return 'to square one.' In other words, you've come back around to a place that you recognize—one that feels dry and unsatisfying and stagnant. But if you can see how this time around is slightly different than the last time; if you can find a way to understand, within the context of your overall progress, that this particular stuck place is the latest example of a *category* of stuck place, but it's not the *same* stuck place you encountered before—this can help you stay motivated and avoid the disillusionment that comes with feeling you're going nowhere.

Post-Attainment Depression

Let's look at some other ways to understand and experience stuck points and obstacles that we encounter in the Great Work. One of the most important is the experience of coming to a new understanding—a moment when you feel like you've finally gotten your head above the clouds. You've had a profound mystical experience of some kind, or a breakthrough in a line of work you're pursuing. And inevitably (because you're a human being) you come back down from that exalted state into the mundane world. You must now go to work, deal with your family, and otherwise resume outer life. Sure enough, the mundane world hasn't parted like the Red Sea in front of you to be a problem-free environment. You get disillusioned. You have glimpsed a higher truth, and it's depressing not to be able to remain in that vision.

Once again, the key is to have some compassion with yourself and understand that the ego, the ruach, is trying to adjust to straddling that gap between the idealized experience and the way that most of life plays out in a mundane fashion. The key to avoiding despair here is to understand the universality of this experience among spiritual seekers. It's completely expectable and completely normal. And it is not a bad sign of anything. You've had your head above the clouds and you'll get back there when the time is right.

Finding Lessons

Another way to look at obstacles, stuck places, and dry spells is to ask what the obstacle is teaching you. Why did you *need* to be stuck right now? Why did you need to be held down in the same place longer than your ego wanted? Often, it will be due to a particular maturation process that you needed to undergo. You needed to slow down, look at something, feel something, or wrestle with something. And I think if you reflect back on the times in your life that have been most transformative you will find that those growth periods were very often accompanied by intense discomfort and challenge. The process of moving toward Knowledge and Conversation of the HGA has many points where it is necessary to be slowed down, to be hindered while we grow in *just* the way we need to grow, and experience *exactly* the trials that we need to in order to become a more perfect vessel for the light that is awaiting us.

Another question to ask yourself when you encounter an obstacle or stuck point is: Do I have an undue degree of lust of result here? How much ego-attachment do I have to whatever goal I'm working toward? And is that tripping me up? All of us find ourselves in this position from time to time, and we must strive to be conscious of such impediments to success.

When Spirit Enters

It is useful to consider the mechanism by which these dark times intrude into our work and our lives. Jungian analyst Robert Johnson has lectured extensively on this process. He discusses the various portals through which Spirit (his term) enters our lives. One of these is through encounters with paradoxical situations. When we encounter a choice point in life—a dilemma that seems to have no rational solution—we're stuck between the proverbial rock and a hard place. We don't know what to do, and no choice seems right.

In these situations, the ego is stymied by the situation, and has nowhere to turn. It can't *think* itself though the problem. And in this ego-breakdown, space is created for superconsciousness to enter. There is an opening for inspiration and intuition. If you trust this process – if you let go of the habitual attachment to thinking your way out of these dilemmas – you will make room for your own spiritually informed conscience to guide you.

Another way that spirit enters our lives, according to Johnson, is through shadow confrontations. When we are tripped up by something unacknowledged or unwanted in ourselves, we are facing our shadow. For example, we may have a tendency toward excessive emotional attachment to people or things, an addiction, a conflict between our magical goals and the external life we have set up for ourselves, and so on. These are things that we'll likely want to push away and not think about, yet in facing them we open up some of the truest opportunities we'll ever have for growth and transformation.

If we embrace the shadow we can allow the voice of spirit to be heard. This voice deep within us is urging us *not* to ignore the totality of who we are; *not* to carve out a part of ourselves, demonize it, and refuse to look at it. If we've been doing that, it's going to come find us. And the sooner we embrace the disowned aspect of self rather than run from it, the sooner we will begin to grow.

Practical Suggestions

Here are a few final, practical suggestions for getting unstuck. One of them is as much a cognitive-behavioral therapy principle as it is a magical principle: Just do *anything*. When you feel stuck, lost, or overwhelmed, simply *take action* so that you can see you're not actually immobilized. There's no way you're going to be able to tell yourself, "I'm stuck, I can't do anything" when you've just gotten up to do a banishing, a few minutes of meditation or some other task. Write in your diary. Take a walk. Pick a random book off the shelf and read it for a few minutes. Don't worry about which thing you choose. Just do *something*.

One of the big traps that people get into is overthinking, or getting perfectionistic with their magical choices. They feel that if they don't pick just the right thing to do, it must be the wrong thing to do. They fear that choosing the 'wrong' ritual or practice will drastically impede their progress along the path. In almost every case, however, these choices are not so critical, so don't make it harder on yourself by thinking in this manner. We usually learn more from our magical mistakes than our easy successes, in any case.

Another way to get unstuck is to perform a divination. Consider your situation, and make a conscious decision *not* to rely purely on the ego to find a solution. Do a Tarot spread, throw the I Ching or even simply flip a coin. It's a good way to loosen the ego's grip and shake up your thought process.

Conclusion

No matter which methods you choose to help yourself get through the challenges of the magical path, you will inevitably gain insight into your most common problem patterns. Your hard-earned experience with embarrassing screw-ups, frustrating stuck places, and depressing 'dark nights of the soul' will be the very fuel for your future attainments. And each time you make another pass around that upward spiral, you will be more empowered to find effective solutions to the challenges you find there.

25

DREAMWORK

As a Jungian psychologist, dreamwork has been an important part of my personal work and my professional practice for many years. It was one of the things that most intrigued me about Jung's approach from the very beginning of my career. Much like psychotherapy, dreamwork can be an important tool for the personal development of the magician, enhancing self-knowledge and the magical power that comes with it. I highly recommend dreamwork as a daily practice for the magician at every stage of the path.

Carl Jung called dreams "the royal road to the unconscious." His theory emphasizes the importance of balancing the conscious and unconscious minds, and it posits that dreams are sent from the Self as messages intended to bring balance and wholeness. Dreams are designed to be heard by the Ego, the conscious mind, and the intention is always to promote wholeness and growth. Dreams attempt to communicate information the ego needs to know in order to be more self-aware, and to balance out the predispositions in the conscious mind—to integrate shadow material and other unacknowledged or repressed aspects of the psyche. We can readily see much overlap here with the other symbolic processes used by the magician, such as scrying, pathworking on the Tree of Life, working with symbolic elements in ritual and similar techniques. Dreams are ready-made containers for these same symbol sets. The more rich and diverse we make our symbolic repertoire through memorization of magical correspondences, mythological exploration, and understanding of comparative religious systems, the more meaning we will be able to extract from our dreams.

Nevertheless, we must be appropriately skeptical about the nature of dreams. As noted above, Jungians tend to argue that dreams are a definite attempt on the part of the unconscious to deliver specific messages. In contrast, many contemporary cognitive scientists believe that dreams are simply random firings of neurons, devoid of any particular meaning. Regardless, even if dreams are random neuronal fireworks—even if the very existence of some kind of purposeful subconscious dream-wisdom is a fallacy—I find dreamwork to be an extremely valuable tool to get 'outside the box' of everyday rational thought, by dealing with these more or less irrational symbol sets. Dreamwork forces us to explore certain aspects of ourselves, via these symbolic contents, that we might not have hit on if we were just living in the rational world of our everyday minds. At the very least, much like with divination or scrying, we will get unique views of ourselves, and some invigorating mental calisthenics out of the bargain.

When working with dreams, it is very important to use *your own* symbol sets. Avoid at all costs those dream symbol cookbooks offering predigested interpretations of common symbols. There is a time and a place for moving beyond your own personal interpretations into more mythological and archetypal themes, but for the most part you should rely on your own associations. Another very important consideration is that in the Jungian approach, everything in the dream is some aspect of *you*. If you dream of having a conversation with your mother, it's not a dream about your relationship with your actual mother. Rather, it pertains to the interaction between your ego and that part of you that is best *symbolized* by your mother. A house may refer to a 'location' or state of being within you; a storm may symbolize a tempestuous process within you, and so on. Don't give in to the temptation of overly concretizing and externalizing the characters, places and processes in a dream.

In his seminal book *Inner Work*[46], Jungian analyst Robert Johnson describes the basic Jungian approach to dream analysis in a concise, four-step process.

Step One: Write down everything you can recall about the dream content itself—the story, the location, the characters, the emotions you felt, and so on. The next step is to make associations to each specific element of the dream content. Let's say you dreamed about a house that you lived in when you were 14 years old, and in the dream you were having a conversation with a childhood friend. In step one, you will just

---

[46] Johnson, R. (2009). *Inner Work*. New York: HarperCollins.

associate to that house. What age were you when you lived there? What was your life like then? What was your emotional state? What are the good and bad things you remember from living in that house? Make associations to the childhood friend as well. What were the personality characteristics of the friend? How would you describe the friend to someone that didn't know him/her?

Be careful not to get into 'chain associations' where thinking about the friend reminds you about a bike you had and the bike reminds you about the car that you got later, and so on. Rather, you should keep tying your associations back to the basic symbol as it actually appeared in the dream. For the major symbols in the dream, it may help to do this graphically. Write the word, draw a circle around it, and then draw lines to point to the different associations related to the symbol, so you end up with a 'map' of symbolic associations.

Step Two: Connect the dream images to your own inner dynamics, and 'amplify' the images and symbols via traditional sources. Occasionally, dream contents may strike you as being what Jung called *numinous*; that is, they have a certain quality that seems to resonate beyond the specific content you *personally* associate to the various symbols. For example, I remember once having a dream in which I was living in some sort of culture that lived on the slopes of an active volcano. Obviously, this is not something from my personal life! Jungians might refer to this as a 'big dream'—a dream that practically screams, "There is more to this than your little individual existence!" In amplifying this dream, I found it useful to look at myths involving volcanoes and similar themes. Most of the time, however, you will be connecting your dream images to inner dynamics in more direct ways drawn from your normal waking life and identity. So, in our example about the childhood friend, you would have perhaps identified that this friend was caring, a good listener and loyal in Step One. Maybe the house brought back pleasant and loving memories of your family during the time you lived there. Here in Step Two, when you are connecting dream images to inner dynamics, that friend is the caring and loyal part of you, and the house might represent the state of mind in which you nurture yourself and when you slow down and enjoy your time with people and so on.

Step Three: Weave these inner dynamics together to create an interpretation of the entire dream. The goal is to tell a story based on what you've determined to be the inner aspects of yourself that are referred to in the dream. You are looking for a 'click,' as Johnson would call it. When you 'try on' different interpretations, some of them may not resonate with you, but some will click. Turn on your bullshit detector.

217

Did you learn something that you didn't already consciously know? If you didn't learn something new then chances are it's not the deepest message available in the dream. After all, in the Jungian theory of the psyche, if the ego already knows something, the unconscious doesn't need to tell it to us—there is no imbalance to correct. Are you at least *slightly* uncomfortable with the interpretation? Does it sting a little bit? Do you feel energized by the interpretation, as if it freed up some energy that was bound up in keeping certain things unconscious? All of these experiences may be hints that you have hit on a correct interpretation.

In our example with the friend in the house, the dream might be suggesting that you need to set aside more time to check in with yourself about your emotions and your general well being; that you need to create the inner equivalent of that positively remembered family home where you can more deeply listen to yourself. Essentially, you are being asked by the unconscious to act out the story of the dream, which is to be your own caring, loyal friend and occupy your own symbolic house of comfort and self-nurturance.

Step Four: Perform a ritual to honor the dream and to make it concrete. The theory here is that the more concrete you make the message of the dream—the more you enact some sort of behavior that signals to your unconscious that you are taking it seriously, and that you really understood the message of the dream—the more healing it can be. In our present dream example, you might pay a visit the old family home in the dream. Take some of the dirt from the front yard, put it in a vial or jar and perform a ritual with it. Set the jar on the mantle and keep it with you as a reminder of the truth of the dream that you discovered. The possibilities are endless, and as with all ritual, the more you customize it to your own symbols and the specifics of your inner situation, the more effective it will be.

Interestingly, and perhaps not surprisingly, this four-step process mirrors the Qabalistic doctrine of the Four Worlds. In Step One, where you are making specific associations to the dream content, you are identifying the basic seeds from which everything else springs (Atziluth.) In Step Two, we are giving primal form to those seeds by fleshing them out with our associations and connecting them to archetypal forms through amplification of the symbols. This is much like the world of Briah, where the superconscious *form* is shaped. In Step Three, we translate these archetypes and higher dynamics into apprehensible and fully conscious thought-forms—bringing the content down into the world of Yetzirah. Finally, in Step Four, we do the ritual of honoring the dream. It is easy to see how this relates to the world of Assiah, where everything above is manifested in the physical world—in this case, by our behavioral enactment of the message of the dream.

A related technique you may find useful is *active imagination*, which Jung described as "dreaming the dream onward." In this technique, you enter into a quasi-meditative (but waking) state, and reengage with characters from the dream in order to obtain more fodder for interpretation. You might set up a ritual space, do a banishing, call forth a character from a recent vivid dream—especially a dream that was confusing, or perhaps notably vivid or important—and then interact with the being from the dream. Ask it for more information; ask it what its message is for you; ask it if there are other things you need to know about the content of the dream. One easy method of recording this is to sit at a computer and type your questions in lower case, then switch to all caps for the response of the character with whom you are interacting. Once you have obtained a satisfactory amount of additional information, plug it back into the context of the original dream and revisit the various steps of the interpretive process described above.

Let me close with a few general suggestions:

1. Keep a nice dream journal. The same principle that applies to your magical diary or ritual implements applies here. That is, if you have a beautifully constructed blank book that you treasure, it will tend to empower your work.

2. As you are going to sleep, tell yourself that you will remember your dreams upon waking; then write them down or dictate them into a recording device as soon as you wake up. On advantage of dictating your dreams is that you will more readily get across the emotional tone of the dream and your response to it, which will help you later when you are trying to analyze it. Plus, you tend to get more detail when dictating, as opposed to stumbling to your pad and paper to write it all down in your pre-coffee morning stupor.

3. You will likely notice that the more intensely and regularly you engage with your dreams, the easier it will be to remember them in detail, and the more you will notice a narrative continuity from dream to dream.

4. You may notice interesting patterns in the vividness and intensity of your dream activity in general. For example, you may find that when you are actively engaged with a series of ritual workings, and therefore wrestling with symbolic material in fairly direct ways, you won't remember as many of your dreams. The converse is often true as well; that is, when you are less engaged in such intense symbolic work, the dreams may seem to be under more 'pressure' to make it into conscious awareness, thus making it more likely that you will remember them upon waking.

26

RELATIONSHIPS

This chapter will explore a few perspectives on interpersonal relationships in the life of a Thelemic magician. The primary focus here will be on romantic relationships, but much of this material applies equally well to other types of relationships. That is, we strive to maintain maximum mutual respect for our friend or partner, including (and especially) respect for the other person's inherent divinity—for the star that they are. We do our best not to interfere with their True Will as best we understand it, and to stand up for our own autonomy when or if that is threatened. This is true of any relationship, but romantic relationships present other particular considerations I will review here in some detail.

As you might expect, much of what I say here is informed by my own clinical practice in psychology, and I do a significant amount of couples therapy. A few years ago, I encountered a wonderful book by Dr. David Schnarsch called *Passionate Marriage*.[47] This book, more than any other book on relationships I've ever seen, embodies a set of values that approximate the principles of Thelema. Much of what I'm going to say in this chapter is drawn from my own experience, but I will also present a number of Schnarsch's ideas. As with all of the information in this

---

[47] Schnarch, D. (1997). *Passionate Marriage*. New York: Henry Holt.

book, you should feel free to experiment with these ideas, and disregard them if you find them not to be in accord with your own will.

Thelemic "Values" in Relationships

So, what exactly *are* the Thelemic values we can bring to bear on our relationships? The first principle that I would nominate is the concept of *individual responsibility*. In our society at large, it seems that a great deal of the focus is on the importance of making *the other person* happy. This is where we really get off track. We get obsessed with making the other person happy, or with how the other person is doing at making *us* happy, and we measure our success as a partner by how well we are doing in this regard. I encourage you to examine carefully your own assumptions and expectations in this area. I am always telling my patients that when problems, conflicts, or obstacles arise in a relationship, we should not be asking, "why is the other person not doing the thing that I want them to do? And what can the other person do to make me happier?" Rather, we should be asking, "what am I doing to make *myself* happy?"

If we are feeling lonely or un-nurtured in a relationship, our first line of exploration should be "Have I nurtured *myself* ?" "Have I taken responsibility for *my own* level of satisfaction today?" If we're feeling like our own needs are not being met in the relationship, we should ask ourselves about our own priorities *before* we go to our partner and insist that they do a better job of prioritizing what we need! As you may have detected, this is an area that is ripe for projections—when our own limitations and weaknesses are projected onto our partner. Essentially, we scapegoat them, treating them as the cause of whatever problem we may have, rather than acknowledging our own role in the matter.

The second principle to consider is that *the basic unit in a relationship, contrary to the conventional wisdom in our society, is the individual.* Ideally, relationships exist for the growth and development of the individuals in them. It is through the growth and development of the individual that the health of the relationship is maintained. This flies in the face of the way mainstream culture views relationships, and frankly, it overturns the way many contemporary couples therapists view relationships as well! I should emphasize that the free will and autonomy of each partner is of paramount importance. This doesn't mean that there are no compromises, or that shared goals don't exist—and this certainly doesn't mean the individuals in the relationship should not seek to foster their partner's health and happiness. It would be awfully drab and depressing if relationships had none of this! But both partners tend to move toward greater health quite naturally when they come into a relationship for the purpose of working on *themselves* as individuals, and with the intention to respect each other's efforts along the same lines. In this sense, a romantic relationship is simply one of many opportunities we have in life to unite with others to benefit ourselves, our partners, our community, our extended family, or any other unit of society.

Another important principle to keep in mind is that *relationship problems are good for you.* (Yes, really!) When you are physically wounded, the pain draws your attention to the place that needs healing. Similarly, in a relationship, when partners are in conflict, grating against each other's comfort zones, there is discomfort or pain. The partners are being challenged to stretch in some way, and where there is stretching, there is growth. The appropriate response is to allow ourselves to stretch —to relax into it rather than fight it. We must recognize that we have rigidity in some aspect of self and we're reluctant to unclench the emotional muscles surrounding it. We should say, "this problem is showing me some way I need to grow," not, "this problem is due to something wrong with my partner that *they* need to change." If your primary focus is your own growth and learning, you are also supporting the growth and self-knowledge of your partner. This is quintessentially Thelemic. Taking responsibility for ourselves promotes health and healing for all concerned.

Facing Challenges

Let's turn our attention to some specific types of challenges that may occur in relationships. One sort of challenge relates to magical practice itself: when should a couple work together on magical rituals, and when should they work separately? Balance is the most important factor. For example, if you only performed *Liber Resh* with a partner present you would lose some of the experience of doing the ritual solo. Likewise, if you never experimented with doing it with another individual, you might lose something of that experience. Any of you who have been in a room full of Thelemites doing *Liber Resh* together can attest that while you lose some of the specific intensity of your own solo practice, there's something else entirely to be gained by approaching it as a group ritual: the sense of fellowship with kindred spirits, the amplification of intensity of worship due to all those wills being pointed at the singular goal, and so on. So, keep a balance between doing these rituals individually and doing them with partners or friends.

Another category of problem that can arise in a Thelemic relationship is when the partners are at different places in their personal magical path. For example, if they are both working in a particular order, but one holds a more advanced degree than the other, then they're very likely to have different practices, different reference materials, perhaps different magical implements and similar things that can't be shared with the partner. This is an opportunity for issues of secrecy and trust to emerge. If you feel yourself on the untrusting end of this sort of situation, feeling upset that your partner is off doing something they can't tell you about, I think your first questions for yourself ought to be: "What is this challenging in me? What insecurity is this making me confront? What am I afraid of losing? What would it mean if my partner couldn't share everything with me?" If you do a thorough self-examination with questions like these, you may come up with some important insights into yourself; and by the time you've done that, you will likely find your worry about this whole situation has dissipated somewhat. If you're on the other side of this equation (being unable to share something with your partner) you'll want to be as patient and compassionate as possible. Clarify that there are many things you *do* share with them, but that this particular set of practices may not be among those for the time being. And of course, you should both keep in mind that the main point of having personal practices is for the growth and spiritual development of each individual, not to provide entertainment for the couple!

An even more delicate situation is a relationship where one person is on the Thelemic path and the other isn't; or when one person is a practicing Thelemite and the other person isn't magically inclined. Perhaps they are even actively opposed to magical practices. Assuming the couple decides to stay together, the core issue is effective communication. The partner who is not involved must be given a clear understanding of the basic aims of the magical path. It may take quite a bit of time to help the non-magician understand the fundamental reasons for doing these practices, so they can perceive that it is fundamentally a path of self-development and spiritual growth.

Of course, there are times when you may discover that your path really is diverging from that of your partner. This can be a painful awakening. It doesn't take long being in the work before you encounter some broken relationship among your friends and fellow Thelemites. In the process of getting in tune with your True Will, you may discover that the will has led you away from being able to be harmoniously partnered with a particular person. This is equally true in terms of occupations, alienation from family members, and so on. But before you conclude that you simply must leave this relationship, I hope that you will stop and ask yourself: How you are hindering your own progress? How might you be projecting your own obstacles, your own procrastination, your own self-negativity, and your own lack of belief in what you are doing? Whatever you think the other person is doing to block you or to hinder your progress—stop and ask how you are doing that to yourself. Watch out for these projections, because believe me if you don't do this, and you preemptively end a relationship on these grounds without this self-examination, there's a fair chance you will end up regretting it.

Relationship Advice from the Prophet

To conclude this chapter, I could do no better than to offer a few passages from Aleister Crowley's essay called "Duty," which is a wonderful examination of the implications of the Law of Thelema as applied to our relationships with other individual humans, with society, and with the earth itself.[48] Here are some selections that appear especially relevant to our discussion in this chapter.

Your duty to other individual men and women.

To bring out saliently the differences between two points-of-view is useful to both in measuring the position of each in the whole. Combat stimulates the virile or creative energy; and, like love, of which it is one form, excites the mind to an orgasm which enables it to transcend its rational dullness.

Abstain from all interferences with other wills.

([...]love and war[...]are of the nature of sport, where one respects, and learns from the opponent, but never interferes with him, outside the actual game.) To seek to dominate or influence another is to seek to deform or to destroy him; and he is a necessary part of one's own Universe, that is, of one's self.

Seek, if you so will, to enlighten another when need arises.

This may be done, always with the strict respect for the attitude of the good sportsman, when he is in distress through failure to understand himself clearly, especially when he specifically demands help; for his darkness may hinder one's perception of his perfection. (Yet also his darkness may serve as a warning, or excite one's interest.) It is also lawful when his ignorance has lead him to interfere with one's will. All interference is in any case dangerous, and demands the exercise of extreme skill and good judgement, fortified by experience. To influence another is to leave one's citadel unguarded; and the attempt commonly ends in losing one's own self-supremacy.

Use men and women, therefore, with the absolute respect due to inviolable standards of measurement; verify your own observations by comparison with similar judgments made by them; and, studying the methods which determine their failure or success, acquire for yourself the wit and skill required to cope with your own problems.

---

[48] Crowley, A. (1992). Duty. In I. Regardie (Ed.), *Gems from the Equinox*. Scottsdale, AZ: New Falcon Publications.

27

QABALISTIC COPING SKILLS

In this chapter we'll review a set of tools based on Qabalistic principles, which you can use to cope with any number of everyday challenges, including physical, emotional, mental or spiritual difficulties, as well as interpersonal conflicts. You can even use some of these tools when you find yourself in the position of mediating a dispute between friends or brethren. Before reading further in this chapter, be sure to review Chapters 1 and 19, where I discuss the Qabalistic 'parts of the soul'. An understanding of these doctrines will be essential if you wish to get a full grasp of the material in this chapter.

The coping model we'll present here, which is based on the Tree of Life, has one particularly interesting characteristic: the process we must undertake in order to cope with any given challenge mirrors the path of evolution. That is, it involves movement *up the Tree*, symbolically speaking. All the action we will examine here is *toward* Kether, and why would we expect otherwise? Any given moment in life can be a microcosm of the entire path of return if we approach it mindfully and with an intention to grow. In any particular instance of difficulty, we are given an opportunity to stretch toward a more evolved viewpoint from which to attack the problem. Just as the Tree of Life represents the microcosm of human consciousness, the macrocosm of universal creation, and the path of evolution from base matter to full attainment; so is it also a map of how to deal with *any moment of life* in a growth-oriented and constructive way. The coping model we'll discuss here is based on this 'holographic' characteristic of evolution toward Kether.

Let's use the following situation as an example. You've had a very difficult time at work. You've had conflicts with a coworker, and you're feeling overwhelmed. The first step of the coping model is to start at the bottom of the tree. Check the *guph*—the physical body in Malkuth. The health and well-being of the physical body is the basis of everything else you are experiencing, and if there is something wrong with the physical body, your perception and experience will be greatly influenced by this state. Are you ill, tired, hungry, underslept, or hung over? Look at all of these possibilities and understand that if you don't address these first, it will be difficult to move much beyond a physically reactive level of functioning. As Abraham Maslow taught us with his model of the 'hierarchy of needs,' if the basic physical needs are not met, it is very difficult to put any constructive attention on more refined psychological needs, to say nothing of the even more rarefied spiritual needs.

After you have checked in at the physical level, move further up the Tree toward Kether, to Yesod. Here, we review potential stuck points or other problems in the *nephesh*. Look for psychological projections, unconscious blockages, and emotional tides that are manifesting in the way you perceive the world at a primal level. You may be going through your workday being battered about by the winds of your unconscious and your emotions without even realizing that it's spilling over into how you perceived your coworker's words or actions. In terms of projections, ask yourself: Were they displaying a trait I really don't like in myself, so I was particularly bothered by it? Were they doing something that I try not to do, so I was 'policing' their behavior? And so on.

Also in terms of subconscious issues, look for 'secondary gain' from patterns of failure. Is there some sort of psychological benefit to being stuck? For example, in our hypothetical situation, you may discover that you are keeping yourself in a victim role. Is there a benefit to your feeling of helplessness? Is it enabling you *not* to change or grow—to avoid facing some inner challenge that is uncomfortable? Is it easier to blame others than to take responsibility yourself?

Laxity in magical practice can also be disruptive at the nepheshic level. It is important to keep up with daily magical hygienic practices such as the pentagram ritual, as well as energy-raising rituals such as *Liber Resh* and Middle Pillar-type exercises. Many initiates have found that sloppiness in the details of ritual and astral work can be similarly disruptive. Examples of this include carelessly drawn pentagrams, or failure to be conscientious in pulling back all of the externalized astral substance into the physical body. If these issues are chronic, they may be experienced as a drain of energy, or a general feeling of being 'off'.

The aim, as always, it to *make the unconscious conscious*—to raise our level of awareness of nepheshic influence on our perception and emotional reactivity. By undertaking this self-scrutiny, we evolve—in that very moment—to a level of awareness that transcends the animalistic response patterns of the nephesh.

Once you have examined the condition of the guph and the nephesh, it's time to move up the tree to the *ruach*. Here, we look for ego traps, blind spots, and habitual modes of thinking that narrow our perception of the situation, and our awareness of the range of emotional and behavioral responses to it. Returning to our hypothetical situation: perhaps you are driven by competitive urges, and the office conflict is stemming from some sort of rivalry with the coworker. Maybe you are afraid of being embarrassed or humiliated, or you have a sense of fear of a social stigma related to the outcome of the situation. Anything that involves the ego's wants and needs can become a source of blockage here. This usually involves issues of personal comfort, superiority, stability of circumstances, self-esteem, social standing, and so on.

Once you have identified the source of the problem, what do you do about it? One option is to use thoughtfully crafted rituals to invoke those complementary forces that balance the energies of which you have an excess, and vice-versa; don't try to 'banish away' characteristics you feel you have in excess; instead, invoke the complementary force. For example, if you have too much aggression and anger, invoke Chesed rather than banishing Geburah. If you are feeling fuzzy-headed and confused in your view of a situation, do a Hod ritual to invoke the forces of mental clarity and stability. If you are feeling spiritually dry and unmotivated, as if your spiritual 'batteries' are not fully charged, invoke Netzach to fire up your aspiration and devotion to the Great Work. If you are overthinking things and you want more intuitive guidance, invoke Yesod. If you simply want to invoke spiritual force itself, or inspire yourself regarding your magical goals, or the aspiration to the HGA, invoke Tiphereth or Kether. There are an infinite variety of options, limited only by your creativity and the breadth of your knowledge of correspondences and ritual forms.

Aside from these ritual approaches to attacking the problem at the ego level, there are a few common-sense things to try as well. Review your magical diaries and see if there are clues about what may be tripping you up. What are the recent trends in your thoughts and emotions on a daily basis? Can you detect patterns of emotional upset, interpersonal friction, and the like, that point you to a source of the problem? It may be useful to talk to one or more other people to get some ruach-level input from outside your own head. Ask a friend. Also, ask someone who you know or suspect does *not* like you. As a mental exercise, sit with their advice for a while, as if it is 100% true, and assemble your own arguments in support of their input. Then let the pendulum of skepticism swing the other way, and review the counter-arguments. None of this advice will be something that you have to slavishly follow if it doesn't feel right to you, but it will be one good source of data.

There is an important guiding principle underlying all of this. Once you have identified the level at which the conflict is occurring, your attempts to discover the solution will involve intentional operation from one or another of the other levels *above the level at which the conflict is occurring.* For example, fairly obviously, if you are dealing with physical problems or emotional conflicts or complexes, you have to bump it up a level to involve your ego. The ego has to come in to remind you to sleep or eat, or to stop worrying so much about what that coworker thinks of you, and examine out your projections. You must kick it up to a higher level so that a more enlightened part of you can have a view of the situation. Likewise, if you have a conflict at the level of the ego, the solution will typically involve moving up to a higher level of *spiritual connection* (neshamah/superconsciousness). In such circumstances, you must aspire to, and consciously identify with, the higher self to the extent that you can.

Here are practical tips for this level of work. Perform an invocation of the HGA—or a prayer appealing to the HGA for clarity on the situation. Often, when we consciously feel stuck—like we are between a rock and a hard place, or a paradox that feels un-resolvable—it is because *it is not the ego's job to fix it.* We need something more—something trans-rational and transpersonal—and at those moments of ego conflict, blockage, and stuckness, re-establishing a connection to the divine, superconscious wisdom within us is an essential step.

In addition to coping with you own issues, you can use these tools to deal with conflicts with others as well. The same guiding principle applies here: determine the level of conflict and approach it from at least one level above that. Let's say you have two friends having a conflict that is highly emotional in nature. They are rolling around in the muck of anger, perhaps fueled by unconscious projections, and that is clearly at the nepheshic level. Your task, therefore, is to come into the situation as a problem solver at the *ego* level—to stand in for the frontal lobes they aren't using much at the moment! You are helping them to elevate themselves above the nepheshic level of functioning. An even more primal example is when people are actually physically fighting. Clearly it's not usually constructive to rush in and physically fight with them—that simply results in more people fighting! You must move to a higher, ego-based viewpoint to inject some sense into the situation.

Suppose your friends are in conflict at the ego level, due to competitive strivings that are manifesting in your local Thelemic community. Perhaps they disagree strongly on how a problem should be solved, or each person doesn't want to admit any errors in judgment or behavior. Since this conflict is already at the ego level, you must move up to a spiritual level. If you are all in the same magical order, for example, you may want to appeal to their fraternal bonds. Remind them that they are magicians on the path, and that you can see from the outside that they are stuck in an ego-based conflict. Perhaps they are both right in their own ways, or perhaps there is another solution available that honors the perspectives of both parties? Essentially, you bring a more nuanced and enlightened perspective to the situation by purposely and consciously taking it above the ego level of conflict.

When fully conscious contact with the HGA is attained and stabilized at the Adeptus Minor grade of A∴A∴, many other resources become available. Your HGA will teach you everything you truly need to know. In fact, all along the path toward K & C you will have developed many tools to do much of what I have described in this chapter, in your own unique fashion. An important effect of developing these tools is that your progress toward attainment of the K & C will be accelerated, because your energy will not be bound up in lower levels of psychological functioning. If energy is stuck there, it is unavailable to devote to aspiration to higher purposes. Furthermore, even after the attainment of K & C, each successive stage of attainment beyond Tiphereth beings with it a broader and more nuanced understanding of who you are, what you are here to do, and what powers and potencies are the most appropriate solutions for any difficulties you encounter.

The Qabalah is much more than a source of arcane wisdom and magical techniques. If you conscientiously use the tools presented in this chapter, you will find that the Qabalah is equally beneficial as a source of guidance in coping with the challenges of everyday life outside your temple.

28

PSYCHOTHERAPY

When I first conceived of writing this book, I knew I'd want to address the issue of psychotherapy and its relationship to the magical path. As you might expect, I have some bias in this regard. I have a strongly favorable opinion about the utility of psychotherapy as we progress in magical work – but I'm not alone in this. We don't have to look very deep into the writings of some of our esteemed predecessors, such as Israel Regardie, Soror Meral and others, to see that there's quite a precedent for recommending psychotherapy as a prerequisite or adjunct to the magical path.

Aleister Crowley himself appears to have been fairly well-read in regard to contemporary psychotherapeutic practices, but naturally, his perspective on the nature and utility of psychotherapy was necessarily limited by those forms of therapy that were actually in existence during his lifetime—classical Freudian psychoanalysis and its offshoots, such as the work of Carl Jung. One of the most interesting writings of Crowley's on this topic is the essay called "An Improvement on Psychoanalysis," which was most recently published in *The Revival of Magick*.[49] In this essay, Crowley opines that Jung's theories come closer to the essence of Thelema in one very important sense: whereas Freud conceptualized the

---

[49] Crowley. A. (1998). *The Revival of Magick and Other Essays.* Scottsdale, AZ: New Falcon Publications.

233

will of the individual as springing from the sex drive, Jung theorized just the opposite—that the sex drive arises from the will. This intrinsic drive (will) of the human psyche toward health and wholeness is, according to Jung, the primary motive force, and it's not hard to see how this perspective would have impressed Crowley. That said, it seems that Crowley's exposure to Jung's more mature work, such as his advanced treatises on the psychology of alchemy and other esoteric topics, was minimal. This is a shame, because in my mind the work of these two men continued to converge as they matured, and I think it is quite likely that Crowley would have appreciated the direction Jung took in his later work.

Why would you want to undergo psychotherapy as a preliminary or adjunct to the magical path? I think there are several good answers to this, depending on your unique situation and psychological makeup. First and foremost, you may have specific symptoms that need to be addressed, such as depression or anxiety issues that interfere with your day-to-day functioning in life, or at least impede your happiness and peace of mind. Advances in psychotherapy over the past few decades have taught us how to treat many such issues quickly and effectively, and this is certainly a valid reason to seek out psychotherapy prior to beginning magical studies, or early in your magical career. You don't want such symptoms to be a distraction, or to sap energy that might otherwise be devoted to your spiritual work.

Aside from alleviating specific symptoms, psychotherapy is broadly useful as a means of self-exploration. Most magicians place a high value on self-understanding, so it should be no surprise that undertaking such work in therapy could be quite helpful. This goes beyond the sort of understanding that arises from self-analysis. There is simply something uniquely valuable about sitting in a room with someone who is not entwined in your personal life, and having them assist you to identify your strengths and weaknesses, your blind spots, and other personality issues and behavior patterns that might elude you. Even if you have a very well developed ability to introspect and discover your own quirks, I strongly recommend that you spend at least a few months in psychotherapy with a competent therapist you trust.

When you "front-load" your magical work in this way, fortified by the self-knowledge derived from therapy, you reduce the likelihood of truly debilitating personality patterns undermining your spiritual path later on. There is a tendency for all of us to play to our own strengths and avoid facing (or even becoming aware of) our weaknesses. Therapy is one tool to help ensure we have done this work consciously, and with due diligence. It won't remove the obstacles from your spiritual path, but it will increase the chances that you will be armed with enough self-knowledge to work though them effectively. Therapy is a tool, much like proper education and nutrition—and it would be foolish to avoid using any such tool at our disposal.

Along the same lines, Crowley, in his discussion of the work of A∴A∴, emphasizes the importance of balancing the natural predispositions of the personality—not allowing ourselves simply to cater to our own preferences, choosing only those practices that naturally appeal to us. We enforce this policy in A∴A∴ by insisting that aspirants rigorously engage in the diverse aspects of the curriculum, *especially* those in which they are not naturally gifted. Psychotherapy can help uncover these personality predilections in preparation for the deeper work of the advanced magician.

Let's assume that you have decided to pursue psychotherapy. How can you find a therapist that will be a good match for you? It is crucial to do a good bit of research. You don't want to waste your time with someone who is not a good match for you. Call several therapists, and ask them to tell you about their approach to therapy—often referred to as their *theoretical orientation.* Ask about their training and experience. If you're looking for deeper exploratory work, rather than mere symptom reduction, you're probably going to want to look for someone who self identifies as Jungian, transpersonal or humanistic. These therapists are more likely to have a holistic view of the human psyche, and to integrate spiritually themed topics into the therapy process. Ask them if they are comfortable discussing non-mainstream spiritual approaches, and explain that you are seeking to integrate your psychological and spiritual exploration. Naturally, this doesn't mean you will be relying on them for magical advice—few therapists will be equipped to suggest an appropriate incense for your upcoming Chesed ritual! Nevertheless, you'll want a therapist who can support you when you are in a stage of exploration where meditation, pranayama, or some other practice is especially important to your daily routine, and who can help you integrate this into your other therapeutic work.

If you are primarily looking for symptom reduction, or if you have more troublesome and intrusive symptoms, you may wish to seek out a cognitive-behavioral therapist. Research has shown this approach to be very effective in providing relief for many of the common symptoms of depression, anxiety and related issues. Psychiatrist David Burns' book, *The Feeling Good Handbook,* is an excellent self-help resource based on the tenets of cognitive-behavioral therapy.[50] The tools of mental self-control described in the book are absolutely foundational, and I strongly recommend it as a component of your library, whether or not you pursue

---

[50] Burns, D. (1999). *The Feeling Good Handbook*. New York, NY: Penguin Group.

formal psychotherapy. See Chapter 30 for much more on cognitive therapy approaches that may be useful for practicing magicians.

Thelemites often ask me, in the context of my background in psychology, about the difference between a visionary state or magical experience that might involve an interaction with a spirit or some other entity, and a pathological psychotic state. One iconic view on this issue was offered by Joseph Campbell in his book *Myths to Live By*: "The mystic, endowed with native talents...and following...the instructions of a master, enters the waters and finds he can swim; whereas the schizophrenic, unprepared, unguided, and ungifted, has fallen or has intentionally plunged and is drowning."[51] How do we differentiate these, and convey to the therapist that you have not lost your marbles? Isn't the therapist just going to conclude that you are "hearing voices" and must be psychotic? *Probably* not, as long as you are judicious in how you talk about these things. A true psychotic disorder involves a great deal of mental dysfunction and disorganization, and any competent therapist is trained to look for this. If you go into a therapy session and explain that you performed an evocation where a spirit spoke to you, but you also are coming across as a reality-based, functional, competent adult who is integrating such experiences into your spiritual path, it is unlikely that your therapist will be too alarmed. Of course, it is important to work with a therapist who will not be put off by your use of the language of ceremonial magick, such as references to invoking archangels or summoning spirits into triangles. Help them understand that you are attempting to describe certain experiences in poetic and somewhat archaic terms, as a means of deepening your self-awareness. Now, there are *some* therapists out there who are simply not going to respond in an open-minded way to discussions of these sorts of things, hence the importance of the initial screening process.

Magicians also frequently express concerns about how to talk with their therapist about their magical path without breaking oaths of secrecy. Often, these folks are simply over-thinking the situation, or rationalizing an underlying resistance to participation in psychotherapy. It is not that difficult to "translate" your oath-bound experiences into different terms. To give one intentionally ridiculous example: Rather than say that you took such-and-such degree in a certain magical order, and you had to promise not to eat oatmeal, you can simply say that you've decided it's very important for you not to eat oatmeal, and you want the therapist's assistance in this regard. At other times, you may be able to reduce the amount of detail discussed with the therapist, and easily avoid infringing upon your oaths of secrecy.

---

[51] Campbell, J. (1972). *Myths to Live By*. New York, NY: Penguin Group.

Another issue that inevitably arises any time we are looking for a healthcare practitioner of any kind is how to pay for it. If you are fortunate enough to have health insurance, that's the place to start. Get a list of providers that are in your area and on your insurance panel, and then start calling and interviewing them as described above. If you do not have insurance, there may be publicly funded options available to you. This varies a lot from place to place, but you can start by checking with your city or county to see what services may be offered. Additionally, some therapists in private practice may have sliding fee scales, or be willing to see some clients *pro bono*, so be sure to ask about this when you make your initial round of phone calls. Believe me, most magicians are just the kind of clients that therapists enjoy working with —intelligent, creative, and insightful—so you stand a good chance of persuading a therapist to take you on, even if you have financial constraints.

Aside from professional therapy options, our Thelemic communities are increasingly composed of leaders who have received at least rudimentary training in pastoral counseling techniques, via workshops such as the one I developed with the Psychology Guild of O.T.O. Don't hesitate to approach your local body leaders and clergy for assistance— they are there for you as contact points to discuss issues of concern. While this isn't psychotherapy and shouldn't be construed as a replacement for professional help, it is an important resource within our growing communities. Many of our leaders also try to be aware of local resources for professional mental health care, and they may be able to help connect you with these resources.

The issue of psychiatric medication often arises when symptoms are more severe. Understandably, many people have concerns about the potential for over-reliance on these medications within the medical establishment. Others have moral qualms about the very concept of taking prescribed medication to change our mental state. I can't deny that over-prescription of medications such as anti-depressants is rampant in our society. Nevertheless, I have seen many of my patients benefit tremendously from judicious use of these medications, especially when their symptoms severely impair their day-to-day functioning. If it is genuinely needed, the proper medication, at the proper dosage, is unlikely to impair the ability of a magician to perform their Great Work with a clear head and open heart. Indeed, for those suffering from a true psychiatric disorder, it may be one of the tools that makes the Work more attainable.

In the final analysis, you must take responsibility for your own choices in this regard, as with any medical care. Your psychotherapist will have valuable insights into the potential benefits of psychiatric medication, based on your actual history and symptoms. If you decide you want to pursue a medication evaluation, your therapist can assist you and coordinate care with the medical practitioner of your choice. For most people dealing with straightforward anxiety or depression, this is often a primary care physician, although some clients seek out a psychiatrist to receive specialized care.

Recommended Reading:

Assagioli, R. (2000). *Psychosynthesis: A Collection of Basic Writings.* Amherst, MA: Synthesis Center.

Bourne, E. (2005). *The Anxiety and Phobia Workbook.* Oakland, CA: New Harbinger Publications.

Brenner, C. (1974). *An Elementary Textbook of Psychoanalysis.* New York, NY: Anchor Books.

Burns, D. (1999). *The Feeling Good Handbook.* New York, NY: Penguin Group.

Campbell, J. (1971). *The Portable Jung.* New York, NY: Penguin Group.

Frager, R. (1999). *Heart, Self and Soul.* Wheaton, IL: Quest Books.

Gendlin, E. (1982). *Focusing.* New York, NY: Bantam Dell.

Hillman, J. (1996). *The Soul's Code: In Search of Character and Calling.* New York, NY: Random House.

Johnson, R. (1986). *Inner Work.* New York, NY: HarperCollins Publishers.

Johnson, R. (1991). *Owning your own Shadow.* New York, NY: HarperCollins Publishers.

Jung, C.G. (1964). *Man and His Symbols.* New York, NY: Dell Publishing.

Rogers, C. (2004). *On Becoming a Person.* London, UK: Robinson Publishing.

Kubler-Ross, E. (1969). *On Death and Dying.* New York, NY: Scribner.

Lerner, H. (2005). *The Dance of Anger.* New York, NY: Harper Perennial.

Lemesurier, P. (1993). *Healing of the Gods.* New York, NY: HarperCollins Publishers.

Moore, T. (1994). *Care of the Soul.* New York, NY: Harper Perennial.

Palmer, P. (2000). *Let Your Life Speak: Listening for the Voice of Vocation.* San Francisco, CA: Jossey-Bass, Inc.

Schnarch, D. (2009). *Passionate Marriage.* New York, NY: W.W. Norton & Company.

Sherman, C. (2001). *How to Go to Therapy.* New York, NY: AtRandom.

29

THE ANIMA & ANIMUS

Success in the Great Work depends on thorough self-knowledge. After all, how can we transform ourselves if we don't understand the raw material? How can we judge our own work if we don't have the proper tools for its inspection? Accordingly, any tool that can aid us in self-knowledge is a worthy tool for the magician. The psychological concepts and processes described by Carl Jung are one such set of tools, and in this chapter we'll be focusing on one particular aspect of his system, known as the *anima* or *animus* complex. Put simply, anima is the unconscious feminine aspect of one who consciously identifies as male. Conversely, animus is the unconscious masculine aspect of one who consciously identifies as female.

Jung's model of the psyche is in many ways rooted in the concept of the union of opposites; most importantly the union of the conscious and unconscious minds. Jung felt the striving for the ego to unite with the anima/animus was a particularly important expression of an underlying drive toward intrapsychic balance. This is essentially a 'hydraulic' model of the psyche. That is, when we push contents down into the unconscious (i.e. repression), this results in an equal and opposite push back *from* the unconscious. The push comes in the form of dreams, intuitions, and other forms of feedback. When we attend conscientiously to these messages from the unconscious, we move toward balance and wholeness; when we ignore or continue to repress these messages, the unconscious tries ever harder to get our attention, resulting in obsessions and misdirected drives.

We can find similar doctrines expressed as magical principles in our Thelemic Holy Books, confirming that we must unite the higher and lower, the light and dark, the conscious and unconscious, in order to be healthy and whole. As we read in *Liber Tzaddi*:

> 33. I reveal unto you a great mystery. Ye stand between the abyss of height and the abyss of depth.
> 34. In either awaits you a Companion; and that Companion is Yourself.
> 35. Ye can have no other Companion.
> 36. Many have arisen, being wise. They have said «Seek out the glittering Image in the place ever golden, and unite yourselves with It.»
> 37. Many have arisen, being foolish. They have said, «Stoop down unto the darkly splendid world, and be wedded to that Blind Creature of the Slime.»
> 38. I who am beyond Wisdom and Folly, arise and say unto you: achieve both weddings! Unite yourselves with both!
> 39. Beware, beware, I say, lest ye seek after the one and lose the other!
> 40. My adepts stand upright; their head above the heavens, their feet below the hells.
> 41. But since one is naturally attracted to the Angel, another to the Demon, let the first strengthen the lower link, the last attach more firmly to the higher.
> 42. Thus shall equilibrium become perfect. I will aid my disciples; as fast as they acquire this balanced power and joy so faster will I push them.
> 43. They shall in their turn speak from this Invisible Throne; their words shall illumine the worlds.
> 44. They shall be masters of majesty and might; they shall be beautiful and joyous; they shall be clothed with victory and splendour; they shall stand upon the firm foundation; the kingdom shall be theirs; yea, the kingdom shall be theirs.[52]

The basic theory of the anima/animus is that a person whose outward and conscious identification is primarily of one gender will have a less expressed, mostly unconscious aspect embodying the other gender's characteristics. Jung described the anima and animus as being archetypes of the collective unconscious, existing independently of a person's

---

[52] Crowley, A. (1983). *The Holy Books of Thelema*. San Francisco, CA: Weiser Books.

individual experience. There is certainly a danger of societal gender stereotypes coming into play whenever we try to talk about universal masculine and feminine traits, and Jung himself likely fell into this trap based on the views of gender that were prevalent in his time. Yet, we can understand this more flexibly as an expression of a fairly obvious fact: *whatever* a person's conscious gender identification may be, the complementary aspects with which he or she does *not* so much identify will embody an unexpressed and largely unexplored aspect of self.

Jung felt that the development of the anima/animus reflected specific, successive levels of psychological growth for the man or woman. For the man the levels are said to reflect a deepening connection with emotion, intuition, and spirituality. For the woman, they show a maturing relationship to various forms of power. Again, there is the danger of falling into gender stereotypes, but the underlying theory may be useful as a way of understanding our deepening relationship with unexpressed aspects of self. The reason that the anima/animus is so important to psychological self-exploration and growth is that the polarity of gender identity is an easily accessible and virtually universal experience in human life. We can identify fairly readily with a striving to actualize under-developed aspects of self via gender characteristics, whereas other areas of exploration may be harder to grasp at first. They will be so alien as to be almost entirely unconscious; we *are* conscious of gender, however, and so the anima/animus is an easier "hand-hold" as we begin this exploration.

Accordingly, we can understand the anima/animus as an expression of the classical 'psychopomp,' the guide to our own personal underworld— the unconscious—that helps us to begin bridging the conscious and unconscious worlds, and ultimately to aid us in building the conscious link between the ego and the Self which is so important to wholeness and health. The corresponding principle of this ego-Self axis, put in terms of the magical path, is the K & C of the HGA. It is very important to understand that I am *not* saying that the HGA is the same thing as the anima/animus. What I am saying is that the HGA ultimately serves as our primary guide to the unexplored realms of our psycho-spiritual selves. The HGA is intimately entwined with the very core of our being, and any influence it exerts upon the everyday ego has the potential to bring vibrant insight into who we really are. In this way, the HGA serves many of the same functions as the anima/animus, but on a more exalted level. Once firmly established and stabilized, the K & C is a direct and open channel to the unconscious, in both its personal and collective manifestations. Given the gender polarity of the anima/animus complex, it is perhaps also important to note that the HGA may or may not be perceived as being of the opposite sex, or of any defined gender at all. The experience of adepts varies widely in this regard.

So, what *is* the relationship between the anima/animus and the HGA, exactly? And how do these tend to function in the unfolding path of the initiate? In one sense, we can see the anima/animus as residing in Yesod. Here, the 'guide' to the unconscious is those initial intuitive and symbolic bread crumbs that are in fact foreshadowed elements of the eventual conscious communion with the HGA. The so-called "vision" of the HGA attributed to Malkuth awakens us to the spiritual reality behind the veil of nature. Most importantly, this is the veil that has blinded us to *our own* spiritual reality, beneath the opaque shell of body and personality upon which we place so much emphasis in mundane life. At Yesod, we begin to get instruction from the HGA as to the *nature* of this spiritual reality, veiled in the language of symbols, dreams, astral experiences, and intuition. In this place, the anima/animus is in a very full sense our guide to further attainment. Jung felt the anima/animus would often appear in dreams as a guide or friend, and we have literary and mythological reference points for this as well. For example, the poet Virgil guiding Dante through the underworld in the *Inferno*; and the role of the god Hermes as the so-called 'messenger of the gods'—one who bridges the human and divine worlds—another metaphor for the conscious and unconscious realms. (Notably, Hermes is often depicted as androgynous, a further connection with the contrasexual nature of the anima/animus.)

One of the most common ways in which the anima/animus is visible and potent in our daily lives is through projection onto our love partners, whether actual or merely desired. The yearning for the other person; the sense that they somehow complete or heal us; the intensity of our desire to possess them; all of these are symptoms of anima/animus projection. The other person symbolizes an unexpressed aspect of self, and if we are not sufficiently aware of this perceived *deficit* in ourselves, the intensity of our desire for them will generally be directly proportional to our blindness! These situations inevitably lead to disappointment, for the object of our desire—a mere human—can never live up to our expectation of perfect, divine love.

SUGGESTED EXERCISES:

1. List your beliefs about the personality characteristics of masculinity and femininity. Not what you think society believes, but what **you** actually believe. If you have trouble coming up with such a list, you can fall back on listing your sense of society's beliefs.
2. Now compare your own personality characteristics to those on your lists, based on your identified gender. Circle those that you

feel you embody, and put a line through those you feel you do **not** embody.

3. Now look at the items you have crossed out. Each day, pick one of these characteristics and make a conscious effort to **live out** that characteristic throughout the day, in interpersonal interactions as well as your private thoughts. Take on a 'magical personality' that fully embodies the trait in question. Note the results in your diary.

4. Now look at the items you've circled. Each day, pick one of these characteristics and make a conscious effort **not** to live it out that day. Note the results in your diary.

5. Pay attention to the less obvious ways in which your daily behavior and experience of yourself and the world change. By living out those aspects of self that are rarely given voice, we open a channel for other suppressed or unexplored characteristics to surface.

6. You might wish to ask a friend or partner what they have noticed about your behavior at the end of the day, as a means of cross-checking the outward expression of your chosen characteristic on a given day.

7. Watch for projections of anima/animus onto partners (or desired partners). List the characteristics of your partner, and reflect on how you might benefit from increasing their expression in your life.

8. Record your dreams for at least a few months, paying special attention to those figures that appear as guides. Start a list of the characteristics of these guides, adding to it each time a new guide appears in a subsequent dream. After a few weeks, you will have a list which may be quite suggestive in terms of directions for personal exploration. How could you be more like these guides? In what ways would this represent growth or change for you?

30

Cognitive Therapy for Magicians

As we have discussed in earlier chapters, the human ego is one of the most important tools in the magician's toolbox. The ego is the lens through which we perceive and organize our experiences; if this lens is distorted, cloudy, imbalanced or unduly skewed by bias, prejudice or blind spots, we will not function optimally. Obviously, as magicians, we deal with a lot of symbolic, archetypal, and unconscious material that does not have much to do with the ego. This material is dealt with on its own plane through ritual, astral work, and other occult practices. Similarly, when it comes to the ego, we must address it on its own plane.

Unfortunately, this is a stumbling block for many magicians. There is a tendency to gloss over common, dysfunctional habits of thinking, and skip to more esoteric work. In the process, many magicians overlook the importance of a balanced psyche, thereby undermining the effectiveness of their magical work. It is a particular manifestation of ego inflation: "I've attained to these lofty states of consciousness, therefore my personality doesn't need any attention." Yet in reality, *all* of us have further growth and development to accomplish, regardless of our magical attainment; and none of us are immune to having some blind spots in our day-to-day lives. Cognitive therapy is simply a technology of daily mental and magical hygiene at the level of the ego that, I believe, is an important weapon in any magician's arsenal.

Cognitive therapy, sometimes called cognitive-behavioral therapy, derives primarily from the work of psychiatrist Aaron Beck. In the 1960s and 70s, Beck developed his seminal theory on this approach, and his ideas have gone on to radically reshape modern psychotherapeutic technique as we know it. Essentially, the theory says that disturbing emotions such as anxiety, depression, and anger, are fundamentally rooted in habitual negative thought patterns that get engrained in us through our upbringing, and through our day-to-day process of taking in information from the environment and making decisions about what it means. We tend to fall into habits that are unduly skewed toward the negative side in our views of ourselves, other people, and the world in general. If we get stuck in a rut in terms of these thought patterns, we are more likely to suffer from depression, anxiety, anger, control issues and all manner of dysfunctional emotions and behavior patterns.

Cognitive therapy is designed to break us out of these destructive habits. We examine our thoughts and emotions, being attentive to distorted, irrational, and maladaptive thinking patterns. We then gradually and progressively replace them with more realistic, positive and constructive thoughts, actually reprogramming ourselves to think differently. Done properly, this results in permanent and substantive improvements in emotion and behavior. Several decades of research now exist to support the efficacy of this approach, and nearly all psychotherapists in practice today have, in one way or another, been influenced by this school of thought.

I should emphasize that cognitive therapy is *not* about pretending bad things have not happened, or talking ourselves out of feeling bad about something that legitimately *should* make us feel bad. Rather, cognitive therapy deals with the various thoughts and interpretive schema we lay over the top of these negative events, thereby exacerbating our negative emotion. Sometimes something bad really has happened, such as the loss of a job. If you feel depressed, angry and frustrated in this situation, that's not a cognitive distortion—that's reality. Often, however we add layers of negative interpretations: "I've lost my job and I'll probably never get another good one. I'll probably never be hirable in the field that I want to work in." And so on. Bad stuff happens, but this kind of self-talk is *optional,* and very likely unrealistic.

Another category of unnecessary negative emotion occurs when we feel bad not because anything at all has happened, but because of what's going on in our head. A classic example of this is when we get upset because we *think* we know what someone is thinking about us. We imagine they are thinking they don't like us, or that they are criticizing us, and so on. We then tend to get mad at them, but the fact is we don't have any evidence about what they are thinking. We have stirred ourselves up into an emotional place just by *imagining* that we know what they are thinking.

Psychiatrist David Burns, who studied with Aaron Beck, is one of the most important contemporary authors and lecturers on cognitive therapy. In his excellent book *The Feeling Good Handbook*, he classifies the most common cognitive distortion patterns into ten categories. Let's review these ten common cognitive distortions and go into a bit of detail about each one, because these are the things you will be working with on a day-to-day basis if you incorporate this approach into your magical toolbox. For each of these distorted thinking patterns, I will describe its basic nature, and then give you some suggestions for ways to overturn the pattern; that is, to punch a hole in the distorted thinking and shift it to a more realistic and constructive set of thoughts.

1. **All-or-Nothing thinking.** A situation is seen in black-and-white terms. If you don't get a perfect score on a test, you tell yourself you've failed completely. If a friend doesn't support you on a particular issue, she is a terrible friend. To overturn this cognitive distortion, ask yourself if there is a gray area—a more moderate way of looking at the situation, without resorting to extremes. Does the situation really have to be seen in terms of extremes, or have I just chosen to think about it this way?

2. **Jumping to Conclusions.** You imagine worst-case scenarios about how an upcoming event is likely to unfold, in spite of the lack of evidence for the negative outcome. The boss gives you a so-so performance evaluation and you conclude you will *never* get promoted. Your partner has been quiet and withdrawn lately, and you conclude that he or she doesn't love you anymore. You jump past facts (or lack thereof) into fears about the situation (the "mind-reading" mentioned earlier is a sub-category of jumping to conclusions). To challenge this pattern, ask yourself if there is any evidence that the outcome is really likely. Has it really happened that often in the past? Once you are aware of a tendency to jump to conclusions, it may be easier to avoid undue anxiety by catching yourself doing it.

3. **Magnification**. This is also known as *catastrophizing*. "If my spouse left me, life wouldn't be worth living anymore. I might as well just end it all." "If I don't get to be Deacon pretty soon, I won't be able to contribute to the Lodge and it's just going to go downhill from here." You underestimate your own strengths and exaggerate the gravity of the situation. To challenge this pattern, ask yourself about evidence for the likelihood of the feared outcome. Also, remind yourself of how you have adapted to similar adverse circumstances in the past. For example, if you fear the loss of a relationship, remind yourself about how you have

bounced back from prior failed relationships. How would you *really* cope if the relationship ended? Chances are, you would hurt for a while, then move on to a better relationship.

4. **Overgeneralization**. The hallmark of this pattern is the use of words like 'always' and 'never.' For example, you are working on a project at your local body and someone comes in late. You think to yourself that they are always late. Well, they are probably not *always* late. Perhaps they are *frequently* late, but if you talk to yourself using words like 'always', you are going to be more upset than if you use more measured terminology. Your choice of words matters, even when you're only talking to yourself! Another example: you make a mistake and you say to yourself, "I can't do anything right." True, the mistake was made; but you are talking to yourself as if the mistake is a pervasive character flaw, and that's almost certainly not the case. With cognitive therapy, you not only teach yourself to respond more positively, but also more realistically and constructively.

5. **Mental Filter**. This is a sort of tunnel vision where you have a negative belief about yourself, another person, or a situation, and you pick out details in your experience that seem to confirm the existing negative belief—nothing else gets in. You get several compliments at work, but then at the end of the day one person has a critical thing to say to you and that's what you focus on all night. You're not thinking about the fifteen people who said nice things to you, you are thinking about the one person who said something negative. To deal with that distortion, ask yourself what you might be overlooking. Challenge yourself to look for counter-examples, to help you see the whole picture in a more balanced way.

6. **Discounting the Positive.** This is similar to Mental Filter. With this pattern you actually take note of positive events, but you explain them away. Someone compliments you, and instead of taking it in as a legitimate observation you brush it off, thinking "They are just trying to get something from me," or "They say that to everybody." You find some way to make it not count. One way to challenge this pattern is to imagine that a friend has come to you and described a similar situation. You would probably reassure your friend that the compliment they had received was genuine and deserved, and you would encourage them to accept it rather than writing it off. Now take your own advice! Another way to challenge this pattern is to remind yourself that, most likely, the *actual evidence* in front of you is the compliment itself, and the negative side is only in your head.

7. **Emotional Reasoning**. You treat feelings as if they are facts. Your spouse is ten minutes late coming home, and you start to worry that he or she has been in an accident. So far, this is simply jumping to a conclusion. However, once your body hears your mind saying something bad has happened, your body starts to pump adrenaline, and you start to feel a very tangible, bodily sensation you associate with fear. Since humans have evolved to interpret these emotional cues in the body as signs of actual danger, you conclude if you're feeling this way, true danger must surely be present. Yet, there is absolutely no evidence of anything being amiss—just a vicious cycle of negative thoughts and fight-or-flight bodily arousal.

One thing you can do is to challenge this pattern is to force yourself to be more factually based in your conclusions. Once again, the magic(k) bullet is to ask yourself what evidence you have that supports your fear. Almost certainly, there will be none. Look for positive counter-examples from the past, or alternate explanations: Your spouse has been late before, and it wasn't a terrible accident; he or she was simply delayed by traffic or errands. Feelings aren't necessarily facts. Now, of course, emotions are *one* piece of data our ego uses to understand and respond to the environment; but when we give *undue* weight to emotional responses, we can easily lose sight of more reality-based perceptions of our situation.

8. **'Should' Statements**. You feel there is something you are obligated to do; or that someone else is obligated to do. You have expectations about the way the world is supposed to work or the way people are supposed to behave. Then, when something doesn't turn out the way you think it should, you react with anger, resentment, or shame. Common self-statements along these lines include: "People should be more considerate of one another," or "I should have done better or known better." The basic remedy here is to remember that just because you think something *should* happen, that doesn't mean that it is a law of nature. This can be a pretty subtle thought process. We build in many expectations in day-to-day living based on what we wish would happen, reflecting calcified beliefs about the way the world ought to work. It takes courage and persistence to root our habitual illusions in this regard.

9. **Labeling**. Labeling is essentially an extreme form of Overgeneralizing. Based on a limited set of behaviors, you apply a label to yourself or to others that is unfairly objectifying or dehumanizing. For example, someone treats you poorly on a given occasion and you write them off as a 'jerk' or a 'bitch'; or you make a mistake and tell yourself you are a 'loser'. These labels limit your ability to see the subtle strengths and weaknesses in yourself or others—to appreciate the

humanity beneath the label. They also make it harder to change your situation, because you have conceived your world in terms of conceptual boxes—one box is full of jerks, and the other box is full of non-jerks. Where is the opportunity for growth or change in such a worldview? Instead of applying a label, ask yourself: what are the specific behaviors I dislike in myself or others? Remind yourself that you, the other person, and everyone else in the world behaves badly sometimes. Maybe you don't need to be so black-and-white in your characterization of the situation. Can you put yourself in their shoes and see how they might behave problematically, without meriting an intractable stamp of defectiveness?

10. **Personalization and Blaming**. Something negative has occurred and you either take it personally (personalization), or assume it *must* be someone's fault (blaming). "My co-worker didn't smile when I spoke to her this morning. What did I do wrong?" "That Mass was really low-energy. That stupid Deacon always screws things up!" There is a natural desire to explain the universe in terms of cause and effect, and sometimes, in the heat of the moment, it is more comforting to conclude that someone is to blame, even if it's ourselves. But once again, conceptual 'boxes' like this make us less likely to consider other explanations for why things have occurred. It makes us motivated to take constructive action, or to understand the subtleties of the problem, and it binds us into a narrow view of the situation. To challenge this pattern, look for alternate explanations: maybe that co-worker who didn't smile at you just got some bad news, and their response had nothing to do with you. Perhaps the Mass was less than stellar because everyone was tired from the initiations the day before, and not because any individual was to blame.

Practical Suggestions
How can you put all these concepts to constructive use as a magician? I suggest that each time you have a strong and significant disturbing emotion—and this is likely to be at least once a day—you make an entry in a 'mood log.' This might simply be included in your magical diary. In the log, you write down the thoughts that are flying around in your head, no matter how irrational they might seem. These will likely include a good bit of distorted thinking. Next, you identify which cognitive distortions are present in the thoughts, and come up with a rational response. Use the challenging questions suggested in the discussion above. Through vigilance and repetition, you will increase your ability to catch the negative thought patterns soon after they arise, and replace them with more constructive, realistic, and positive responses. Eventually, you will truly reprogram yourself, and the rational thoughts

will become your new 'default' mode of operation. In my opinion, every magician, no matter how psychologically healthy they feel, should spend at least a few months doing daily journaling of this kind. You will gain invaluable insight into your thought patterns and the way they affect your emotions; and this becomes an essential part of your scientific record.

You can also use these techniques when you are planning a magical working. It is very important to consider the psychological conditions that led you to the conclusion that a working is necessary. If your ego is unduly clouded with cognitive distortions, your decision to undertake a magical working to change your situation may be skewed as well. Consider whether there are any purely emotional reasons for desiring the goal that you have in mind. Ask yourself if there are upsetting emotions like anger, frustration, or dissatisfaction with your life that are driving your desire to do the magick working. Might these be better addressed directly, on their own plane, through cognitive therapy?

Finally, and perhaps most importantly, if you use these techniques to make sure your mind is as clear and unbiased as possible, you will be maximally enabled to stay tuned in to that most important inner voice—the voice of True Will and deep conscience—the voice of the HGA, which is the one infallible guide along your magical path.

Conclusion

It is my dearest hope that the material in this book will be helpful as you progress along the path of your own unique Great Work. Let me close by reminding you of the advice given earlier in the book: you should above all else *persist* through the challenges, dangers, and discomforts that confront every earnest seeker as they undertake the work. When in doubt, in darkness, or in despair, know that attainment awaits you if you simply keep aspiring to the Light of the Holy Guardian Angel burning ever in your heart. Accordingly, I will leave you with a poem by Soror Meral that beautifully expresses the rapture of union with the Angel.

THE LIGHT OF LIFE (1982)

I love you in all the star wrought graces of the skies,
In the Isis of beauty that about me lies;
Waiting for Thy touch of love to awaken in splendid flame
The ever-coursing thunder of Thy name.

Oh, splendid One, Thou mysterious, unspeakable,
Coursing through my veins in agony unbearable:
Oh, Light of Life in splendrous rapture of delight
Who fills my veins with life in majesty of might.

As a mote in the strong sunbeam dances
So dance I as a creation of Thy fancies.
These words of mine are but chaff upon the wind
Compared to the intensity of Thy glance and Thy mind.

Bind my everlasting passage and path with Thee
From life to life, from aeon to aeon for all eternity.
Bring me closer to Thy Heart that I may be fit symbol
Of Thine encompassing love and hold me lest I tremble.

Ah, Lord, these words are poor that fall before Thy face,
Fill me and lend me still of Thy intoxicating grace
That I may love and pour my heart out in Thy praise
And joined forever with Thee remain a Star ablaze.

--Phyllis Seckler (Soror Meral)

ABOUT THE AUTHOR

Dr. David Shoemaker is a clinical psychologist in private practice, specializing in Jungian and cognitive-behavioral psychotherapy. David is the Chancellor and Prolocutor of the Temple of the Silver Star. He is a long-standing member of O.T.O. and A∴A∴, and has many years of experience training initiates in these traditions.

He is the Master of 418 Lodge, O.T.O. in Sacramento, having succeeded Soror Meral (Phyllis Seckler), his friend and teacher. He also serves as the Most Wise Sovereign of Alpha Chapter, O.T.O., and as a Sovereign Grand Inspector General of the order. David was the founding President of the O.T.O. Psychology Guild, and he is a frequent speaker at national and regional events. He is also a member of the U.S. Grand Lodge Initiation Training and Planning committees, and he serves as an Advanced Initiation Trainer. A consecrated Bishop of Ecclesia Gnostica Catholica, David led the team that developed the Pastoral Counseling Workshops and brought them to O.T.O. members across the U.S.

David is a co-editor of the journals *Neshamah* (Psychology Guild) and *Cheth* (418 Lodge). In addition to his essays in these publications, his writings have been published in the journals *Mezlim* and *Black Pearl*, and his chapter on Qabalistic Psychology was included in the Instructor's Manual of Fadiman and Frager's *Personality and Personal Growth*, an undergraduate psychology textbook. He was the compiler of the T.O.T.S.S. publication, *Jane Wolfe: The Cefalu Diaries 1920-1923*, and a co-editor of the T.O.T.S.S./Teitan Press collections of the writings of Phyllis Seckler, *The Thoth Tarot, Astrology, & Other Selected Writings*, and *The Kabbalah, Magick, and Thelema. Selected Writings Volume II*. His popular *Living Thelema* instructional segments are presented regularly on the podcast of the same name. His record of scrying the Thirty Enochian Aethyrs, *The Winds of Wisdom*, was published in late 2016.

In addition to his work in magick and psychology, David is a composer and musician. He lives in Sacramento with his wife and his son.

www.livingthelema.com

Temple of the Silver Star - Academic Track

The Temple of the Silver Star is a non-profit religious and educational corporation, based on the principles of Thelema. It was founded in service to the A∴A∴, under warrant from Soror Meral (Phyllis Seckler), to provide preparatory training in magick, mysticism, Qabalah, Tarot, astrology, and much more. In its academic track, each student is assigned an individual teacher, who provides one-to-one instruction and group classes. Online classes and other distance-learning options are available.

The criteria for admission to the academic track of the Temple are explained on the application itself, which may be submitted online via the T.O.T.S.S. website. The Temple has campuses or study groups in Sacramento, Oakland, Los Angeles, Reno, Seattle, Denver, Boston, West Chester (Philadelphia-area), Toronto, Japan, Austria and the U.K. Public classes are offered regularly; schedules are available on our website.

Temple of the Silver Star - Initiatory Track

The Temple of the Silver Star's initiatory track offers ceremonial initiation, personalized instruction, and a complete system of training in the Thelemic Mysteries. Our degree system is based on the Qabalistic Tree of Life and the cipher formulæ of the Golden Dawn, of which we are a lineal descendant.

Our entire curriculum is constructed to be in conformity with the Law of Thelema, and our central aim is to guide each aspirant toward the realization of their purpose in life, or True Will. In order to empower our members to discover and carry out their True Will, we teach Qabalah,

Tarot, ceremonial magick, meditation, astrology, and much more. Our initiates meet privately for group ceremonial and healing work, classes, and other instruction. We occasionally offer public classes and rituals.

Active participation in a local Temple or Pronaos is the best way to maximize the benefits of our system. However, we do offer At-Large memberships for those living at some distance from one of our local bodies.

If you are interested in learning more about our work, we invite you to download an application from our website and submit it to your nearest local body, or to contact us with any questions.

totss.org

Do what thou wilt shall be the whole of the Law.

The A∴A∴ is the system of spiritual attainment established by Aleister Crowley and George Cecil Jones in the early 1900s, as a modern expression of the Inner School of wisdom that has existed for millennia. Its central aim is simply to lead each aspirant toward their own individual attainment, for the betterment of all humanity. The course of study includes a diversity of training methods, such as Qabalah, raja yoga, ceremonial magick, and many other traditions. A∴A∴ is not organized into outer social organizations, fraternities or schools; rather, it is based on the time-tested power of individual teacher-student relationships, under the guidance of the masters of the Inner School. All training and testing is done strictly in accordance with *Liber 185* and other foundational documents.

Those interested in pursuing admission into A∴A∴ are invited to initiate contact via the following addresses:

A∴A∴
PO Box 215483
Sacramento, CA 95821
onestarinsight.org

The Student phase of preparation for work in A∴A∴ begins by acquiring a specific set of reference texts, notifying A∴A∴ of the same, and studying the texts for at least three months. The Student may then request Examination. More information about this process is available via the Cancellarius at the addresses given above. NOTE: While our primary contact address is in California, supervising Neophytes are available in many countries around the world.

If you are called to begin this journey, we earnestly invite you to contact us. Regardless of your choice in this matter, we wish you the best as you pursue your own Great Work. May you attain your True Will!

Love is the law, love under will.

Ordo Templi Orientis
and
Ecclesia Gnostica Catholica

Those interested in learning more about O.T.O. and E.G.C. may initiate contact via the following addresses and websites:

In the United States:

Ordo Templi Orientis U.S.A.
PO Box 2313
Maple Grove, MN 55311

Or contact your nearest O.T.O. local body via the U.S. Grand Lodge website: www.oto-usa.org

In other countries:

Secretary General
PO Box 33 20 12
D-14180 Berlin, Germany

Or contact your own country's Grand Lodge or other local representative via the International O.T.O. website: www.oto.org

Other Works by David Shoemaker

As Author

The Winds of Wisdom: Visions from the Thirty Enochian Aethyrs

Various essays, published in the journals *Mezlim, Agape, Black Pearl, Neshamah, and Cheth*

Living Thelema (podcast)

As Editor

Karl Germer: Selected Letters 1928-1962

Phyllis Seckler (Soror Meral): The Thoth Tarot, Astrology, & Other Selected Writings

Phyllis Seckler (Soror Meral): Kabbalah, Magick, & Thelema. Selected Writings Vol. II

Jane Wolfe: The Cefalu Diaries 1920-1923

As Musician and Composer

Elsa Letterseed Original Score

Workings (2000-2010)

Last Three Lives (self-titled)

Last Three Lives: Via

23553225R00157

Printed in Poland
by Amazon Fulfillment
Poland Sp. z o.o., Wrocław